AF632178

Yoga-Tantra and Sensuousness in Art

Tantra in Contemporary Researches

1. Impact of Tantra on Religion and Art; by T.N. Mishra (ISBN 81-246-0073-2)

2. Lalitā-Sahasranāma — A Comprehensive Study of One Thousand Names of Lalitā Mahā-tripurasundarī; by M.L. Joshi (ISBN 81-246-0104-6)

Tantra in Contemporary Researches, no. 3

Yoga-Tantra and Sensuousness in Art

T.N. Mishra

D.K. Printworld (P) Ltd.
New Delhi

Cataloging in Publication Data — DK

Mishra, T.N. (Tej Narain), 1945-
Yoga-tantra and sensuousness in art.
(Tantra in contemporary researches : no. 3)
Includes bibliographical references (p.)
Includes index.

1. Yoga. 2. Tantrism. 3. Sensuality in art.
I. Title. II. Series: Tantra in contemporary researches : no. 3.

ISBN 81-246-0239-5
First Published in India in 2003
©Author

All rights reserved. No part of this publication may be reproduced or transmitted in any form or by any means, electronic or mechanical, including photocopying, recording, or any information storage or retrieval system, without prior written permission of both the copyright owner, indicated above, and the publisher.

Published and printed by:
D.K. Printworld (P) Ltd.
Regd. office : *'Sri Kunj'*, F-52, Bali Nagar
New Delhi - 110 015
Phones : (011) 2545-3975; 2546-6019; *Fax* : (011) 2546-5926
E-mail: dkprintworld@vsnl.net
Web: www.dkprint.com

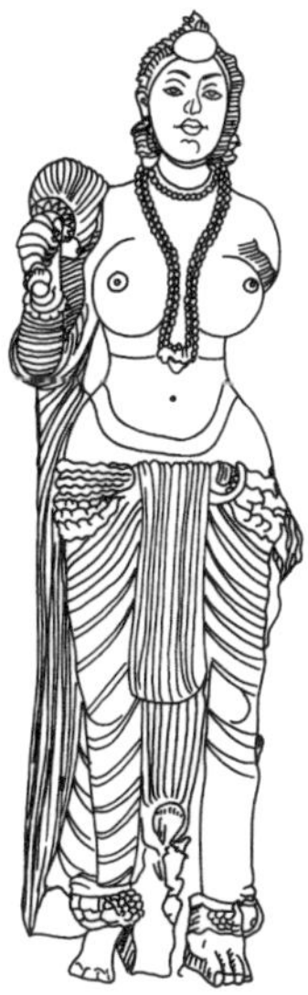

Preface

THE word *yoga* perhaps received the highest attention of readers among other Sanskrit words and the word is being interpreted, globally. In this book the author makes a humble attempt to explain the word *yoga*. During the course of exploring the meaning, certain related aspects needed discussions. These include an analysis of the philosophy of *yoga-tantra*, a clear-cut understanding of *Ulṭā-Sādhanā* or Regressive Process, etc. The moral and philosophical annotations of the word *yoga* also calls for an intensive introspection of the yogic *sādhanā* of Sahajīyas and the yogic *sādhanā* in Buddhism. The present writer made a thorough research on the aforesaid issues and the outcome of this book is his personal realization of the subject. Finally, an attempt has been made to understand the concept of Yoga and Tantra as reflected in Indian art through the ages and how such concepts moulded Indian art and introduced the philosophy of Yoga-Tantra, on the one hand, and the evident yet, subtle sensualism, on the other, in the religious as well as secular art of India.

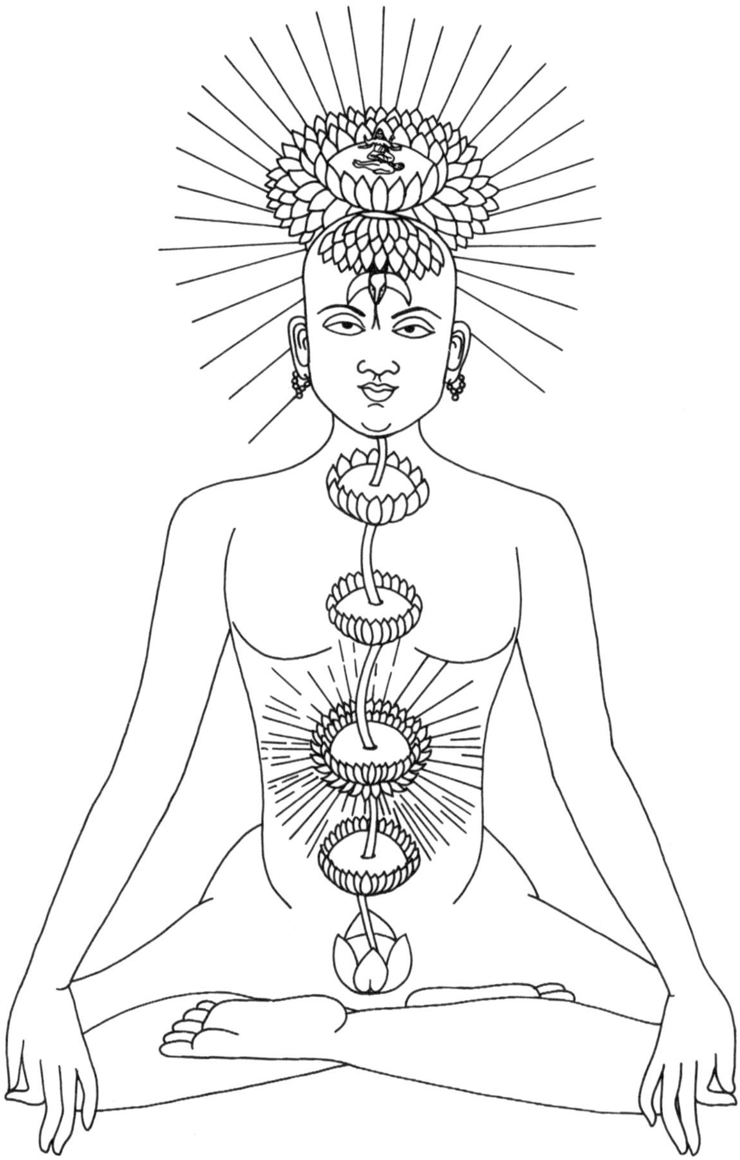

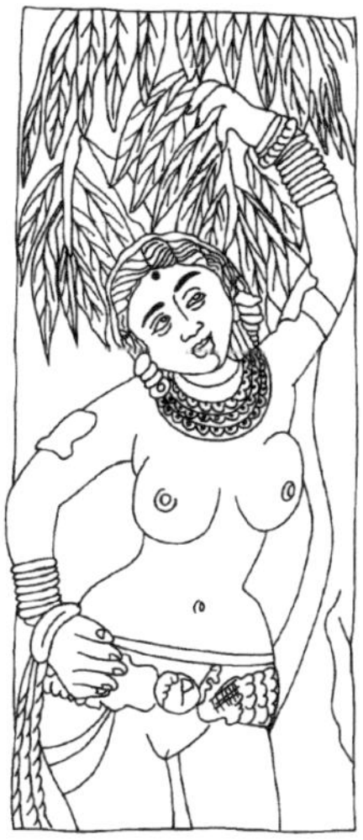

Contents

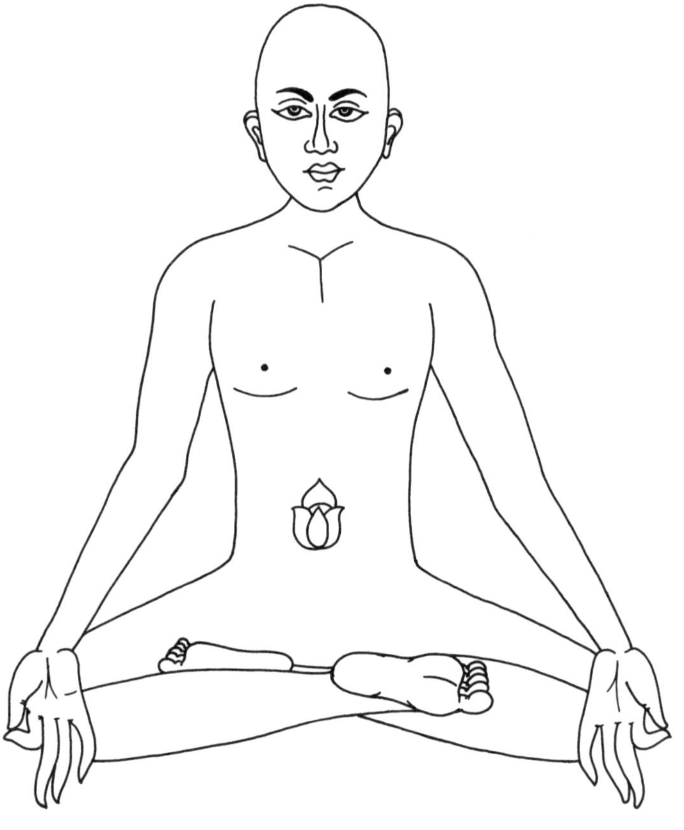

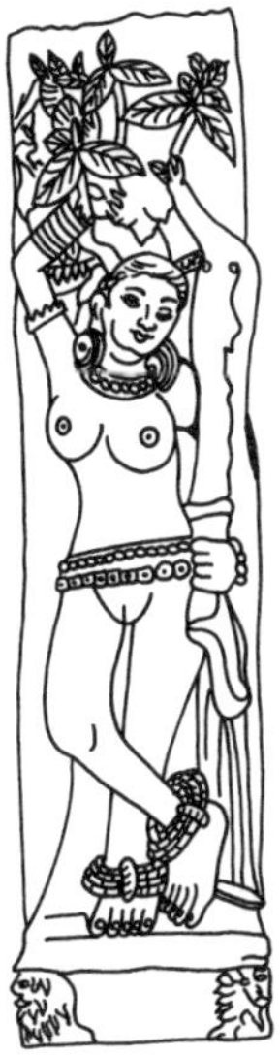

Acknowledgements

FOR the collection of relevant materials for this volume, I am very much indebted to my spiritual teacher for his spiritual guidance. I am equally grateful to other *ācāryas*, saints and *yogīs* for their blessings, guidance, suggestions and useful dialogues but they wanted to remain anonymous. I am grateful for the help and for the reply to certain querries and suggestions to Prof. (Miss) Krishna Banerjee, Department of English (M.M.V.) and to Dr. T.K. Biswas, Joint Director, Bharat Kala Bhavan, Banaras Hindu University who has gone through the manuscript and made invaluable suggestions. I am obliged to Prof. Deena Bandhu Pandey, Head of the Department of History of Arts, Banaras Hindu University and all my colleagues of Bharat Kala Bhavan, B.H.U., who gave me encouragements in the preparation of this book. I want to thank Dr. Sakuntal Mauriya, S.R.F. for the help in the preparation of the line-drawing (*yogi*) for this volume.

My thanks are due to Bharat Kala Bhavan Library, Philosophy Department Library, Malaviya Bhavan Library, Central Library of B.H.U., Saraswati Bhavan Pustakalaya, Sampurnananda Sanskrit Visvavidyalaya, Varanasi.

I also wish to mention here the moral support I received from my wife Vandana and my daughters Kavita, Pratima, and Jyoti in the course of the preparation of this book.

T.N. Mishra

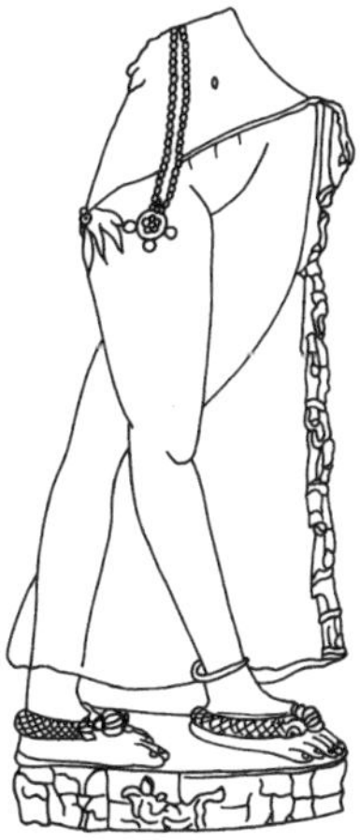

List of Illustrations

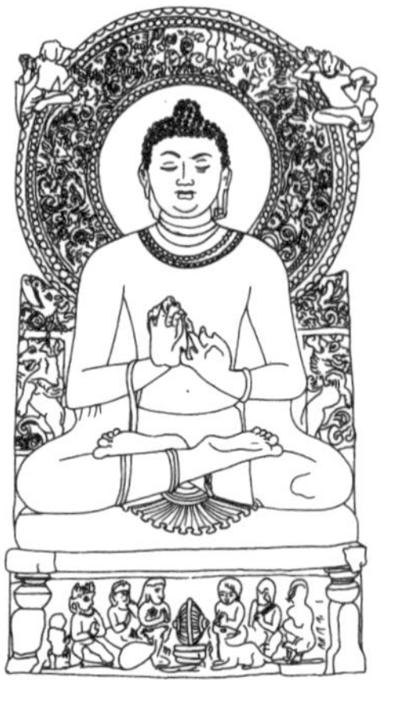

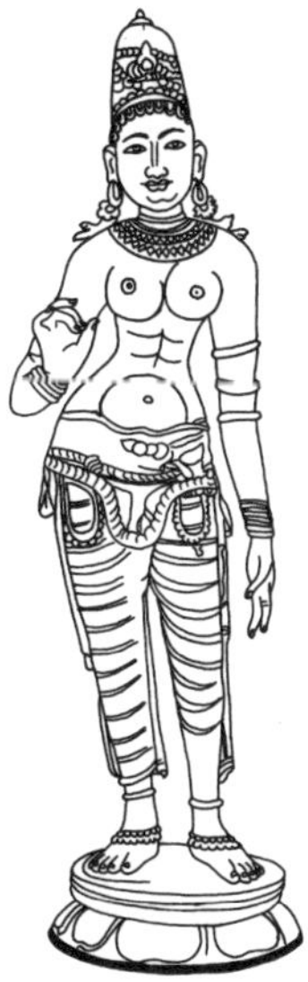

Introduction

THE word 'Hindu' has become very common as an appellation of our race and religion. This word 'Hindu' was used by the ancient Persian to mean river 'Sindhu', so Sindhu became Hindu. That man who does not believe in the most marvellous infinite power, from which everything has come, in which everything lives and to which everything must, in the end, return, cannot be called Hindu. We believe in nature, a being without beginning and end. There are certain great principles in which, I think, we are all one, and whoever calls himself a Hindu believes in those principles. 'Hinduism' is a blanket term derived from Hindu, a word that originally had no religious association. The spirit of tolerance and assimilation has been the hallmarks of the Hindu civilization.

Except the Hindu religion, every other religion in the world, depends upon the lives of a personal founder. It naturally follows a good deal of fight — what they call historical evidences that centre round these great personalities. Hinduism escaped this fate because this religion is not based upon persons but upon principles. Hinduism has survived all sorts of vicissitudes, because it was, from the very ancient times, held aloft the banner of renunciation. People of different races, languages and religions, with their rise and fall, played their part on the stage of the history and disappeared, leaving some faith behind. Thus, the Hindu religion is not in the books, nor in the theories; neither in the talking or even in the reasoning — it symbolizes being and becoming.

True religion is all about respecting the life, as such. All the religions regard values such as love, tolerance, kindness, fraternity and helpfulness as the principles of a true creed. No religion has ever been able to establish its superiority to all others. This truth has been expressed in the *Ṛgveda — ekaṁ sat viprāha bahudā vadanti* (the truth is one, the wise call it by many names).

Let us walk together with a common goal. Let us converse with a common purpose. Let our mind meet together in the quest of true knowledge. Let the religion of the world unite for peace in a common endeavour.

In Indian religion, there is a common element that makes every stage and every movement an expression of the concept of religion in its totality. The religion, in the form of literary records that have come down to us, is that of the Indians. A man's religion is something integral to his nature. There are systems of thought, like Sāṁkhya, Yoga and Mīmāṁsā which cultivate a spirit and attitude to which it would be difficult to deny the name of 'religion', even though they may not accept any belief in the God or the Gods, superior to oneself. A *yogī* may adopt other methods for achieving salvation from the cycle of birth and death. It is the spirit in man that is responding to the spirit in the universe; the high vision of those, who have penetrated into the depths of being and their very sense of the divine in all their exaltation of feeling and enrichment of personality, which has been the source of the noblest of works in the world.

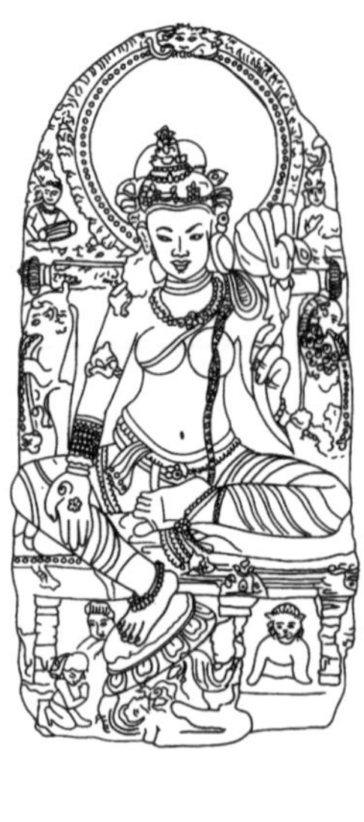

In fact, what is final, is one's own experience itself, though its expressions may change if they are to be relevant to the growing content of knowledge. The experience is, what is felt by the individual in his deepest being, what is seen or heard by him, and this is valid for all times. The relation between the vision and its expression and, the fact and its interpretation is very close on the fundamental,

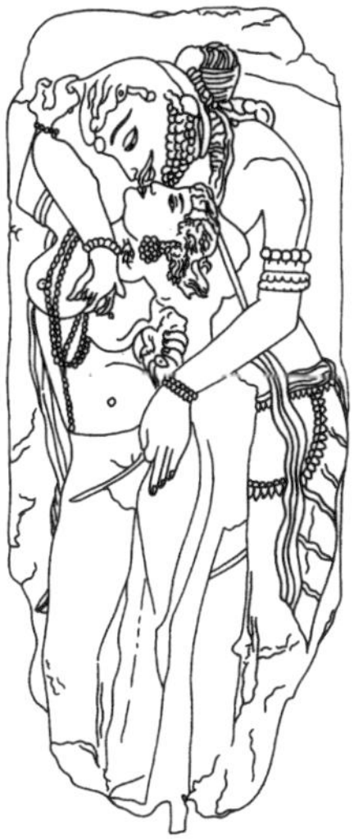

metaphysical and religious issues. Different commentators have given different interpretations. It is referred to in the Upaniṣad that 'The soul enters into the all. The heart is released from its burden of care. The sorrows and the errors of the past, the anxieties of the unsatisfied desire, and the suddenness of resentment are no more.'

If *Brahman* is the eternal reality and we are non-different from it, birth cannot be our beginning, nor death, our end. The soul is eternal, though, it appears to be born, and later, appears to die. Birth and death relate to the integration and disintegration, respectively, of the elements that compose the physical body. These are changes that affect the body, like the growth and the decay. It is because we identify the soul with the body, on account of ignorance, that it suffers and becomes a victim of *saṁsāra*. *Mokṣa* is the final goal of man. According to the doctrine of non-duality, one need not wait till death for the attainment of salvation. *Mokṣa* is the eternal nature of the self. What prevents the soul from realizing it, is its own ignorance (*ajñāna*). When ignorance is dispelled through wisdom of the nature of self, one attains *mokṣa*. This is known as *jīvan-mukti* or *parā-mukti*.

It is said that the true nature of the self is 'Pure Consciousness'. But, unfortunately, this is not how we see ourselves. We, through ignorance, identify the body, mind and the intellect along with their functions and modifications as the true nature of the self and say, this is the Reality.

Inherent tendencies that we carry with us (*vāsanā*) are termed as impurities of the mind and these manifest themselves in the form of likes and dislikes in the world of sense objects. The purpose of Yoga is to firmly establish one's true self and is different from the practice of meditation, which helps purify the mind by eliminating the past tendencies of impurities and habitual errors.

The word *yoga* is applied in many senses in the *Bhagavad Gītā*, which, itself, is described as the Yoga-Śāstra and each chapter of this is called *yoga*, for example, Abhyāsa-Yoga, Karma-Yoga, Jñāna-Yoga, Bhakti-Yoga, etc. The word *yoga* can be traced as early as in the *Ṛgveda* (V.81.1) where it speaks of concentrating the mind. This word *yoga* occurs in some of the Upaniṣads and *Brāhmaṇa*s in the same sense in which it is employed in the Yoga-Śāstra. *Yogatattvopaniṣad* and *Śiva Saṁhitā* speaks of four *yoga*s, viz., Mantra-Yoga, Haṭha-Yoga, Laya-Yoga and Rāja-Yoga. All these occur in the system of Patañjali, but each emphasizes some particular aspect of the Yoga discipline. There are only two main systems of the Yoga, viz., the one expounded in the *Yoga-Sūtra* and its *Bhāṣya* by Vyāsa and the other, dealt with in such works as the *Gorakṣaśataka* and the *Haṭhayogapradīpikā*. The difference between the two is that the *yoga* of Patañjali concentrates all its efforts on the discipline of the mind, while Haṭha-Yoga mainly concerns itself with the body (perfect body is disciplined by Yoga), its health, purity and the freedom from decay and disease. Patañjali defines *āsana* as a kind of posture that concerns with *Sthirasukha,* while Haṭha-Yoga describes many *āsana*s to remove diseases as well as deals with such processes as *dhauti, basti* and *nauli* about which Patañjali is silent. There are other differences between the Haṭha-Yoga and the Patañjali Yoga. *Haṭhayogapradīpikā* speaks about the rousing of *kuṇḍalinī* and takes it through the several *cakra*s to *brahmadvāra,* while *Yoga-Sūtra* hardly ever dilates upon *cakra*s and *nāḍī*s.[1] The ultimate aim of Yoga concerns with the final arrest of mind and this has often been admitted also by the Haṭha-Yoga.

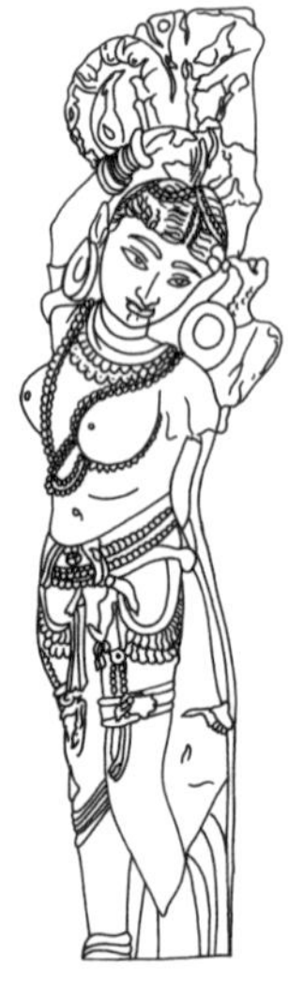

In the *Mahābhārata,* the term *yoga* has been defined as the art of following right action. Generally, right action is identified with *yama* and *niyama,* the primordial virtues propagated by each and every religion as the foundation

1. *Yoga-Sūtra,* III. 29-31.

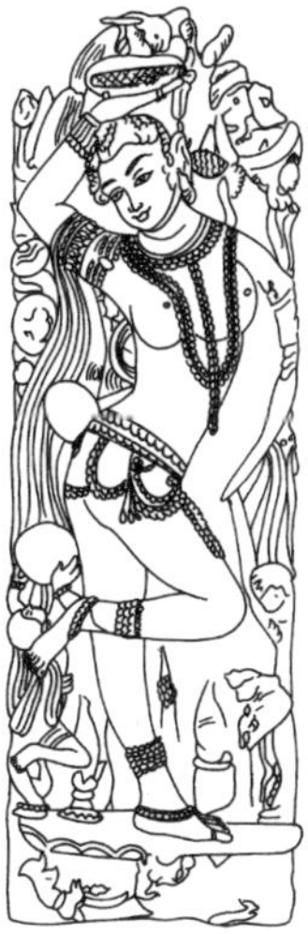

stone of spiritual life. These are based on the widely accepted universal values. *Yama* includes non-violence, truth, non-stealing, celibacy and non-acceptance of favours whereas *niyama* prescribes steps for purification of the body and the mind, and to attain contentment, penance, taking lessons in self-realization and surrender of ego to the Absolute.

According to Buddhism, right action led by right thoughts gives rise to right mindedness and right concentration. Constant observation of the self and surrounding as a non-reactive witness is the right mindedness which produces right concentration on the part of the subject and all object like thinking, feeling, willing and right sensations and sights. This awakens within us a conducive orientation and attitude to action.

The root cause for all our sufferings lies in blinding attachment to the cherished expectations of life. All relationships are transitory. No relationship lasts forever. Our relationship with our body is not eternal. Similarly, our relationship with a particular space and time is transitory. Relationship with another individual is also not lasting. Every union ends in separation. Despite we realize this truth, we continue to suffer in sorrow. This is because we know it only verbally, without having experienced its truth. Hence, practice of *niṣkāma karma* Yoga is the way to liberate the soul from human bondage of the body and the mind. While our endeavour with an eye to the effect of the same is wrong actions which lead us to bondage, right actions, without any attachment to the fruit of the *karma* (action), unfold and faciliate flowering of our true self. At this stage, action and inaction both lose their significance in life and elevate us to a state of meditation.

In India, a highly well-developed civilization had been flourishing for centuries. It is the religious life, in the period between 750 BC to 320 BC which displayed certain characteristic features. The first and the foremost is the introduction of the image of Gods for worship and meditation of the Supreme Being was thought possible only when He was endowed with a form. There was the belief that the form of Supreme Being, as He manifests Himself, should be worshipped according to the rites prescribed. The Vedas were considered as the infallible source of spiritual truth, and the rituals prescribed therein, were considered as the sole means of salvation or emancipation. The essential elements common between the two theistic religions, viz., Śaivism and Vaiṣṇavism, are *bhakti* (devotion) and *prasāda* (divine grace). *Bhakti* means intense love and devotion of the worshipper to his beloved god, even to the extent of complete self-surrender. There, *bhakti* is aimed at for a higher cause. Devotion is essentially of the nature of love. It is not a mere physical attraction to a person or thing nor is it just an intellectual appreciation of the qualities of the desired object. The abode of love is not the body or intellect, it is the heart. That is why it is not possible to understand the nature of love by intellectual analysis or by logical reasoning. *Bhakti* is devotion to a higher cause. It uplifts us and makes us unselfish. It helps us rise above petty limitations and sacrifices even the ego (the sense of 'I' and 'Mine') for the object of love. Where there is love, nothing else is required. Devotion to the Absolute is the nectar of this knowledge. The *prasāda* means the grace of god which brings salvation to the devotee. This is known as the Bhakti-Yoga or Bhāva-Yoga.

India is a land of many religious faiths, and even within the same faith, there have been many sects and sub-sects, often, in sharp differences with one another, irrespective of beliefs and tenets. All the Indian religions are known to have adopted common norms for the expression of their thoughts and beliefs through art. Religious differences have hardly been able to divert these norms from their logical course. The norms remain the same for all religions

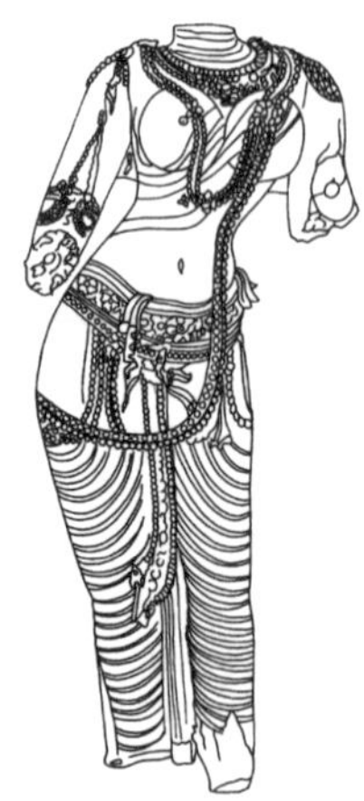

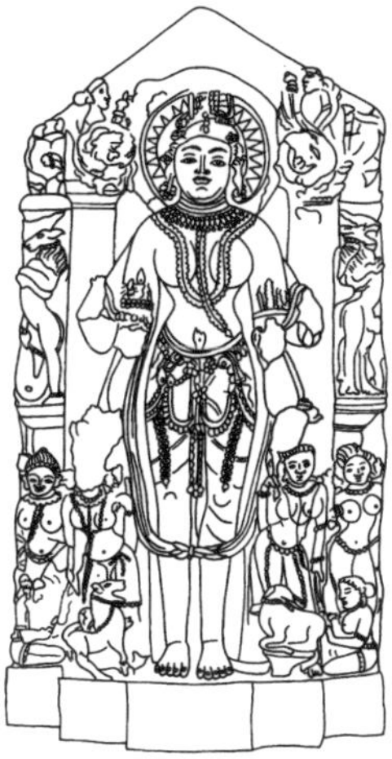

irrespective of the subjects depicted. Indian art depicts life as interpreted by religion and philosophy. Art, in all periods of development, was closely associated with the rhythm of life, including the life of the gods and all the living beings on earth.

The image or icon or any visible deity has been the medium through which a devotee could transfer his devotion to his god. The deities are a product of psychic exercises of the most subtle character and visualized by the worshipper in the course of intense meditation. The psychic exercises are called *sādhanā* which has a special bearing on the history and evolution of icons. The *bhakti* gives a significant impetus to the construction of images and houses of gods. Emotional attachment with the God was considered as the road to salvation (*mokṣa*), the easiest one, and a path open to all. Devotion popularized image-worship, as meditation of the unmanifested Absolute was considered a difficult process.

Indian art is so intimately associated with Indian religion and philosophy that it is difficult to appreciate fully unless one has some knowledge of ideals that governed the Indian mind. Yoga has played an important role in the formation of the imagery of the gods and goddesses and is common to Hinduism, Jainism and Buddhism. All the Jaina *tīrthaṅkara*s and the historical Buddha always represented as ideal *yogī*s engaged in meditation, seated or standing. More significantly, since Yoga is considered the best means of attaining control over both body and the mind, the relaxed body of a perfect *yogī* is considered the best ideal form for the sculptor. They exude a vitality that emanates from inner tranquillity rather than physical power and the achievement of this inner harmony is one of the principal aims of *yoga*.

However, secular and religious sculpture reflects an ambivalence that is characteristic of all Indian mythology, literature and art and seemingly appears as a celebration of the sensuous even though the intent is spiritual. The gods and goddesses are spiritual entities but their forms are often sensuous, if not erotic; youthfulness is also regarded as an essential feature, and indeed, this is true of all the Indian gods and goddesses. The glorification of youth and sensuousness remained pivotal in all religious sculptures. Perhaps, the semi-nude form of the female is desirable and seen more to celebrate life than to renounce it. The frank eroticism of some images, particularly *yakṣīs*, (celestial nymphs) and *mithuna* (lovers in dalliance) play a pervasive role in embellishing the temple. It may be noted that an architect of an ancient temple did not take the *mithuna*s to mean only a human couple but sexual pairs of all kinds of being were in his mind. But this symbol was generalized, in most cases, and was accommodated in all the three religions, the Hindu, the Jaina or the Buddhist. From the very earliest times, the *mithuna*s have been appropriated by the Buddhist builders at Sāñcī, Bharhut, Karle, Kanheri and Nāsik. Their presence in numerous Hindu temples did not make it peculiarly a Hindu (brāhmaṇa) conception, either. The temples of Rājpūtāna offer numerous evidences of motifs by the Jaina builders.

The disciplined body and conquered mind happen to be the characteristics of the art of the Gupta period. The relief sculptures of a little earlier date in Amarāvatī and, particularly, of Nāgārjunakoṇḍa revealed all the dramatist personae as seemingly engaged in enjoying their life for the last time before entering into a stage of detachment and discipline. The treatment rendered in art is, no doubt, artistic and poetic. But we must remember that such amorous motifs were all placed just next to Buddhist scenes. There must have been something in the social climate of the time that encouraged the use of erotic motifs as a form of embellishment in religious art. The idea was to indicate the impermanence of physical beauty and futilities of worldly attachments. The quest was for the ultimate truth, beauty.

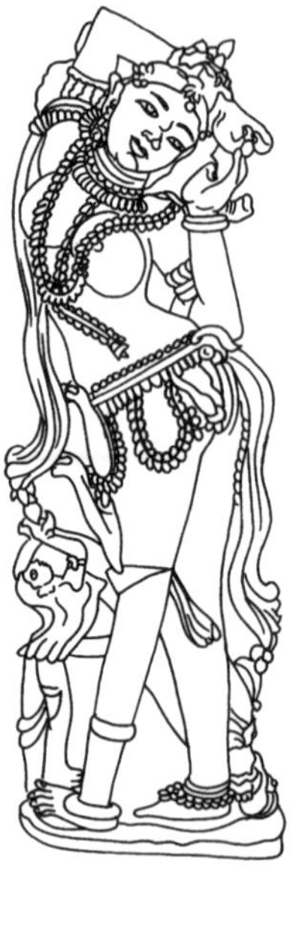

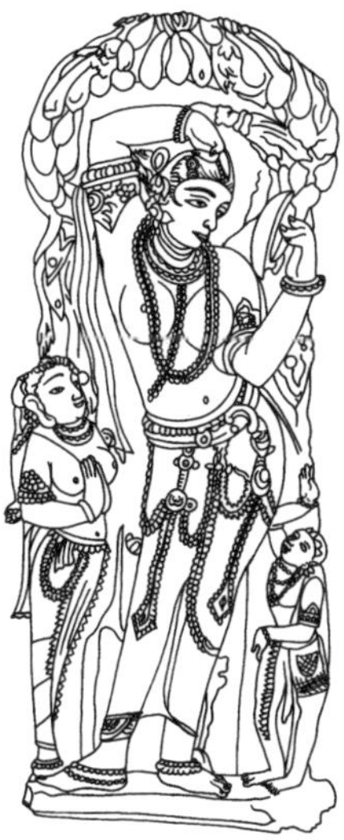

The relationship between nature and art, in this context, may be relevant. It can be stated that the primary concern of the Indian sculpture is with the human body, mostly as a divine manifestation. Whenever a form in nature is employed in sculpture, it is used as a symbol; almost every deity is placed upon a lotus; flowers and their petals often served as the symbol of grace and beauty or of fertility. Generally, when a tree is associated with woman, whether mortal or divine, it announces the intimate relationship between nature and the woman and also functions as a fertility-symbol.

Many religious and philosophical movements contribute their different hues to the multi-coloured canvas of the ancient culture of India. The ultimate aim of life is to attain salvation (*mokṣa*) and art is one such means of attaining this aim. So much ado has been made about the frank eroticism of the sculptures of the religious shrines that, perhaps, now the time has come for a valid observation. A creative sensuousness has always been regarded as an important source of energy, of vital urge in life, and this is as much true in religious and spiritual quest as in the quest for expression; and the *maithuna* idea of this *sādhanā* finds most creative expression. Indeed, it was accepted as a normal and essential expression of life without any compunction, attached to it, as depicted in the temples of Purī and Koṇārka, where, admittedly, the eroticism is not only in the sensuous suggestiveness but the sexual act has been expressed in a wide variety of poses and postures. Perhaps, the artists got the inspiration from Vātsyāyan's *Kāma-Sūtra* which appears to have influenced the art of that period and no creative imagination had remained unaffected by the tenderness, brought to human relations. Certainly, the odour and sweat of sex is made sacred, and no shame is attached to it! This blissful condition comes to be epitomized in the word *ānanda* and in the Upaniṣads the essence of all human knowledge is comprehended under this concept, identified with the Ultimate Reality.

1

Yoga

THE word *yoga* occurs in the *Ṛgveda* in many senses, such as yoking or harnessing, achieving the unachieved, connection and the like. The word *yoga,* however, became gradually rarer and rarer in its original meaning as it began, more often, to be used in the sense of yoking the senses.

With the development of philosophic ideas in the *Ṛgveda,*[1] we find that religious austerities were gaining a prominent place among the thinking people. In the Upaniṣads,[2] we get the word *tapas* in the sense of austerity and meditative abstractions, productive of mighty achievement. In the light of the growth of these ideas of asceticism and self-control, it is easy to understand that, when the force of the flying passion was felt to be as uncontrollable as that of a spirited steed, the word *yoga,* which was originally applied to the control of steeds, was applied to the control of the senses. The senses were regarded as uncontrollable, as evident from passages of *Kaṭha*[3] and *Maitrāyaṇī Upaniṣads*.[4]

Yoga means a permanent state of concentration which removes all our afflictions and eradicates all mental

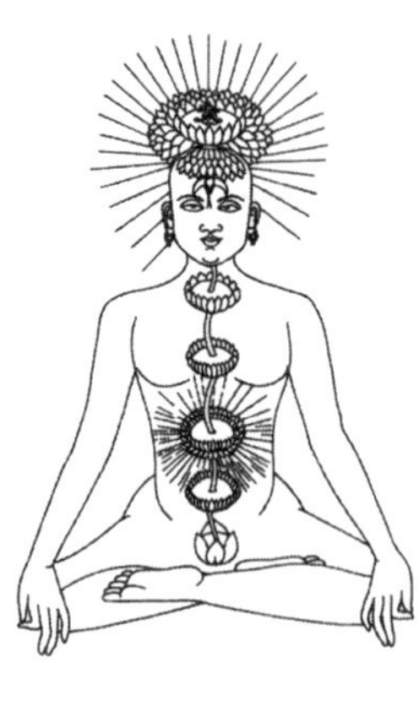

---

1. *Ṛgveda*, X.129.
2. *Chāndogya Upaniṣad*, 3.17; *Kaṭha Upaniṣad*, 6.11 and 18; *Śvetāśvara Upaniṣad*, 2.8 and 2.11; *Bṛhadāraṇyaka Upaniṣad*, 1.2.6, 3.8.10 and 4.4.12; *Taittirīya*, 1.9.1, 3.1.1, 3.2.1, and 3.3.1.
3. *Kaṭha Upaniṣad*, 3.4.
4. *Maitrāyaṇī Upaniṣad*, 6.2.

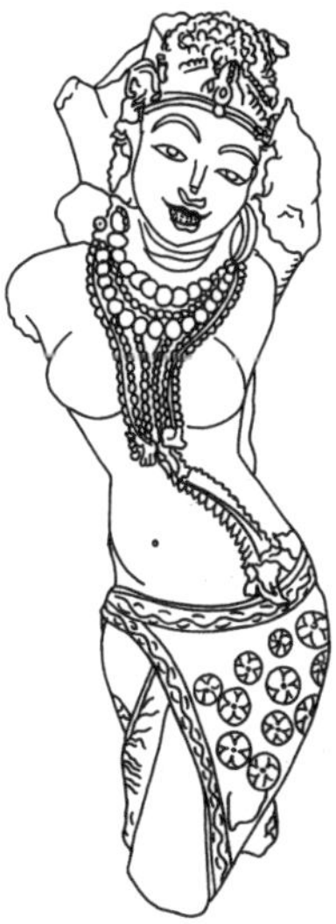

complexes and root-instincts, that serve as the seed for further recurrence of life and suffering.[5] *Yoga* is the art of opening unconscious parts of our being, which will enable us to feel the direct touch of our cosmic consciousness and, sometimes, inspire us with the touch. *Yoga* makes our dynamic nature finer and more rhythmical and, naturally, a vaster comprehension and a wider power is the result. But the goal cannot be attained unless there is a greater concentration or consciousness. This alone can help us to achieve its transcendent-power. Generally, in the Upaniṣads, *yoga* is treated as a preliminary discipline for concentration and clarification of the mental being. But, it soon reveals finer psychic movements towards enriching life and unless the seeking soul distinguishes between the values of conscience and power, the soul could be carried away by the power. Hence, a constant watch and a strict discipline for the absolute Truth alone can keep the seeker safe and save him from the domination of the power. Knowledge provides the surest anchor to save us from the labyrinth of power.

Therefore, one can say that *yoga* is a term for those physical and psychical processes which are used to discover man's inner essence. It is the method by which the mental and intellectual feeling (*cittavṛtti*) is controlled and conditioned so that the aspirant is able to dissolve his own self into the absolute, the supreme reality as conceived by him, and this state is called *samādhi*.

The *yoga* which, after weakening the hold of the afflictions and causing the real truth to dawn upon our mental vision, gradually, leads us towards the attainment of our final goal. This is possible only for the last two kinds of minds. Here, also, there are two kinds — first *samprajñāta* (cognitive) and the second *asamprajñāta* (ultra-cognitive). The *samprajñāta yoga* is that in which the mind concentrates

5. *Tattva-Vaiśāradī*, 1.1.2.

upon some object, external or internal, in such a way that it does not oscillate or move from one object to another, but remains fixed and settled in the object that it holds before itself. At first, the *sādhaka* holds a gross material object before his view, but when he can make himself steady in doing this, he tries with the subtle *tanmātra*s, the five causes of the grosser elements, and when he is successful in this, he takes his internal senses as his object and, last of all, when he has fully succeeded in these attempts, he takes the great egohood as his object, in which state, his object gradually loses all its determinate character and he is said to be in a state of suppression in himself, although devoid of any object. The second stage, like the other previous states of the *samprajñāta* type, is a positive state of the mind and not a state of mere vacuity of objects or negativity. In this state, all determinate characters of the state disappear and their potencies only remain alive. In the first stage of a *yogin* practising *samādhi*, the conscious state of the lower stages often intervene but, gradually, as the mind becomes fixed, the potencies of the lower stages are overcome by the potencies of this stage, so that the mind flows in a calm current and, at last, the higher *prajñā* dawns, whereupon the potencies of this state also are burnt and extinguished, and the *citta* returns back to its own primal cause, *prakṛti* and *puruṣa* attains absolute freedom.

The goal of life means a long course of discipline to reach it. This discipline is presently briefly referred to in the Sāṁkhya system but it is fully described in the system of Yoga. The discipline comprises of what are described as the eight *aṅga*s of Yoga (Yogāṅgas). These Yogāṅgas not only remove the impurities of the mind but help it further by removing obstacles in the way of attaining of the highest perfection of discriminative knowledge. These are (1) *yama* (self-restraint), (2) *niyama* (observance), (3) *āsana* (posture), (4) *prāṇāyāma* (regulation of breath), (5) *pratyāhāra* (withdrawal of the senses of obstruction), (6) *dhāraṇā*

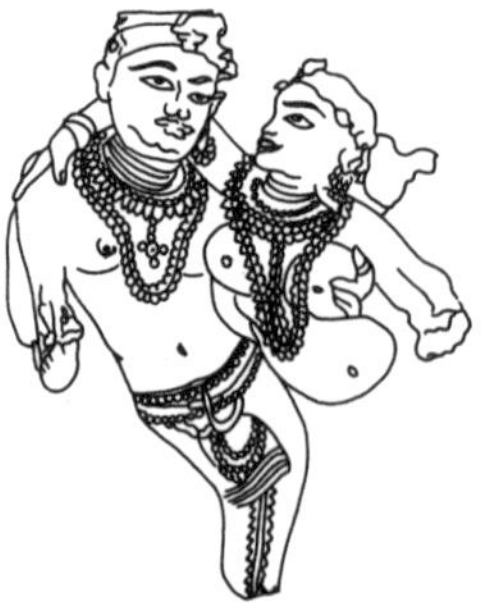

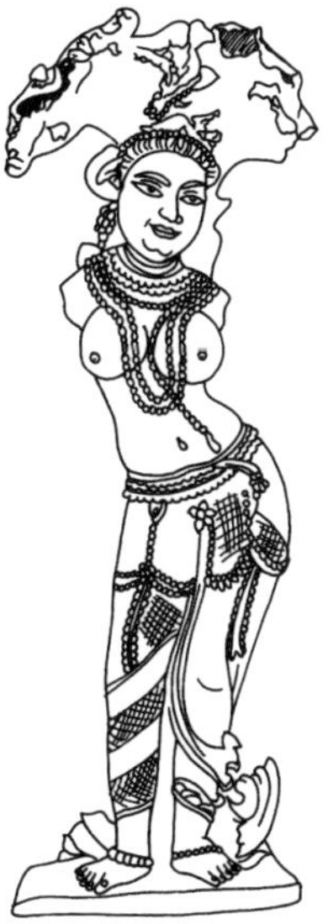

(steadying the mind or concentration), (7) *dhyāna* (contemplation or meditation), (8) *samādhi* (trance-contemplation).

In order to understand these better and ascertain their relative values for a man striving to attain the highest perfection of *yoga*, the following observations are made :

The first is concerned with the right direction of the will and represents the attainment of the goal, as distinguished from the ultimate. It relates to the acquisition of virtues comprised of in the first two stages of *aṅgas* of yogic discipline, namely *yama* and *niyama*.[6] The former is mostly negative and consists of non-injury (*ahiṁsā*), truth-speaking (*satya*), abstention from stealing or misappropriation of others' property (*asteya*), celibacy (*brahmacarya*) and disowning of possessions (*aparigraha*). The latter is mostly positive and includes purity (*śauca*), contentment (*santoṣa*), right aspiration (*tapas*), study (*svādhyāya*) and devotion to God (*iśvara-praṇidhāna*).

The second stage of discipline, consisting of the remaining six *aṅgas*, is for specific cultivation of the power of the mental concentration. Of the six *aṅgas*, the first three are devised to secure control of the physical frame with a view to faciliating the control of the mind. They refer to right body-posture, regulation of breath and withdrawal of the senses from their respective objects. Of the succeeding three, two assist in getting a direct but gradual mastery over the ever-fitful mind.[7] The object chosen for meditation may be any in this stage. The last consists, essentially, in the direct meditation on the Sāṁkhya truth. When success, in this fianl stage, is achieved all operations of the internal

---

6. These *yamas* and *niyamas*, to be described, are called *karma/kṛyā-yoga*, by the performance of which men become fit to rise, gradually, to the sate of *jñāna-yoga* by *samādhi* and to attain *kaivalya*.

7. The first five are known as exterior methods (*bahiraṅga*) mainly concerned with the body and the last three are inner methods (*antaraṅga*) employed for development of mind.

organs are suspended and the spirit returns to its true self, so to speak. The disciple, then, becomes a *jīvanmukta*. He may, thereafter, continue to live on the earth but, virtually, divorced from *prakṛti* and, therefore, remains far from passion, pain and guilt.

The *yoga* can, therefore, be best described as a manual of psychological ethics, intended for developing the powers of the mind with the ultimate object of seeing through the futility of exercising them in spiritual interests. Once it is recognized that the soul is different from matter in all its form, unconscious and pseudo-psychical, there will be no inclination to attend to the objects of nature or to indulge in any kind of thinking, feeling or action. The object of *yoga* psychology was to teach the way to self-knowledge and everything else, including devotion to god, was subservient.

The Yoga system of achieving salvation is a bold man's creed although there is a theistic reference in the system. The ultimate effect of all processes of thinking does not differ very much from that in the Buddhism and the Jainism where the theistic implication is absent. The Yoga system insists on certain fundamental traits for achieving success in spiritual culture. These are *śraddhā* (faith in the efficacy of concentration), *vīrya* (increased effort or energy, arising out of the belief), *smṛti* (mindfulness or capacity to call up the desired object before the mind repeatedly by that energy), *samādhi* (concentration of the mind on a single object with a view to stopping all dispersiveness) and, lastly, *prajñā* (insight into the nature of things by concentration).[8] This list, is to be found in Buddhistic enumeration also and, apparently, comprised of those factors, which were regarded as indispensable for narrowing down thought to a single object. They are not processes but faculties which the

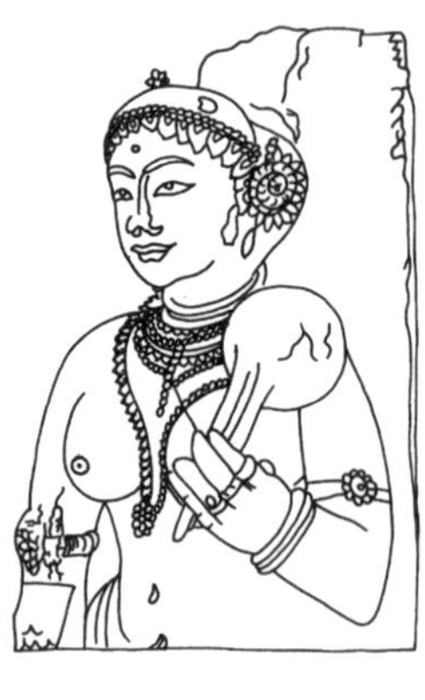

8. S.N. Dasgupta, *Yoga-Philosophy* (in relation to the other systems), New Delhi, reprint, 1979.

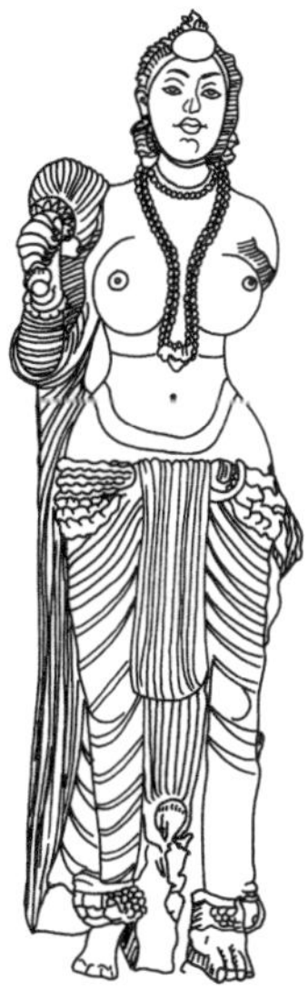

individual must possess in order to attain discriminative knowledge.

The Yogāṅgas (help to *yoga*) represent the method of getting rid of the distempers of the soul in a progressive fashion. Therefore, bodily infirmity, unsteadiness of the limits and breathing upset the mind and render concentration difficult or impossible — these must be controlled and eradicated. Cleanliness (*śauca*) of the body, as of the mind, is, therefore, necessary for concentration. Then, again, the *yogin* must learn to control his limbs — he must try to sit straight like the trunk of a tree (*sthāṇu*), with the spine, the neck and the head, in one line, and assume certain postures (*āsana*) that are favourable to concentration. The *Yoga-Sūtra* recommends the practice of controlled breathing (*prāṇāyāma*) with the ultimate object of suspending it for as long a period as possible. The breathing (both in and out) should affect as small an area as possible, its frequency should be diminished and its duration should be expanded.[9] It must be remembered that while *prāṇāyāma* is practised, the mind must be fixed by *dhyāna* (contemplation) and *dhāraṇā* (fixed attention) to the same object, external or

---

9. Originally breath was controlled because it disturbed the attention and the control of breath not only made the mind attentive but also scoured away the *karma* (activity) that veiled discriminative knowledge. Still, even in the *Yoga-Sūtra* an exaggerated importance is given to breath-control for purposes of concentration and ultimate salvation is noticeable. This may be reminiscent of the Upaniṣadic view that man is continually offering sacrifice to the gods through breathing and that all the scriptures were breathed out by the Absolute Being; in fact, in later literature, we are told that, when inhaling, a man makes the sound *saḥ*, and when exhaling, he emits the sound *haṁ*, and, in this way, he is unwittingly repeating the formula (*ajapā-japa*) that the *jīvātman* is identical with the *paramātman* (*so'haṁ*, or *haṁ saḥ*) without intermission. Thus the regulation of breath was not the primary motive of *prāṇāyāma* in the *Yoga-Sūtra*.

10. *Maitrāyaṇī Upaniṣad* (Cowell's edition, Ch. VI, p. 129) where the six *aṅgas* are described as *pratyāhāra*, *dhyāna*, *prāṇāyāma*, *dhāraṇā*, *tarka* and *samādhi*.

internal. When the *sādhaka* almost loses himself in the object, the ultimate goal of the process of concentration is reached, namely, *samādhi*[10] (concentration). The distinction of these three (*dhyāna, dhāraṇā* and *samādhi*) is so small that the *Yoga-Sūtra* calls the three together *saṁyama* (constraint) and lays down that, in proportion, as constraint becomes stable, concentrated insight (*samādhi prajñā*) becomes clear. These three represent the direct aids to conscious-concentration (*samprajñāta samādhi*) as compared with the other five aids, namely — *yama, niyama, āsana, prāṇāyāma* and *pratyāhara*.[11] Therefore, the Yoga can be described as a manual of psychological ethics, intended for development of the mental powers.

In the Yoga psychology, there have been five planes of minds which are technically known as the five *citta-bhūmis*, also described by the *Bhāṣya* and there are commentaries upon their fitness for *yoga*, leading to *kaivalya*.[12] These are:

(a) *Kṣipta* (wandering), *rajas*

(b) *Mūḍha* (forgetful), *tamas*

(c) *Vīkṣipta* (occasionally-steady)

(d) *Ekāgra* (one-pointed)

(f) *Niruddha* (restrained).

The *kṣipta* state is the ordinary unsteady state of mind which is always changing from one object to another by the rise of passion, because it is being always moved by the *rajas*.

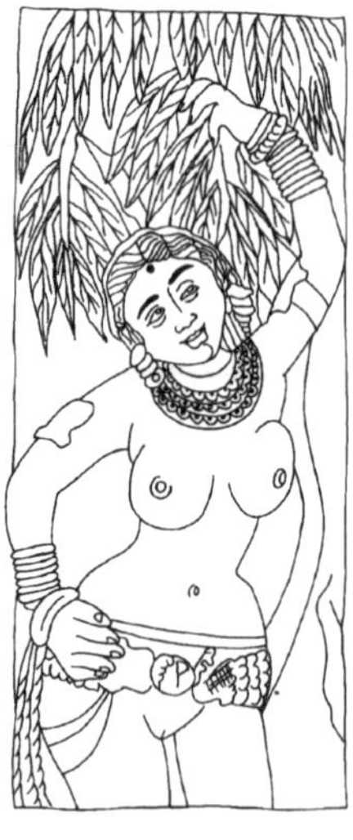

11. It will be observed that in the Patañjali system *yama, niyama* and *āsana* are physical and moral discipline for the control of the mind and *pratyāhāra, dhāraṇā, dhyāna*, etc., are purely psychological processes for the final concentration and arrest of the mind, all these processes are associated in the Nātha cult with the process of retaining the *mahārasa* and the yogic regulation of its secretion for transubstantiation of the body and thus attaining a life eternal.

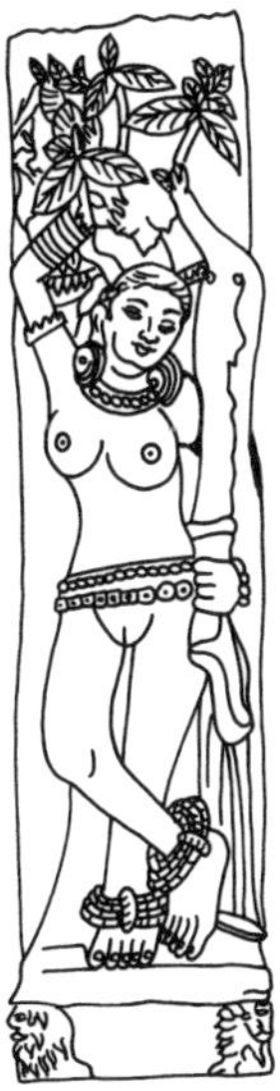

The second state is *mūḍha-citta,* in which the mind, under the sway of some strong sensation of emotion, lies infatuated, as it were. In this state, *citta* is overpowered by *tamas* or passion (the gross material stuff) like that of anger, when the mind falls asleep or swoons, as it were.

The third state is the state of *vikṣpita* or occasionally-steady *citta* or distracted. It is that mind, which is distinguished from the *kṣipta* state by the possibility, therein, of temporary arrest of the mental states.[13] It is the momentary steadiness that the mind may have amidst its unsteady changes.[14] None of these three — *kṣipta, mūḍha* and *vikṣipta citta* can hope to attain that contemplative concentration, called *yoga.*

Ekāgra (one-pointed) is that kind of mind in which true knowledge of the nature of reality is present and affliction, due to nescience or false knowledge, is occurs and the mind is better equipped to attain the *nirodha* (restrained) state. All these come under the *samprajñāta*[15] type (concentration on a subject of knowledge). This *ekāgra* state leads to the next stage which is the state of final arrest (*niruddha*).

The *niruddha* or restrained mind is that in which all

---

12. *Kaivalya,* absolute independence or oneness; Hajari Prasad Dvivaidi, *Nātha Sampradāya* (in Hindi), Allahabad, 1950, pp. 114 onward.
13. The exponent of Yoga have admitted the fact that it may be possible to attain a state of arrest even through some strong sensation or emotion, but that kind of arrest of mind is very transitory and, as such, falls far short of the final state of *samādhi. Samādhi* of *yoga* proper does not mean a temporary arrest of mind.
14. Surendra Natha Dasgupta, *Yoga as Philosophy and Religion,* New Delhi, 1978, p. 92.
15. The *samprajñāta* (cognitive) *yoga* is that in which the mind is concentrated upon some object, external or internal, in such a way that it does not oscillate or move from one object to another, but remains fixed and settled in the object that it holds before itself.

mental states attain an oneness in deep concentration on some particular object of meditation. This leads to *kaivalya*.[16]

Now, of the five planes (*bhūmi*) of the mind, only the last two are recognized as the *bhūmi* of *yoga* proper. Temporary arrest may be possible in the *mūḍha* and *vikṣipta* planes also, but they cannot be recognized as states of *yoga* as there is the possibility of their relapse to ordinary active state at any moment on any movement.[17] The exponent of *yoga* has admitted that it may be possible to attain a state of arrest even through some strong sensation or emotion; but that kind of arrest of mind is very transitory and, as such, falls short of the final state of *samādhi*. *Samādhi* of *yoga* proper does not mean a temporary arrest of mind, and it cannot be recognized as a state of *yoga* proper. In Yoga philosophy, it is said that when the states and processes of the mind are arrested, the *yogin* remains in his 'own true nature' (*svarūpa*), all the subjective and objective disturbances of the mid are absolutely lost in supreme realization of the bliss; we attain our true self, which is the pure state of *yoga-samādhi* (state of *yoga* arrest).[18]

16. Ordinarily, our mind is engaged in perception and inference these mental states are natural processes. These ordinary mental state are full of *rajas* and *tamas;* when these are arrested, the mind flows with an abundance of *sattva* in the *samprajñāta samādhi*. Lastly, when even *samprajñāta* state is arrested, all possible states become arrested. It is a state which is without beginning and end, a state which is free from duality. When this state is attained, the objective world disappears from view and all the aggregate elements and senses merge in it. The *sādhaka* then find himself to be the sole reality, identical with the universe, a being who is ever free.

17. If we examine the state of *samādhi* described, particularly, by the Kāśmīra School of Śaivism, we shall be tempted to say that many of these states can be classed as the *mūḍha* state of mind and only a few of them fall within the state of *ekāgra*.

18. The state of complete *samādhi* is called *para-saṁvit* (pure-consciousness). There are two degrees of *samādhi* — *savikalpa* and *nirvikalpa*. *Savikalpa* is that in which the mind is yet to transgress the limit of worldly existence and *nirvikalpa* is that in which it has been achieved with the effect that it becomes one with the subject of its contemplation.

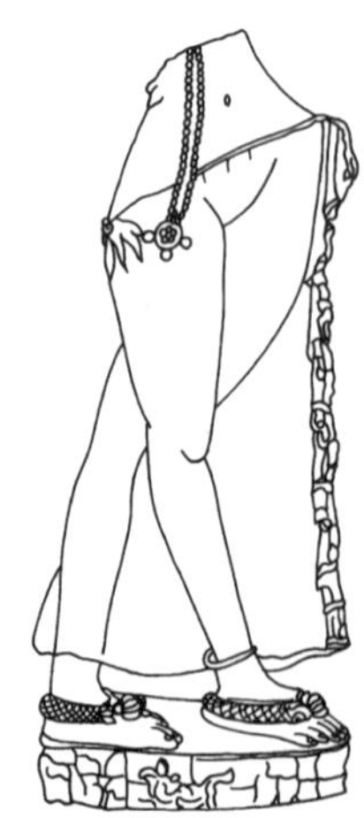

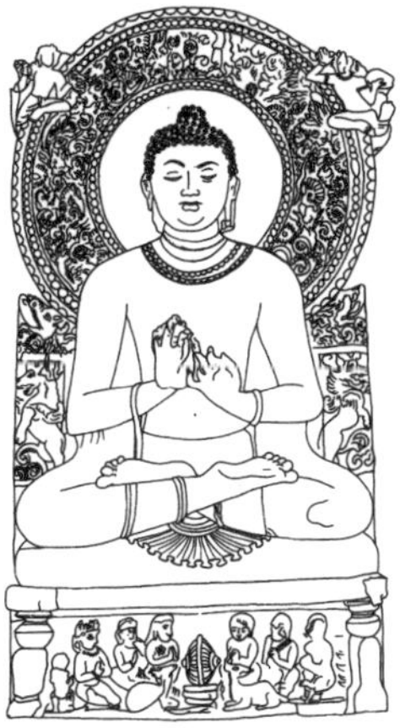

2

Practice of Yoga

Kāya-Sādhanā

KĀYA-SĀDHANĀ is a slow and gradual process of continual purification, rejuvenation and transubstantiation of the body through various yogic processes. It has been said that, through the fire of *yoga* or purifying processes of *yoga*, the ordinary body of change and decay is burnt away and from the process of purification and rejuvenation results a new immutable divine body as a transformation of the old. It has been said in *Yoga-vīja* that the perfect body of the *yogin* is subtler than the subtlest, yet grosser than the grossest; a *yogin* can transform his body according to his will and his form is above all disease and death. He can assume any form by his incomprehensible power. Liberation is not that of soul. It is of body which can be attained within the span of human life. The *sādhaka*s used the term *jīvanmukti*. It means the attainment of immortality which is possible by disciplining the body (*kāya-sādhanā*).

The principle and practice of *kāya-sādhanā* is common to all schools of esoteric Yoga. *Yoga*, in general, involves psycho-physiological processes; it is said, therefore, that higher kinds of *yoga* should never be attempted without a mature or perfect body.[1] It has been referred in a few yogic

1. What is the perfect body? It is an indestructible spiritual body, absolutely free from the principle of defilement or the principles of *aśuddha-māyā*; but it is associated with principles of *viśuddha-māyā* which prevents it from becoming absolutely static and acts as the absolutely purified dynamic principle for its further evolution through subtler stages to lead it to the final state of *parā-mukti*.

texts, that the body is of two kinds, viz., *apakva* (unripe) and *pakva* (ripe). The unripe body is the body not disciplined by *yoga*, and the ripe body is the body disciplined by *yoga*. Through the fire of *yoga* the body becomes supra-material and above all sorrows and sufferings, it is called *yoga-deha* (*yoga*-body), while the unripe material body of all ordinary persons becomes the cause of all sorrow and sufferings. A *yoga*-body, bereft of all limitations and bondage, is limitless like the sky but, purer, even than the sky. For this purpose of making the mature or perfect body, the practices of Haṭha-Yoga are to be adopted. In the *caryā*-songs, we find frequent reference to the strengthening of the *skandha*s of the elements whose aggregate constitutes the body.[2]

As this perfect body is produced through the burning away of one's physical body, through the fire of *yoga*, there is no further death (in the physical form) for him. He has no duty for his own, he is liberated, while living, and is always living in his true body, which is bereft of all defilement. Such a ripe body helps the *yogin* attain the final state of *parā-mukti*.[3]

2. The entire world is made up of the five great elements (also known as five *skandha*s); they are — Earth, Water, Fire, Air and Ether. These elements are not elements in the chemical sense, rather they are states of matter. The earth-element predominates in everything that is solid in the universe, the water-element in that which is liquid, and the air-element in gases. The Ether-element is the space in which things occur, and the fire-element is the force which changes solid to liquid, and liquid to gas and vice versa. Everything in the manifested world, including the human body, is made up of these five elements. The essence of *yoga-sādhanā* is the purification of the five elements, to cleanse the impurities and make it steady.

3. Pre-eminently, a Śaivite School in Nātha Cult aims at the attainment of Śivahood or the State of Maheśvara. Immortality is recognized to be the quintessence of the ulitmate nature of the Lord; to attain the state of *parā-mukti* in and through the state of *jīvan-mukti* is, therefore, virtually the same as to attain the state of Maheśvara.

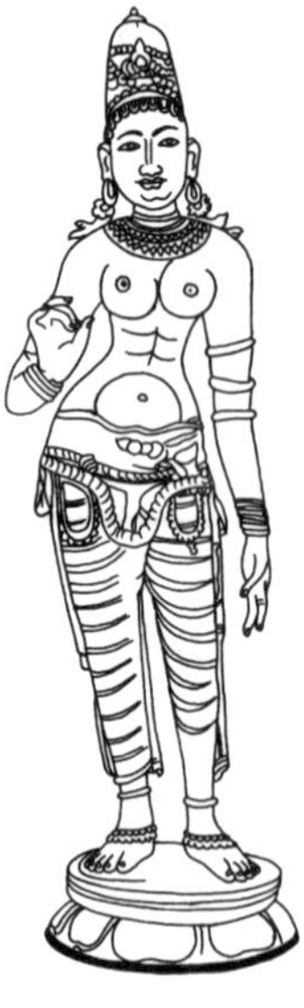

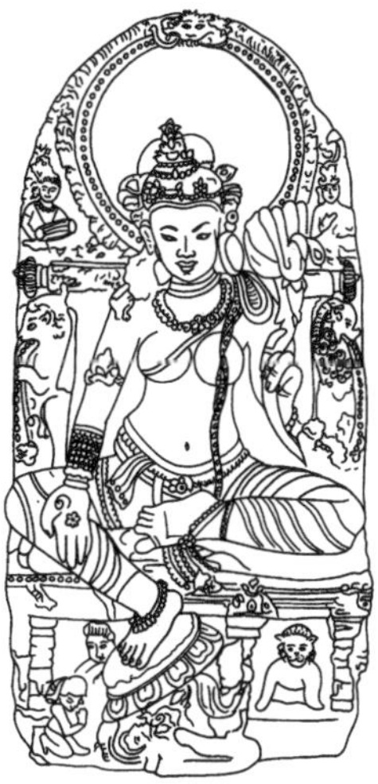

Yoga is, generally, classified into four categories — Mantra-Yoga, Laya-Yoga, Haṭha-Yoga and Rāja-Yoga.[4] Each of these forms has eight subservient parts, called eight limbs of Yoga, which are known as *aṣṭāṅga-yoga*. They are *yama, niyama, āsana, prāṇāyāma, pratyāhāra, dhāraṇā, dhyāna* and *samādhi*. The first five are known as the exterior methods, mainly concerned with the body and the last three are the inner methods, employed for the development of the mind.

Yama is abstinence from evil propensities by which the mind is disturbed while *niyama* is commitment to certain moral values by which the mind is elevated and conditioned for some higher attainment. *Āsana* is the posture of body, a physical disciplinary method to make the body fit for controlling senses while *prāṇāyāma* is breath-control needed for the same purpose. *Pratyāhāra* is restraint and subjection of the senses to the mind. *Dhāraṇā* is the holding or fixing the mind on a particular object of thought. *Dhyāna* is concentration of the mind through which is acquired mental realization. These are of two kinds — *saguṇa* (meditation on a form) and *nirguṇa* (in which the self is its own object). *Samādhi* is the ecstasy resulting from the union of the individual soul with the ultimate reality. The state of complete *samādhi* is called *parā-saṁvit* or pure-consciousness.[5] There are two degrees of *samādhi* — *savikalpa*, in which the mind is yet to transgress the limit of worldly existence, and *nirvikalpa* in which this has been achieved with the effect that it becomes one with the subject of its contemplation.

---

4. In *Yogaśikhopaniṣad*, besides these four Yogas, Bhāvanā-Yoga and Sahaja-Yoga are also added.

5. The Supreme realization, known as *mahā-sukha*, becomes a lulling- sleep of the senses or something like a swoon. It will be a mistake to confuse this state of swoon with the state of *mahā-sukha*. It is pointed out in *Rati-vajra* that, if the body and the mind fall into a swoon while practising of *yoga*, how can there be perfection of *yoga*? Therefore, the *sādhaka* has been advised to acquire a perfect body (*yoga-deha*) before entering on the yogic process for the attainment of *mahā-sukha*.

Mantra-Yoga

Mantra means the mystic sound or the ultimate reality in the form of sound.[6] As the Mantra-Yoga contains all the secrecy of the potency of sound, this can be awakened and perceived through a variety of practices. It comprises all those forms of *sādhanā* in which the mind is controlled by means of its own object. The universe is *nāma-rūpātmaka*, made up of name and form, and the nature of mind is to adjust or modify itself into the form it perceives. In Mantra-Yoga the aspirant is selective about the object of his contemplation. This is called *saguṇa* or *sthūla-dhyāna* of the gods in images, emblems, pictures, *maṇḍala, yantra, mudrā*, etc. It is the simplest form of Yoga.

The *japa* of the *mantra* does not mean the mere chanting or the muttering of *mantra,* it is as per the School of the Mantra-Yoga, a yogic process for controlling the vital sound with the help of *mantra*s. In Mantra-Yoga some *mantra*s, as for example, *oṁ,* containing within it the parts of *a, u* and *ṁ*, are divided conveniently into three parts of the process of *prāṇāyāma*, viz., *pūraka, kumbhaka* and *recaka*. Thus, here, in the *pañca-karma,*[7] the *japa mantra* is *oṁ, āḥ, huṁ* and to mutter them in the yogic process, according to their meaning, is called *vajra-japa*.[8] It is said in Yoga that the *oṁ* creates all beings,[9] *āḥ* preserves them and *huṁ* destroys them;

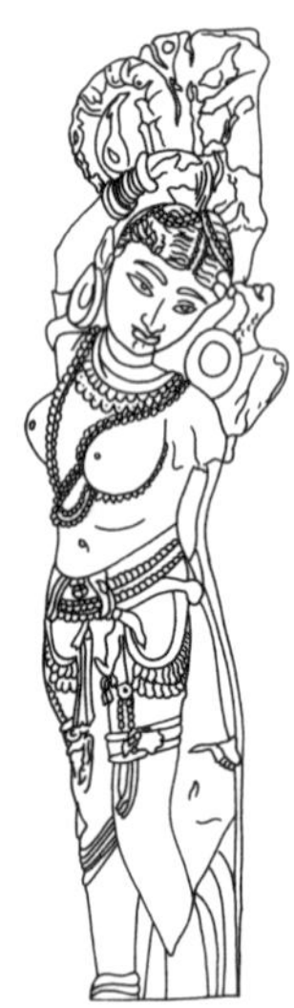

6. Mysticism, by its very nature, transcends sectarianism and regionalism in the highest stages of its development.

7. In the *pañca-karma,* the vital wind has been described as the vehicle (*vāhana*) for our defiled nature (*prakṛti*) and the *vāyu* (wind) is described as the root of all the principles of defilement and as such the root cause of the *saṁsāra* or the cycle of birth and death.

8. In the *Vajra-japa,* we find that *mantra-tattva* is nothing but the *vāyu-tattva* (air element or the science of the vital wind). This *vāyu-tattva* comprises within it the five *tattva*s (which, when combined together, constitute the ultimate truth).

9. *Oṁ,* the cosmic sound, is a combination of three syllables *a, u* and *ṁ*, that represent three phases of the cosmic cyle —

→

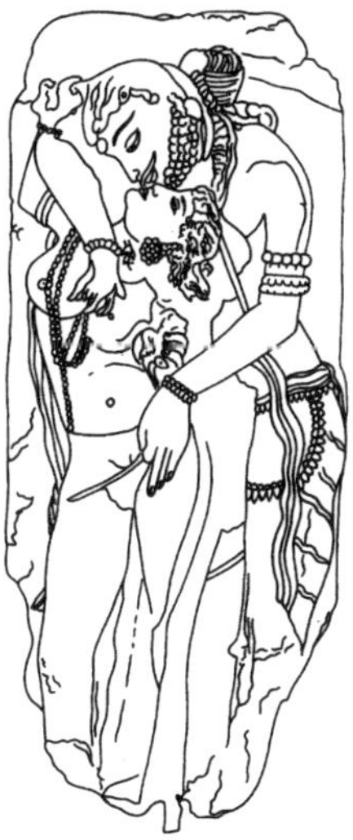

therefore *oṁ* will mean the inhalation, *aḥ* the suspension and *huṁ* the exhalation. Thus the *vajra-japa* seems to be nothing but *prāṇāyāma,* associated with the Mantra-Yoga for the control of the vital sound; the control of the vital sound is to control the mind, and to control the mind and to destroy it is to realize the essencelessness of the *dharma*s.

The realization of the meaning of the *mantra*s (as pure negation) helps the *sādhaka* to realize, in pure intuition, the nature of the *dharma*s as essenceless. But through this negation of all meanings of the *mantra*s a unique transcen-

→ creation, preservation and dissolution — condensed into a single unit, *oṁ*. This word first appears in the Upaniṣad as a mystic monosyllable and is regarded as the object of the most profound religious meditation. In *Māṇḍūkya Upaniṣad,* it is stated that this syllable is all that has been and that which is said to be, and, that all is *oṁ*. *Oṁ* is taken to be made up of three letters or quarters, the *a*; is *vaiśvānara,* the spirit of the waking soul, in the waking world, *u* is *taijasa,* the spirit of the dreaming soul in the world of dreams and *ṁ* is *prajñā,* the spirit of sleeping and undreaming soul; and the whole *śabda* (word) is said to be unknowable, unspeakable, into which the whole world passes away; above duality. It is usually called *praṇava.* The primal sound is the basis of cosmic evolution. The *oṁ* is the symbol of seven *tattva* located in the seven *cakra* on the *suṣumnā* line, inside the back bone. The *oṁ* represents in the different stages of creation from the subtlest to the grossest. These seven stages of creation are *a, u, ṁ, nāda, bindu, kāla* (time) and *kālātīta* (timelessness). The *a* of *oṁ* is *pṛthvī-tattva* (earth-element) and its seat is in the *mulādhāra-cakra* and it is identical with the creative principle of the universe. The *u* of *oṁ* is *jala-tattva* (water-element) and its seat is in the *svādhiṣṭhāna-cakra* and it is identical with the sustaining principle of the universe (Viṣṇu); the *ṁ* of *oṁ* is *teja-tattva* (fire-element) and its seat is in the *maṇipūra-cakra* and it is identical with the destructive principle of the universe (Rudra), the *nāda* or *oṁ* is *vāyu-tattva* (air-element) and its seat is in the *anāhata-cakra* and it is identical with *īśvara* (god); the *bindu* of *oṁ* is *ākāśa-tattva* (space-element) and its seat is the *viśuddha-cakra* and it is identical with Maheśvara; the *kāla* of *oṁ* is the *prajñā-cakra* and it is identical with Paraśiva, and *kālātīta* of *oṁ* is the *sahasrāra* and it is identical with *Para-Brahman*. The seven *cakra*s, mentioned here, are the seven stages of realization of all-embracing *oṁ*. The object of realization of *mulādhāra-cakra* is the awakening of the *kuṇḍalinī śakti* and the means to attain this *śaktī* is Mantra-Yoga.

dental, immutable meaning is revealed to the heart of the *sādhaka*; this immutable nature is the real nature of all things.

As per *Yoga-Śikhopaniṣad*, in Mantra-Yoga, it is said that when inhaling, a man makes the second *saḥ*, when exhaling he emits the sound *haṁ*, and in this way he is unwittingly repeating the formula (*ajapā-japa*) : the *jīvātman* is identical with the *paramātman*; *so'haṁ* or *haṁsaḥ*, without intermission.[10] It is the ultimate reality in the form of sound.

Belief in the potency of sound or mysterious power of the sound is a social heritage with the Indian masses from the past. The term is used in Yoga or Yoga-Tantra in a variety of senses. It is the manifestation of the consciousness of the Supreme Being revealed as sound.[11] This sound is known as *nāda*. *Nāda* is conceived as *Brahman* in the form of primordial sound. The Mantra-Yoga concerns itself with the sound (*mantra*). It believes that certain special mystic forces are generated by reciting certain words (*śabda*)[12] in a certain

10. Hajari Prasad Dvivedi, *Nātha Sampradāya* (in Hindi), Allahabad 1950; pp. 127-29.

11. In the Indian philosophical tradition, sound (*śabda*) is the quality (*guṇa*) of space (*ākāśa*). This sound, when unlettered, is known as *dhvani* or *dhvanyātmaka-śabda* and, when lettered, is known as *varṇātmaka-śabda*. By mental action, such sounds are co-ordinated into words (*pada*) and sentences (*vākya*), from which a meaning (*artha*) emanates; the mind becomes the subject and the object in the cognitive process (that is, *grāhaka* and *grāhya*), revealer and revealed (*prakāśaka* and *prakāśya*), denoter and denoted (*vācaka* and *vācya*).

12. *Śabda* has four states called *parā*, *paśyanti*, *madhyamā* and *vaikharī*. *Parā* is motionless, casual sound, conceived as existing in the *kuṇḍalinī* in the *mūlādhāra-cakra* in a dreamless state of deep-sleep (*suṣupti*). *Vaikharī* is the gross-sound, the uttered-speech by which the ideas are expressed. *Paśyanti* and *madhyamā* are in between these two, the former representing a non-particularized motion (*sāmānya spanda*) and the later a cognitive aspect of mental movement.

It is said that consciousness moves as Śakti, at first, in a subtle form of mind, which, in itself, is the motionless, casual sound (*parā-śabda*); then, it assumes a general undifferentiated

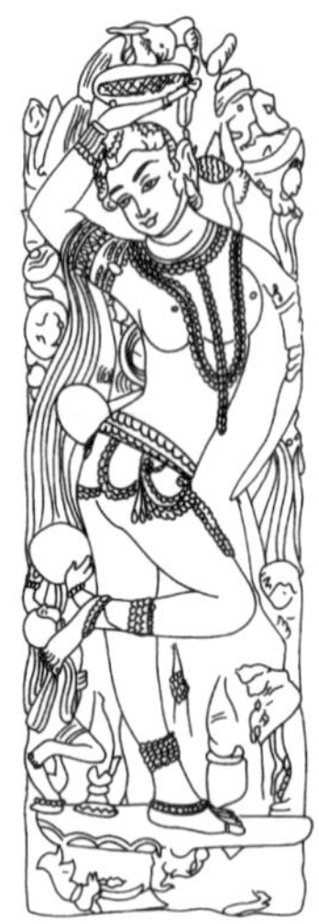

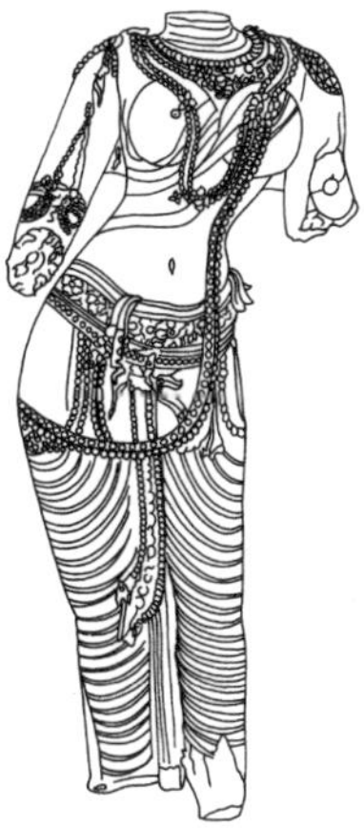

manner and they can help one to obtain, whatsover one desires, including emancipation. Thus, in respect of the muttering of these *mantras* (*śabda*), the ultimate void (*śūnyāta*) will transform herself into the particular form of god or goddess and confer infinite benefit on the reciter. This kind of belief in a syllable representing a god or goddess is a very old belief from the time of the *Āraṇyaka* and the Upaniṣad. The Mantra-Yoga is idealistic in the philosophical outlook and, therefore, lays the greatest emphasis on the final arrest of the mind and the attainment of liberation.

It is held in Yoga that when all the senses are closed and nerves controlled and the breath suspended through the yogic process there arises a spontaneous sound within, which is known as *anāhata-dhvani*. The yogic nerves are fully under control and vibration of the spontaneous sound rises tremendously.

It is held that through the practice of Mantra-Yoga and after getting success, in *sādhanā*, one's faith advances towards Haṭha-Yoga. After this, the *sādhaka* proceeds to Laya-Yoga.

Laya-Yoga

Laya means absorption of the mind or deep concentration or the state of absolute bliss. Therefore, it lays the greatest emphasis on the final arrest of the mind. The aim of this *yoga* is exclusive dissolution (*laya*), return of the seeker to the state of undifferentiated existence. It consists only of the methods for achieving this *laya* or the union of the individual with the infinite. It is an experience of eternal

---

→ movement (*paśyanti sāmānya-spanda*); then, it assumes a differentiated movement (*madhyamā viśeṣa-spanda*); and, finally, it is expressed in a clearly articulated speech (*vaikharī-spaṣṭatara-spanda*) in the gross form of language as the expression of ideas and of physical objects (*artha*).

bliss in which the mind totally merges with the Supreme Being.[13]

Laya-Yoga is also a physical process, an exercise of supersensible forces and function of the inner body. Laya-Yoga is concerned with the nerve-plexuses, and it is, thus, used as a means to stimulate the *kuṇḍalinī śakti*. In other words, it is a higher form of Haṭha-Yoga. It is specially connected with the functioning of *kuṇḍalinī*. That is why, Yoga-Tantras lay greatest emphasis on this form of Yoga. The *āsana* and *prāṇāyāma* are used to awaken *kuṇḍalinī* so that life-forces, withdrawn from *iḍā* and *piṅgalā*, may enter into the *suṣumnā* and then go, upwards, towards *brahmarandhra*. The body on each side of the spinal column is devitalized, and the whole current of life-force (*prāṇa*) is infused into it. *Prāṇa-vāyu* (life-force) which exists in the form of vital force, generates heat which causes *kuṇḍalinī* to be awakened and reach her final aim. This is possible through repeated efforts and by a gradual process. It takes years from the commencement of the practice of Laya-Yoga to lead to the union of the individual with the infinite. The *sādhaka* sits in the prescribed *āsana* and steadies his mind by the *khecarī-mudrā*. The upper part of the body is contracted so that the upward breath is checked. By this concentration the air so inhaled is prevented from escape. The air, so checked, goes downwards. This motion is again checked by the contraction of the anal muscle. The air thus stored becomes an instrument to animate the *kuṇḍalinī*. The uncoiled *kuṇḍalinī*, at first, enters the *citriṇī nāḍī* and then pierces, in that *nāḍī*, each of the lotuses, and, thereby, absorbs into itself the *tattva*s which are the five elements and their modifications. In the Laya-Yoga there is gradual process of involution of the gross world with its elements into its cause. Each gross element (*mahābhūta*) together with the subtle (*tanmātra*) from which it proceeds and the

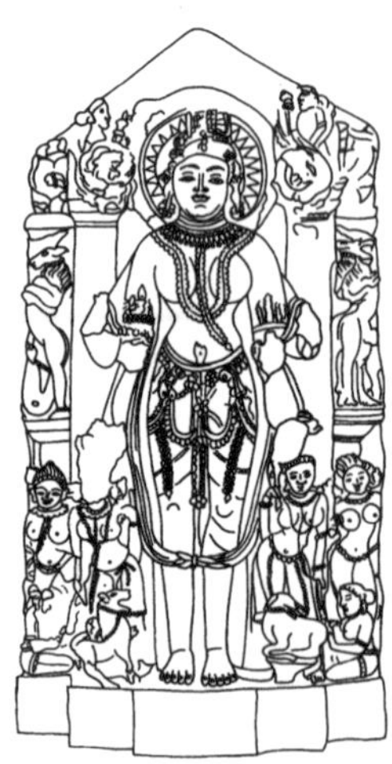

13. *Yogaśikhopaniṣad*, I.134-36; *Haṭha-Yoga-Pradīpikā*, IV.31-34; Hajari Prasad Dvivedi, *Nātha Sampradāya* (in Hindi), p. 127.

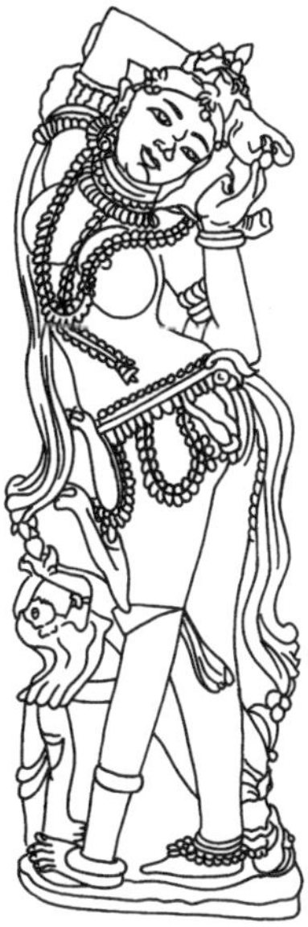

connected organ of sense (*indriya*), is dissolved into the next above it until the last element, space, with the *tanmātra*, sound and *manas* are dissolved in egoism (*ahaṁkāra*), of which they are *vikṛtis*. *Ahaṁkāra* is merged in *mahat*, the first manifestation of creative ideation, and, later, into *bindu*, which is the Supreme Being. This is the Tāntric adoption of Sāṁkhya categories. However, in the upward movement in the *kuṇḍalinī* it absorbs in herself twenty-three *tattvas*, commencing from the gross elements, and then, unites with Paramaśiva whose nature is one with hers. The union is known as *sāmarasya*. The *sādhaka* in Laya-Yoga, thinking of himself as Śakti or the female principle of creation, feels himself in union with Śiva and enjoys infinite pleasure. The union of the Śakti with Śiva in the body of the *sādhaka* is that coition[14] of the *pañca-tattva* (five-*makāra*)[15] which is regarded in the Yoga-Tantra as the best of all unions for those who have already controlled their passions through yogic exercises. On their union, nectar flows, which runs from *brahmarandhra* to *mūlādhāra*, flooding the *kṣudra brahmāṇḍa* (microcosm) or the body of *sādhaka*, who becomes forgetful of all in this world and immersed in ineffable bliss. When, by preliminary *sādhanā*, purity of physical and mental function is gained, the aspirant learns how to open the entrance of *suṣumnā*, which is ordinarily closed at base.

---

14. Sexual union, in terms of *yoga*, symbolically, represents the process of unification of the two breaths, *prāṇa* and *apāna*, *piṅgalā* and *iḍā*, the opposites, sun-moon, into central *nāḍī suṣumnā*. It is believed that, by this process of combining the polar opposites and unifying them in the *suṣumnā*, the *yogī* can transcend the human condition and go beyond the phenomenal world and pass into that non-conditioned and timeless state in which there is neither day nor night.

15. The aim of these practices is not the fulfilment of desire; these practices are said to be undertaken only for attainment of *bodhicitta*, i.e., for the realization of perfect knowledge or for the attainment of the final state of supreme bliss and for the upliftment of all beings.

Laya-Yoga is a term for those mental and psychical processes which are used to discover man's inner essence. It is the method by which the mental and intellectual feelings (*cittavṛtti*) are controlled and conditioned so that the aspirant is able to dissolve his own self into the absolute, the supreme reality, as conceived by him. This state is called *samādhi* or *laya-samādhi*. It defines the unity of the individual soul and the universal soul, that by which the oneness is attained. The whole process is very complex and depends entirely on the mental and intellectual faculties of the aspirant.

Haṭha-Yoga

Patañjali, the great founder of Yoga, also devoted a full chapter of *Yoga-Sūtra* to the different kinds of supernatural powers, (*vibhūtis*) attainable through concentration of mind on different centres of the body. The eight supernatural faculties are well known in the School of Yoga. It is held that, through the practice of Haṭha-Yoga,[16] the gross body begins to acquire something of the nature of the subtle body and to possess something of its relations with life energy; that becomes a greater force more powerfully felt and capable of a lighter and freer and more resolvable physical actions, powers which culminate in the Haṭha-yogic *siddhis*.[17]

16. Patañjali, gives Haṭha-Yoga a subsidiary place — it is resorted to only for gaining a control over the physical and psychological states and conditions, and a perfect control over the psychological state leads to final liberation :

    The word *haṭha* really signifies the union of *ha* and *ṭha*, i.e., *ha* = Sun (Sūrya) and *ṭha* = Moon (Candra).

17. The eight supernatural faculties, viz., *aṇimā* (the power of becoming as small as an atom), *mahimā* (the power of becoming big), *laghimā* (the power of assuming excessive lightness at will), *garimā* (the power of becoming as heavy as one likes), *prāpti* (the power of attaining everything at will), *prakāmya* (the power of attaining all objects of pleasure at Will), *iśitva* (the power of attaining supremacy over things) and *vaśitva* (the power of subduing, fascinating or bewitching) are well known as the power of Lord Śiva himself, who is the Lord of *yoga* (*yogīrāja*).

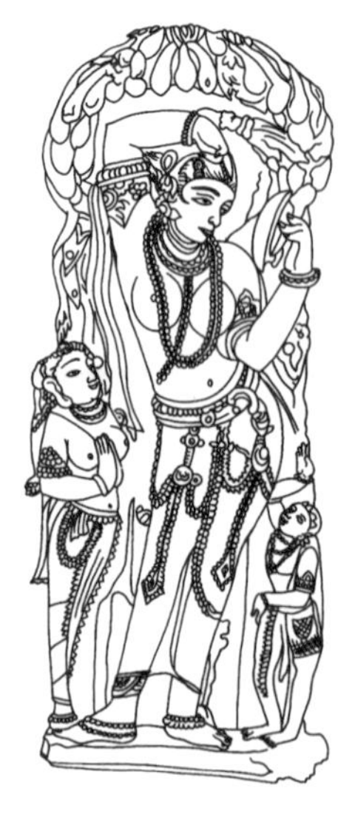

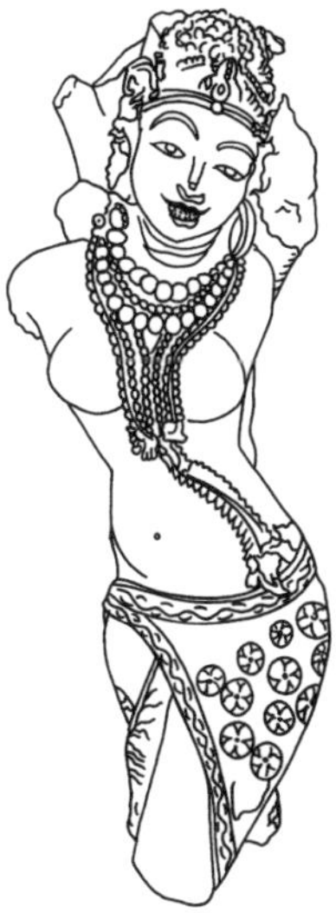

This final aim of Yoga as the final arrest of mind has often been admitted by Haṭha-Yoga. It is generally felt that Haṭha-Yoga is subservient to Rāja-Yoga;[18] but considering the general tone of Haṭha-Yoga it seems that the very approach of Haṭha-Yoga was, somewhat, different from the approach of the other schools of Yoga. Mantra-Yoga, Laya-Yoga and Rāja-Yoga are idealistic in their philosophical outlook and, therefore, lay the greatest emphasis on the final arrest of the mind and the attainment of liberation. In Haṭha-Yoga the conception of liberation itself is different from that of the other schools.[19] Here, liberation means immortality, first, in perfect body (*siddha-deha*) and then, in a divine body (*divya-deha*), and this is perfection (*siddhi*) which the *haṭha-yogin* aspires for.

It is said that by Haṭha-Yoga the body becomes healthy, the eyes bright, the semen hardened, the *nāḍī*s purified, the internal fire increased and *nāda* (sound) heard. According to *Siddha-Siddhānta-Paddhati,* the word *haṭha* is composed of the syllables *ha* and *ṭha* symbolizing the Sun and the Moon,[20] the *prāṇa* and *apāna vāyu*s respectively. The union of these two vital winds in the *suṣumnā* is called Haṭha-Yoga. The practice of Haṭha-Yoga is divided into seven parts — cleansing (*śodhana*), by six processes (*ṣaṭa-karma*), the attainment of strength (*dṛḍhatā*), by bodily postures (*āsana*), of fortitude (*sthiratā*), strength by bodily position (*mudrā*), of steadiness of mind (*dhairya*), by restraint of senses (*pratihārya*), the lightness of breath-control (*prāṇāyāma*), of the realization (*pratyakṣa*), by meditation (*dhyāna*) and of detachment (*nirliptatva*) in *samādhi*.

18. *Haṭha-Yoga-Pradīpikā*, 1-2.

19. The other schools of thought regarded the final dissolution of the body and its final dissociation from the spirit as indispensable for liberation.

20. *Haṭha-Yoga-Pradīpikā*, 3-15, Pāṇini Office, Allahabad, 1915, As per this book, the sun means *iḍā* and the moon represents *piṅgalā*.

Cleansing (*śodhana*) is effected by six processes known as *ṣaṭ-karma* which are — *dhauti* (inner-washing) the clearance of wind, phlegm and bile, in a variety of ways, the most important being filling the stomach with sufficient water and evacuating it by vomiting; *vasti* (contraction and expansion of the anus in water); *neti* (cleaning the nostrils); *lauliki* or whirling of the belly from side to side; *trāṭaka* (cleaning the eyes) and *vāta-karma* (removal of phlegm by inhalation and exhalation or by water drawn through nostrils and ejected through the mouth or the reverse.[21]

Āsanas (bodily postures) are required for strength or firmness; *mudrās* are for *sthiratā* or fortitude, because it removes pain and sorrow.[22] When the physical body is purified and controlled, there follows *pratihārya* to secure steadiness. The next practice is *prāṇāyāma* for lightening of the body. The *sādhaka* sits in the *padmāsana* (posture) inhales (*pūraka*) and exhales (*recaka*) *vāyu*, alternatively, through the left and right nostrils, retaining the breath (*kumbhaka*) for gradually increasing periods. The theory is that the vital air (*prāṇa-vāyu*) should enter the *suṣumnā* and must be united and made to flow through the middle nerve passing through the lotuses in the navel, heart, neck and forehead. And then, this vital wind must be made steady in the lotus between the eye-brows. This is what is meant by *prāṇāyāma*.

The purification of and the control over muscles, sinews, nerves, ducts and nerve-centres through the processes of *āsana* (posture), *dhauti* (washing), *bandha* (different kinds of arrest), *mudrā*, *prāṇāyāma* and other processes of Haṭha-Yoga are generally prescribed to be directed towards the final aim of the transformation and transubstantiation of the body. Closely associated with the question of transubstantiation of the body is the question of attaining full

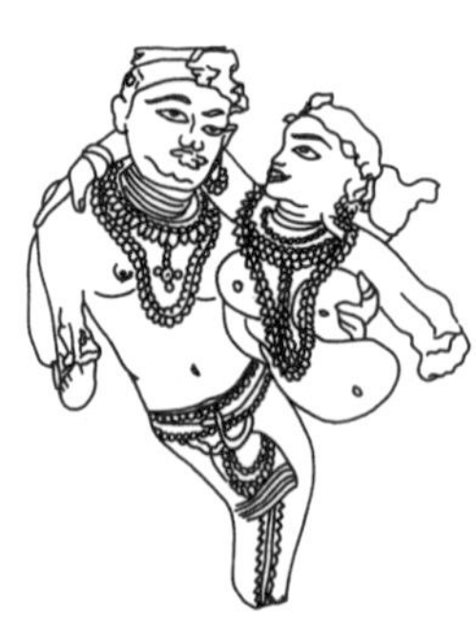

21. *Haṭha-Yoga-Pradīpikā*, III.21, Hajari Prasad Dvivedi, *Nātha Sampradāya*, p. 125.
22. *Haṭha-Yoga-Pradīpikā*, IV.37.

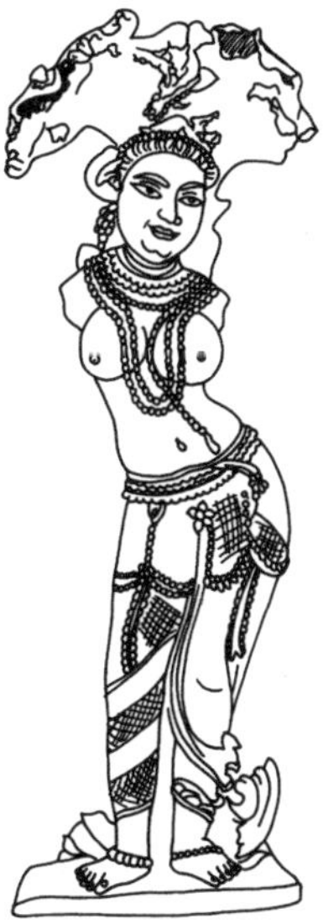

control over the mind. The control of the mind is the *yoga par excellence* and it is held that the vital wind is the vehicle of this mind, and the control of the vital wind through the processes of *prāṇāyāma* leads to the control of the mind. With the arrest of vital wind, the mind becomes arrested, and it is for this reason that the arrest of *vāyu* (i.e., vital wind) has been regarded as very important in the literature of the other schools, containing discourses on Yoga.

Rāja-Yoga

The highest form of *yoga* is Rāja-Yoga. After successful mastery over Mantra-Yoga, Laya-Yoga and Haṭha-Yoga the *sādhaka* steps towards the realm of perfection of Rāja-Yoga. Rāja-Yoga is a form of Yoga in which the mind automatically merges with the *Brahman* just as air merges with the sky.[23] It is free from all dualism. It leads to *nirvikalpa samādhi* in which there is absolute unity of knower, knowledge and the source of knowledge. This *samādhi* is known as Rāja-Yoga *samādhi,* which is also possible by a *kumbhaka* process of breath control, known as *manomūrchā,* which connects the mind with the Supreme Being.[24] It is an easy mode of meditation. It is purely mental exercise in which discrimination between the real and the unreal is possible. It is complete final liberation.[25] It is a term for those physical and psychical processes which is used to discover man's inner essence. It is a method by which the mental and intellectual feelings (*cittavṛtti*) are controlled and conditioned so that the *sādhaka* is able to dissolve his own self into the absolute, the supreme reality, conceived by

---

23. *Prāṇatoṣanī*, VI.3, p. 433.
24. *Gheraṇḍa Saṁhitā*, VII.16.
25. This *samādhi* is also known as *unamanī, manonmanī, amaratva, laya, tattva, śūnya, aśūnya, paramapada, amānāsk, advaita, nirālamba, nirañjana, jīvanmukti, sahaja* and *tūrīya*.

    Haṭha-Yoga-Pradīpikā, 4, 3-4, 4, 29-30; Hajari Prasad Dvivedi, *Kabeer* (in Hindi), pp. 50-51.

him. This state is called *samādhi*. The Rāja-Yoga aims at the unity of the individual soul and the universal soul and thus attain a sense of oneness (non-duality) is attained.

Earlier, we have discussed about the four classes of Yoga, viz., Mantra, Laya, Haṭha and Rāja-Yoga; but the *Yogaśikhopaniṣad* refers to Bhāvanā-Yoga and Sahaja-Yoga. The word *bhāvanā*, used repeatedly in Buddhist scriptures, is a Pāli word, and it means culture on mental development. It aims at cleansing the mind of impurities and mental disturbances such as lustful desires, hatred, ill-will, indolence, worries and restlessness. It aims at cultivating qualitiies like concentration, awareness, intelligence, will and tranquillity. This mental development ultimately leads one to the attainment of the highest wisdom which would help him in the understanding of the nature of things as they are. Buddha gave the world Four Noble Truths — 'Suffering, origin of suffering, cessation of suffering and way to cessation.' This, coupled with his Eightfold Path, is the key to the success amd satiation in this life. Compassion, right action, right livelihood, right efforts and good intentions are the key words around which *bhāvanā* or Bhāva-Yoga revolves.[26]

Sahaja-Yoga

The final state of Yoga is called the *sahaja* state or *sahaja-samādhi* or *śunya-samādhi*.[27] The state of *sahaja*, is a state of pefect equilibrium which transcends all our perceptual knowledge with positive and negative attributes. In that state of perfect quietude the *yogin* becomes one with the whole universe and realizes a non-dual existence. In such a state 'He himself is god, himself is goddess, himself the

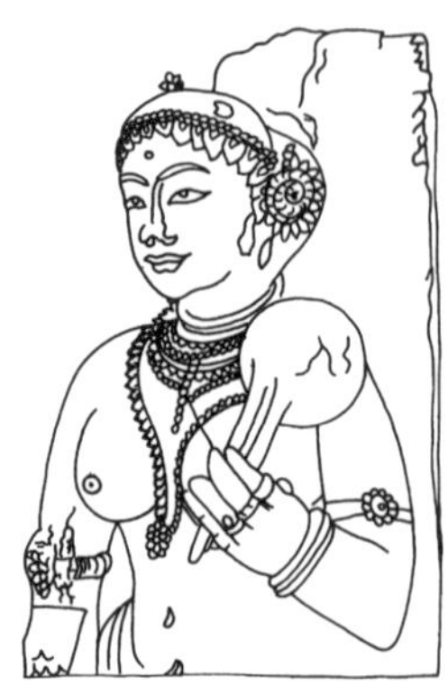

26. T.N. Mishra, *Buddhist Tantra and Buddhist Art*, New Delhi, 2001, p. 1.
27. *Sādho sahaja samādhi bhalī — Kabeer Bānī, pada*, 41; *Kabeer Granthāvalī* (in Hindi), Kāśī, 1928; Hajari Prasad Dvivedi, *Kabeer* (in Hindi), pp. 66-68.

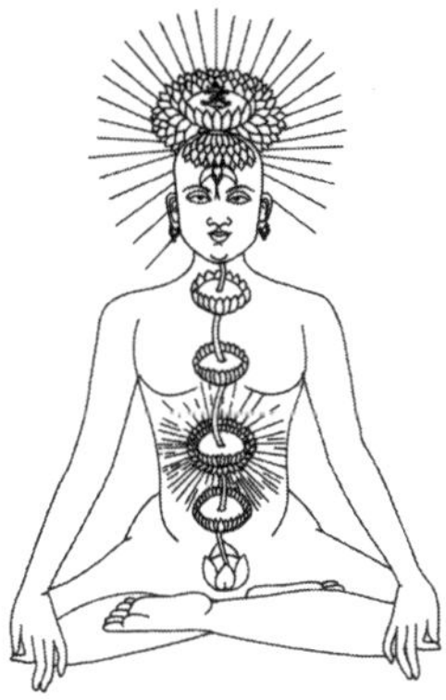

disciple, himself the preceptor, he is, at once, meditation, the meditator and the divinity (meditated upon).'

The exponents of the Sahaja School put the whole emphasis on the protest against the formalities of life and religion. For truth, they affirmed, was a matter of intuition and could never be attained by the artificial and unnatural means. To that end, one must proceed through the natural way, which lies not in discarding the inborn propensities of a human being and the total annihilation of the passion, but in sublimating the same. In the nature of a man, hunger and sex are recognized as the most primitive and fundamental propensities. The Sahajīyas would never prescribe any unnatural strain on human nature, but would take human nature itself as the best help for realizing the truth.

To realize the ultimate innate nature (*sahaja-bhāva*) of the self, what is natural is the easiest and, thus, it is *sahaja*. From its primary meaning of being natural, it acquires this secondary meaning of being easy, straight or plain. This supreme process of Yoga is eternal, it originates from our passion; our passions are part and parcel of our nature and our nature is never transgressible. It is, therefore, wise to transform these passions through the yogic process for realizing the truth. If *sahaja* can be realized, everything is attained, for other rituals and rites are no more necessary. The Sahaja-Yoga is that final state,[28] where all kinds of duality are absorbed in a principle of non-duality.

---

28. *Kabeer Granthāvalī* (in Hindi); edited by Shri Shyam Sunder Das, Kāśī Nāgarī Pracāriṇī Sabhā, Kāśī, 1928, p. 42 (21, 3-4).

3

Philosophy of Yoga-Tantra

YOGA-TANTRA is often used in the singular, which may suggest that it is a uniform formulation of doctrine and discipline. Yoga-Tantras are, however, varied in their theme and expression though the claim is that it has emanated from divine source. Some call it Āgama while others name it as Nigama. Yoga-Tantra being pre-eminently a way to practical realization has necessarily to bear reference to the diverse characters and competencies of different aspirants and seekers. They have, accordingly, designed the framework of their theories and practices, suitably adjusted to the actual conditions prevailing and evolved stages and states in the soul's journey towards chosen ends and values.[1] The soul cannot give up its quest till it realizes all is potential, in meaning and fulfilment, including its own perfections. This highest end has been called *mokṣa,* (liberation) from bondage. Tāntric-Yogic disciples recognize and keep themselves alive to these super-physical and supra-mental forces. The world can never be so bad, materially and spiritually, as to make those forces unavailable for the earnest seeker in his reforming and transforming efforts. The tāntric *yogi*s maxim recognizes that the body is the epitome of the universe and this is also

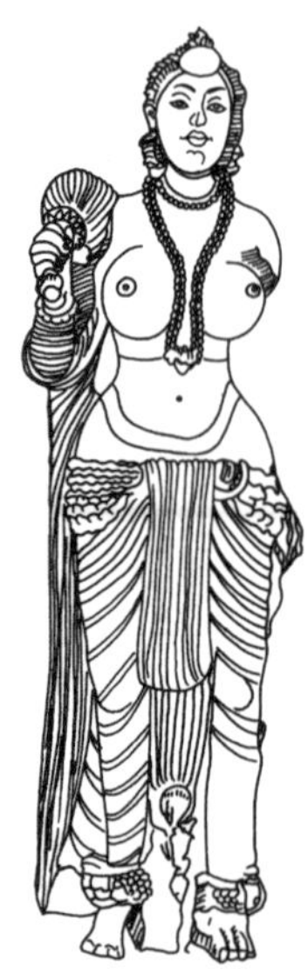

1. John Woodroffe, *Principle of Tantras,* Part I, Madras, 1952, Preface; S.B. Dasgupta, *Obscure Religion Cults,* Calcutta, 1959, p. 34; Baldev Upadhyaya, *Bhāratīya Darśana* (in Hindi), Varanasi, 1966, pp. 429-30; Lalmani Joshi, *Studies in Buddhist Culture of India,* Benaras, 1967, pp. 305-07; Nagendra Nath Upadhyaya, *Bauddha Kāpālika Sādhanā Aur Sāhitya* (in Hindi), Allahabad, 1983, pp. 43-45; T.N. Mishra, *Impact of Tantra on Religion and Art,* New Delhi, 1997, p. 43.

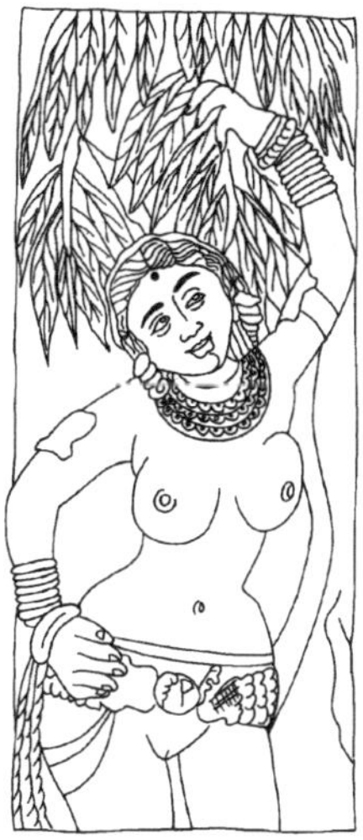

the basis of medical science; it rests on the assumption that the elements, forming the body, cannot be dissociated from the environmental elements and that by applying the law, which governs the latter, the former may be brought into an order. This environmental matter is *prakṛti* in Sāṁkhya and conceived here as the female principle, from which everything in the world is produced. *Prakṛti* is characterized by three qualities which influence and attract a number of forces, conceived as *puruṣa,* and it is only by the union of *prakṛti* with the *puruṣa* the creation starts in different spheres. *Prakṛti* is in constant process of evolution and is subject to the law of cause and effect. The whole cosmos exists in a subtle from in *prakṛti* and becomes manifest in creation and, thus, the unmanifest becomes manifest, the *avyakta* becomes *vyakta*.

According to Yoga-Tantra, the body of the *sādhaka* is the universe which is the abode of the desired (*iṣṭa*) and the goal to be sought (*sādhya*). The unfolding of the power of the self (*ātmaśakti*) is to be brought about by the self-realization (*ātmadarśana*) which is the aim of yogic *sādhanā*. *Śakti* (power), conceived as the female principle, is in the individual and it is only this *śakti* that justifies the existence of the individual. This *śakti* is conceived as existing like the power of 'burning' in fire throughout the created-world of movable and immovable things, through the conscious and the unconscious, through the gross and the subtle. The repository of this *śakti* is regarded as a static principle conceived as the male principle, which is symbolized by the name of God, in any system. The human body is the abode of both these principles, the static Male and the dynamic Female, and the purpose of yogic *sādhanā* is to get these two principles in non-dual and absolute forms. For the *sādhaka* of Yoga-Tantra, there is nothing apart from the body, the functioning of which is considered to belong to the same order as cosmic functioning. Now, in this aspect the whole *sādhanā* is based on the belief that the truth is to be realized, in and through the body.

The belief of the *sādhaka* is that the ultimate truth is not an abstract principle, transcending the universe but is immanent in it, and that the human body is not merely a thing in the universe, the microcosm that exists in relation to the macrocosm. Therefore, there is nothing in the universe which is not in the body of man. There is a perfect parallelism between the physical process of the universe and the biological process in the body of a man; with this idea, the Yoga-Tantra tries to locate the sun, the moon, the stars, the mountains, the islands and the rivers of the external world within the *sādhaka*'s body.[2] The time element of the universe in all its phases of day, night, month and year have also been explained with reference to the course of the vital wind, breath (*prāṇa* and *apāna*). The human body, with its physical structure and biological processes, represents the manifestation of the same energy which is at play in the structure and processes of the vast cosmos. The *sādhaka* should concentrate his attention on himself and realize the truth within, with the clear conviction that the truth, that is realized, within, is the truth that pervades the universe outside (without). According to the *yogī*s (*haṭha-yogī* and *nātha-yogī*), the body is not only the abode of the truth but is also the best medium for realizing the truth. Different plexuses, nerves and nerve-centres represent the different *tattva*s (*tattva* means the science of the cosmic principles or the essential principles), but the *tattva*s, represented by

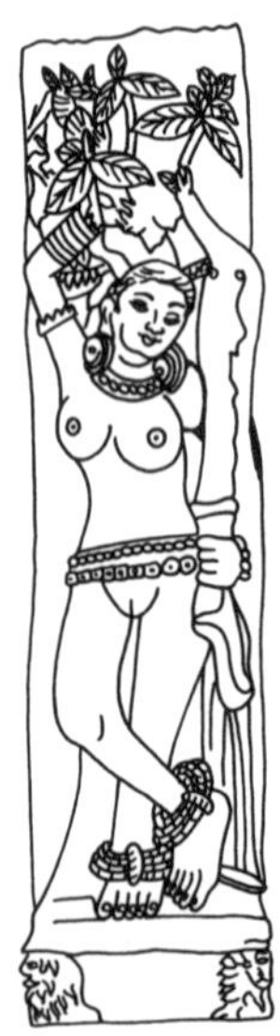

2. In the human body, the central great axis (Mount Meru) is surrounded by seven islands (the vital force, blood, flesh, fat, bones, marrow and so on), as well as seers, sages, gods, goddesses, intelligence, all the stars and planets, sacred places, shrines and presiding deities, the sun and the moon, the agent of creation and destruction. These also move through the body, as do the five great elements of space, air, fire, water and earth. All beings that exist in all worlds are to be found within the body, surrounding the central great axis. Again, the right side of the body is believed to be the region of Śiva and the left, that of Śakti — this is the yogic conception of Ardhanārīśvara (the half-woman and half-man).

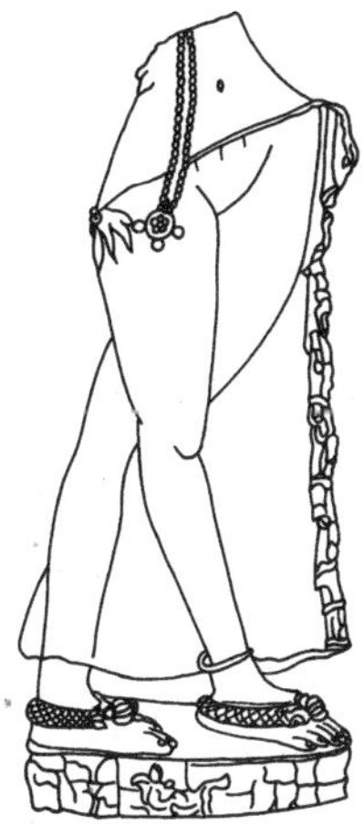

them, lie latent until they are made potent through proper yogic culture and control.[3] Through this, the physical system may be transformed into a perfect instrument for reflecting the truth.

The aim of Yoga-Tantra is *laya*, the return of the seeker to the state of undifferentiated existence. Actually, Yoga-Tantra cannot be termed as a religion but it is a tenet and principle. It consists only of methods for achieving this *laya* or the union of the individual with the infinite. This union is the union of the personal ego, which is known as the female with the absolute (the Male). This is cosmic union of universal dualities. The Yoga-Tantra denotes a cultural discipline in a wider sense, and when used in a limited sense, it is spiritual knowledge of a technical nature. The

3. The centre of power in the human body is not an innovation of Yoga-Tantra. It has its root in the cosmic law of evolution and is revealed to mankind for their salvation. The centre of power is the cause from which the five sheaths arise. These are : sheath of food (*annamaya kośa*), sheath of life (*prāṇamaya kośa*), sheath of lower mind (*manomaya kośa*), sheath of higher mind (*vijñānamaya kośa*) and sheath of bliss (*ānandamaya kośa*). *Ānandamaya kośa* arises from the elements, earth, water and fire. Earth and water produce food, which is assimilated by fire and converted into the substance which forms the body, it nourishes. Earth, water and fire are the presiding elements in *mūlādhāra, svādhiṣṭhāna* and *maṇipūra* centres, respectively. They become the objects of concentration in the first place, as, by awakening the *kula-kuṇḍalinī*, the *sādhaka* first meets *mūlādhāra*, the *svādhiṣṭhāna* and *maṇipūra*. The *prāṇamaya kośa* arises from *anāhata* and *viśuddha* in the centre, in which vital air and space, (ether) respectively, preside, which include the ten senses which form the vital breath. It is a subtle form of manifestation. The *manomaya kośa* is evolved from the *ājñā-cakra*, which is the centre of the mind. The mind is the faculty which discriminates between the physical sensations of the five perceptive senses. The *vijñānamaya kośa* arises from the *bindu* and *nāda*. It directly reflects the intelligence (*buddhi*) of the material body (*kāraṇa śarīra*) or the principle of five senses of man and undifferentiated nature (*prakṛti*). In *sahasrāra* is the *ānandmaya kośa*.

The different kinds of energy that we find working in nature are different expressions of one great energy. This, in scientific terminology, is known as correlation of forces.

tāntric *sādhanā* is also concerned with the ascendancy over the force of nature by the exoteric rituals of the Vedic type as well as by the esoteric rituals involving the yogic practices, the aim being the union of the two pinciples, *jīva* and *ātmā*, Śiva and Śakti, *prakṛti* and *puruṣa*, *prajñā* and *upāya*, and *śūnyatā* and *karuṇā*, *nāda* and *bindu*, etc. The origin and development of the Yoga-Tantra, as a special mode of *sādhanā*, was intimately connected with the rise of Śaivism, with the Sāṁkhya supplying them a philosophical background.

There are three classes in Yoga-Tantra — *dakṣiṇa*, *vāma* and *madhyama*. All the three promulgates profound matters concerning *tattva* and *mantra*. *Tattva* means the science of the cosmic principles, while *mantra* means the science of the mystic sound, *vāmācāra* is based on the profound knowledge of the 'return current' (*nivṛtti*), which seeks to reverse the process of creating and maintaining the bonds of propensities and conventions, in which the *jīva* or the soul has been held as a *paśu*. It must be clearly perceived that, in this path, the aspirant has to make use of certain kinds of rituals (*pañcatava*) which, leading admittedly to some abuse in unsuitable cases and conditions, has made the whole cult of Yoga-Tantra suspect in the judgement of those who do not understand and discriminate.[4] Even those who knew nothing of the 'return-current' (reversing process) got themselves involved in the theory and practice of the left-path.

The end of the *sādhanā* is, to attain pure and perfect *cit* or consciousness. This is also a state of perfect being and perfect bliss in Yoga-Tantra, as also in the Vedānta, the word for this perfect state being *saccidānanda*.

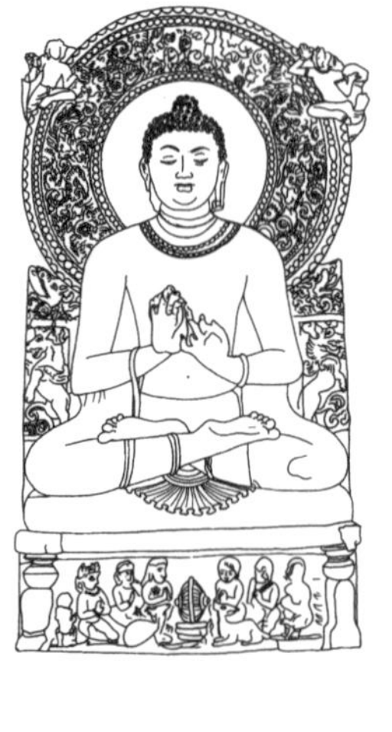

4. The real *yoga sādhakas* naturally enjoy ample balance of mind and alertness (*sattva*) and do not require external aids to *sādhanā*. They utilize the meat of silence, the fish of breath-control, the concentration techniques, the wine of divine love, and coitus of one's ego with the Absolute.

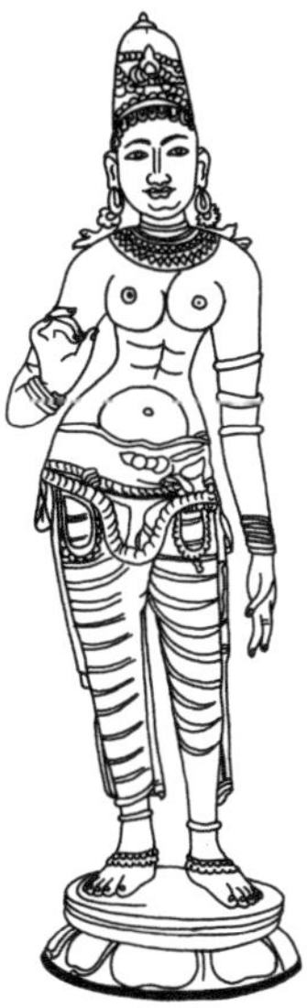

Every kind of duality must be reduced to zero. Man and woman, for example, may be sublimated into cosmic principles, polar to each other in the outgoing aspect of the cosmic process but identified and unified in Śiva and Śakti in reality which is experienced in the reversing of the outgoing current. In reversing the process, we have to bring the two complements (poles) 'together' to reaffirm and realize the identical whole. The so-called 'erotic' symbolism is sublimated as the creative union of Śiva and Śakti, the thrill of the act of union being *nāda*, and the 'seed' that issues from the union is *bindu*. The *vāmācāra* path, which, under very stringent conditions, prescribes to the *sādhanā* or ritual readjustment with woman, that such sublimation of the so-called 'carnal' act has to be effected till the supreme Advaita Śiva-Śakti experience with its perfect *ānanda* or bliss is attained.[5]

According to the Yoga-Tantra, Śiva has two aspects *nirguṇa* (attributelessness) and *saguṇa* (with attributes). As *nirguṇa*, Śiva is transcendent and, therefore, dissociated from *prakṛti* or Śakti, and as *saguṇa*, Śiva is associated with Śakti. It is in the latter, the aspects of Śiva and Śakti emanate, from that, the *nāda* (sound)[6] and out of the *nāda*, the *bindu*. This conception can be put in another way. At the time of final dissolution (*pralaya*), everything is withdrawn into the supreme Śakti. Therefore, when Śakti, which is the substance (*tattva*), approches the light, which is the knowledge (*cit*), there arises in the former and desire to

5. Hara Prasad Shastri, *Advaya Saṁgraha*, Gayakawada Oriental Series, Baroda, 1927, p. 28.

6. This word is a manifestation of sound, and sound exists wherever there is energy. *Sādhanā* which uses the sound (*mantra-yoga*) is part of *nāda-yoga*. In *nāda-yoga* a *sādhaka* worships the *Nāda-Brahman*, the Absolute expressed as the sound, *oṁ*, which emanates from Śiva. Anything, that has sound, has Śakti, and the Śakti has sound associated with it. There are 108 *gatis* (modes) of *nāda*, 108=1+8=9 means *navadvāra* (nine doors). When *kuṇḍalinī* passes through the *anāhata-cakra sādhaka* hears the sound (*nāda*), known as the →

create (*vicikarṣa*). It bursts out and divides itself and, out of that division, arises the *bindu, nāda* and *bīja. Bindu* partakes of the nature of Śiva, (*jñāna*) *bīja,* which is Śakti, and *nāda,* which is relation between the two (Śiva and Śakti) as the stimulator and the stimulated (*kṣobhya*). When *bindu* bursts, an inchoate volume of sound is produced. This sound is called *Śabda-Brahman* or *Nāda-Brahman,* which is the *caitanya* (stress towards manifestation in all beings) pervading all creation, and is the source of letters of the alphabet, of words and other sounds by which thoughts are exchanged. Sounds have meanings and both are inseparable.[7]

The Yoga-Tantra classifies the *sādhaka* under three categories. The *sādhaka,* with divine (*divya*) disposition, (*bhāva*) forms an imporant factor in the process of *sādhanā.* The *sādhaka,* with animal disposition, (*paśu-bhāva*) is the slave of lust, anger, greed, pride, illusion and envy. He can hardly be expected to see, beyond the gross (*sthūla*) or material aspect of the things,[8] the *vīra* is fighting the six enemies (passions) who obstruct the way for spiritual advancement. The *sādhaka* of *divya* disposition is, as a result of his practices in his previous birth, endowed with the qualities which make him almost divine.

Concept of Ṣat-Cakra

Cakra is a symbol of the universe (both macrocosm and

→ *anāhata-nāda.* Which mode of sound (*nāda*) the *sādhaka* hears depends on his *sādhanā.* All rivers go to the ocean of bhāva (emotion). The rivers are *nāḍīs* and the land is human body. First the *sādhaka* follows the rivers into the sea and then the sea will flood the rivers, which will overflow their banks with over-whelming divine intoxication, which is known as *bhāva-samādhi,* followed by *mahā-bhāva samādhi* (intense *samādhi*) which can lead to *nirvikalpa-samādhi.*

7. *Parā* is the motionless casual sound which produces *nāda* and *vāc,* the uttered Speech. The subtle form of these two are, therefore, known as *parā-nāda* and *parā-vāc* and their combination is said to be *parā-śakti,* the source of everything.

8. This kind of *sādhaka* is known as *tāmasika* person. *Tamas* is *viṣa* (deadly poison), which is the essence of water elements.

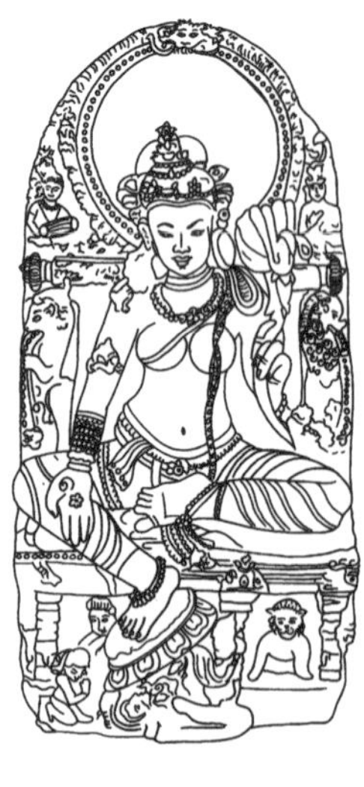

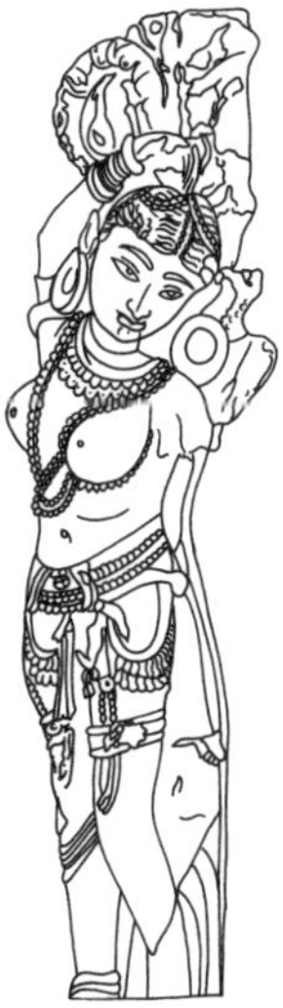

microcosm) and its divine cause.[9] There is an explanation, based, primarily, on the philosophical concepts of the Upaniṣad, according to which the function of *cakra* can be defined as the principle of life and energy (cyle of world process).

It may be pointed out that the *cakra*s were originally conceived in terms of human anatomy for the purpose of physiological study. The *cakra*s, commencing with the *mūlādhāra* and going upwards, were associated with the sacral (Sacrum=Δ), prostatic, epigastric, cardiac, laryngeal and cavernous plexuses and *sahasrāra* with the medulla. At a subsequent stage, in conformity with the tāntric idea that the human body is the microcosm of the universe, worldly objects were connected with these *cakra;* the law of microcosm and macrocosm tells us that there is no real difference between the vast external universe and the limited internal universe of the human body, except that the individual believes himself to be different. A human being is a living microcosm of the universe, and the universe is a living macrocosm of the human being. Each affects the other. Each *cakra* was again thought to represent the gross and the subtle elements.[10] The gross elements of the earth and the subtle elements, like cohesion and stimulation of the sense of smell, arise from the region of *mūlādhāra*. In the *svādhiṣṭhāna,* the gross element is water and the subtle elements include contraction and stimulation of the sense of taste; *maṇipūra* involves the gross element of fire and the related subtle elements are expansion, production of heat and stimulation of sight, sense of colour and form; in

---

9. In the *Ṛgveda*, the word *cakra* is used with reference to the Sun (Sūrya) and the earth, and human body is defined or compared with *cakra*.

   Ṛgveda, 1.164.1, 1.164.13; *Atharvaveda*, IX.9.1-2 and IX.9.11; *Śvetāśvatara Upaniṣad*, 1.4-6, 6.1; *Kaṭhopaniṣad*, 1.33.

10. The entire world is made up of the five great elements; these are — Earth, Water, Fire, Air and Ether. Thse elements are not elements in the chemical sense, rather, they are states of →

anāhata, the gross element is air and the subtle elements connected with it are general movement and stimulation of the sense of touch. In *viśuddha*, the related gross element is space and the related subtle element is the stimulation of the sense of hearing; *ājñā* identifies the gross element of mind; its subtle elements being the mental faculties. These subtle elements, as *tattvas*, are connected with the different organs, main and subsidiary — smell with nose and taste (*rasa*), with tongue and hand, form (*rūpa*) and colour with eyes and anus, touch (*sparśa*) with skin and penis, *śabda* (sound) with air and mouth.

Granthi Bhedana (Piercing of Knots)

The Yoga-Tantra discovers a subtle path which establishes a direct connection between the psychic and the supreme spirit, force and life. The ingress from the central source can filtrate into our whole being through this path. This is called *suṣumnā* or *avadhūti*. In Yoga-Tantra, the three subtle

→ matter. The earth element predominates in everything that is solid in the universe, the water element in that which is liquid, and the air element is gas. The ether element, is the space in which things occur, and fire element is the force which changes solid to liquid, liquid to gas and vice versa. The essence of Yoga-Tantra is the purification of the five elements to awaken *kuṇḍalinī śakti* and this *śakti* can only be awakened, once the elements in our body have become purified. The purification of the five elements is known as *bhūta-śuddhi*. By this *bhūta-śuddhi*, the *sādhakas* allow the *kuṇḍalinī śakti* to travel upwards through *cakras*. *Bhūta-śuddhi* is the essence of Yoga-Tantra.

Kuṇḍalinī śakti sleeps in the *mūlādhāra-cakra* at the base of the spine. She lies under the coverings which prevent Her from remembering Herself? These three coverings are the three *guṇas* (*sattva, rajas* and *tamas*), six tastes (sweet, sour, saline, bitter, pungent and astringent) and five great elements. The *guṇas* control our minds, the elements shape our bodies and the world around us, and the tastes control our internal chemistry, which links our mind and body, together. Together with ten senses — five we all know — plus the tongue, hands, feet, anus and genitals, there are twenty-four limitations which limit the human consciousness. Numerologically twenty-four means 2+4=6, the six *cakra* (energy centres). The six *cakra* (*ṣat-cakra*) are also manifestations of these twenty-four limitations.

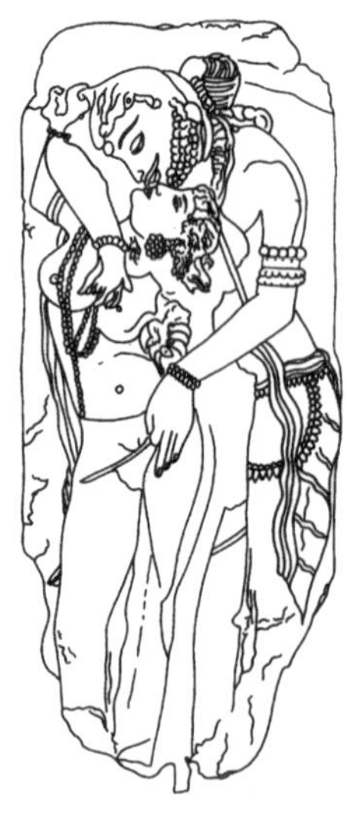

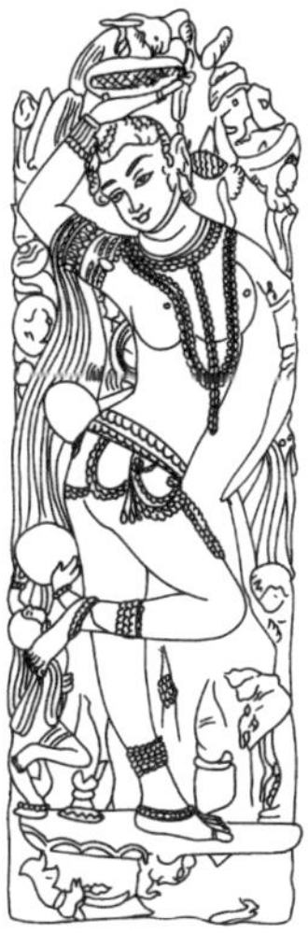

passages are commonly known as *iḍā, piṅgalā* and *suṣumnā* or *lalanā, rasanā* and *avadhūti. Iḍā* is the nerve in the left side and *piṅgalā,* in the right. *Iḍā* can be felt under pressure of inhalation and exhalation. *Iḍā* is active when the inhalation or exhalation gets clear through the left nostril while *piṅgalā* is active when the inhalation or exhalation gets easier passage through the right nostril. The *suṣumnā* is subtle luminous path that opens into vaster spiritual space at top of the brain and connects the *sādhakas* directly with the cosmic depths of existence. It is the path that connects our psychic life with the cosmic life. The psychic and spiritual energy flows through the *suṣumnā*. The Yoga-Tantra discovers many centres but six are supposed to be very important. These centres control our physical and mental systems. The Yoga-Tantra teaches the theory of psychic and spiritual transformation. The presence of an intensive force is felt in those centres and delightful currents are felt there. Thus, these centres act as communicators of the spiritual force to the different parts of our being. They are all connected with one another by a subtle luminous thread.

In general, the nerves are said to be seventy-two thousand in number. Again, thirty-two are said to be more important and, of these thirty-two, again three are very very important. These are *iḍā, piṅgalā* and *suṣumnā*. About the position of these nerves we find in the Yoga-Tantra that inside the passage of the spinal cord flows the nerve *suṣumnā*, which, in reality, is made up of the three nerves, viz. *citriṇī* of the nature of *sattva guṇa* (intelligence stuff), *vajrā* of the nature of *rajas* (energy) and *brahma-nāḍī* of the nature of *tamas* (inertia).[11] All the nerves start from a seat

11. Inside the *suṣumnā*, there is a finer *nāḍī* called *vajrā* which regulates the flow of electric-energy in the human system. It extends from the brain to the second *cakra* (*svādhiṣṭhāna*). Inside the *vajrā nāḍī* the *citriṇī nāḍī*, spreading out like a spider's net, is the vehicle of the auspicious sound *oṁ*. At the lower extreme point of this *nāḍī* is situated the *mūlādhāra*. Through this *citriṇī nāḍī* from the very centre of the *mūlādhāra-cakra*, rises the →

called the *kanda,* which is situated about one inch above the anus and one inch below the penis. The *suṣumnā* seems to be a sort of duct inside the spinal cord and encases, within it, *citriṇī,* which again has an aperture, called the brahma-randhra, running to the *sahasrāra.* The *iḍā* and *piṅgalā,* outside the spinal cord, proceed from the left and the right sides, respectively, towards the nasal region in a symmetrical course, encircling all the *cakra*s.

Another view is that *iḍā* and *piṅgalā* from the right and the left testicles, respectively, pass on to the left and right of the *suṣumnā* in the bent form of the bow. The *iḍā* is also called the moon, as it is of white colour and is the Śakti. The *piṅgalā* is the sun as it is of red colour and is the *puruṣa;* *suṣumnā* is of the nature and of the colour of the fire.[12] The three are again stated to be the rivers Gaṅgā, Yamunā and the Sarasvatī,[13] respectively, and the three meet at a point at the root of the penis, which is regarded as the Triveṇī or the confluence of the three rivers. Through these *iḍā* and *piṅgalā* blow the vital winds, *prāṇa* and *apāna.*[14]

→ subtlest of *nāḍī* called *brahma-nāḍī.* It passes through all the *cakra*s to *sahasrāra.* It is the vehicle of a *nāda* (*anāhata dhvani*) which is finer than sound. It is the medium of the subtlest flow of energy in creation and is the cause of desire that is responsible for downward (centrifugal) and upward (centripetal) current, ever present in the system. The downward flow leads to animality and the upward flow to spirituality, viz., *nāda* to *brahmapada.*

Hajari Prasad Dvivedi, *Kabeer* (in Hindi), pp. 45, 46 & 47.

12. In Indian tradition, colour has always been understood as vibration.

13. In Vaiṣṇava Sahajīya cult and in *Āyurveda* (Faculty of Indian Medicine), we find *iḍā, piṅgalā* and *suṣumnā* equated with *vāyu, pitta* and *kapha.*

14. There are five varieties of *prāṇa* in the body of the *sādhaka* — *prāṇa,* which takes things in and concentrates around the heart region and is responsible for respiration; *apāna,* which throws things out; *samāna,* which assimilates; *vyāna,* which circulates and distributes; and *udāna,* which is expressed, especially, in speech. *Sādhaka* will never be able to raise *kuṇḍalinī* until he can →

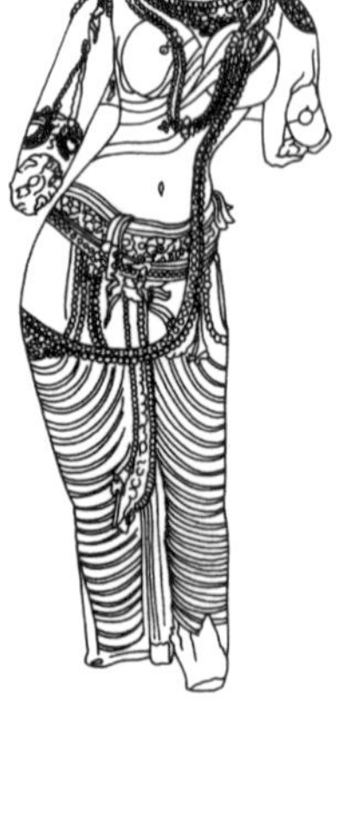

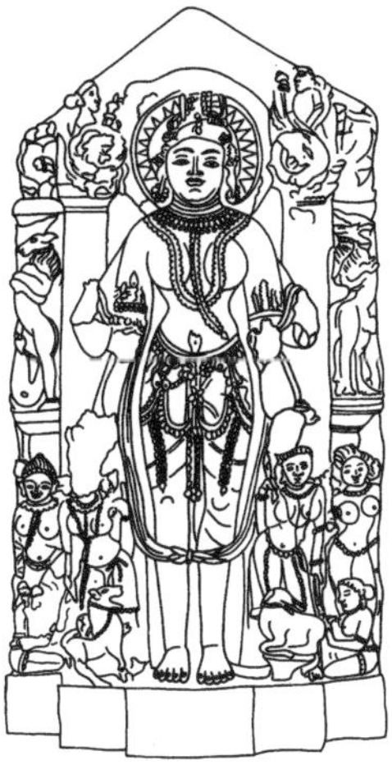

The expression of energy (*śakti*) in the physical body is *prāṇa*, life force, the power which keeps body, mind and the spirit functioning together as a living unit. Seventy-two thousand *nāḍīs* act as conduits for *prāṇa*, numerologically 72,000 means 7+2=9; the nine doors through which *prāṇa* can enter or leave the body. Most of the *nāḍīs* begin or

---

→ control the movements of the *prāṇa* in his body. *Kuṇḍalinī* can only leave the *mūlādhāra-cakra* when *prāṇa*, which, ordinarily, moves upwards, is made to move downwards and *apāna*, which usually moves downwards, is made to move upwards. When *prāṇa* and *apāna* meet and touch, only then *kuṇḍalinī* begins its upward motion.

Prāṇāyāma, the science of breath-control, concentrates on the extraction of the *prāṇa* vitality — essences from the inhaled air. It has sense-contact with the nose, and is associated with the sense of smell.

Udāna concentrates around the throat region, and is responsible for the flow for liquids and secretions. It has sense-contact with the skin, and is associated with the sense of touch.

Apāna concentrates in the genital region, and is responsible for the lower (gastro-intestinal and urinary) regions. It has sense-contact with the tongue, and is associated with the sense of taste. According to the theory of *rasa* (taste) elements, herb or compound is to be classified according to one of the six primary tastes — sweet, sour, saline, pungent, bitter or astringent. Combination of these primaries produce either a harmonious (healthy) or inharmonious (unhealthy) reaction in the body-hormones (*tridoṣa*) of *vāyu prakopa* (space and air aggregate), *pitta-doṣa* (fire aggregate) and *kapha-vikāra* (water and earth aggregate). Through the *apāna-vāyu* the three-fold materiality — bases can be modified through the *rasāyana* preparation, which are 'elixirs and rejuvenators' of alchemic reference. According to *Āyurveda* and *nātha-yogī* (the view of *raseśvara siddha* and *nātha siddha*), the first three tastes — sweet, sour and saline — pacify the *vāyu-prakopa*; sweet, bitter and astringent pacify the *pitta-doṣa* and pungent, bitter and astringent pacify the *kapha-vikāra*.

Samāna concentrates around the navel region (*jaṭhara-agni*), the element is fire and it is responsible for digestion. It has sense-contact with the eyes and is associated with the sight.

Vyāna concentrates around the body, mainly around the head, is responsible for the bodily movements and postures. It has sense-contact with the ears and is associated with the sound, the subtle form of which *śabda* exists as 'uncreated energy'.

terminate at these doors, which are the sense-organs — the two eyes, two nostrils, two ears, the mouth, the anus and the genital organ.[15] *Prāṇa*, moving with the breath, enkindles the body's fire, and the mind is carried through these doors by *prāṇa* so that it can experience the world. Of these thousands of *nāḍī*s three are quite important — the *sūrya nāḍī*, the *candra nāḍī* and the *agni nāḍī* (*suṣumnā*). The right nostril is related to the *sūrya nāḍī* and the left nostril to the *candra nāḍī* and *suṣumnā* (the fire channel) is closely associated with the spinal cord. The sun heats things up while the moon caresses to cool them. If a *sādhaka* is to observe his own body he will find that each nostril works for about an hour and a half, at a time. Continuously, throughout the day and night the *sādhaka*'s body fluctuates from excitation to relaxation and, back. *Yogī*s control this breath by performing *prāṇāyāma*. The *sādhaka* will never be able to arouse *kuṇḍalinī* until he can control the movement of the *prāṇa* in this body. *Kuṇḍalinī* can only leave the *mūlādhāra cakra* when *prāṇa* and *apāna* meet or are combined together in one place. Then *kuṇḍalinī*'s motion begins.

So *suṣumnā* holds the key to psychic opening and different layers of psychic existence. This psychic opening exhibits the different knots (*granthi*) of our being in our physical self and mental self or higher mental self. When these knots are released, our consciousness attains freedom from the insistent urges of these currents and their forces. An adept (*sādhaka*) knows these secrets and becomes free, because he can feel his transcendence and achieve mastery over these forces.

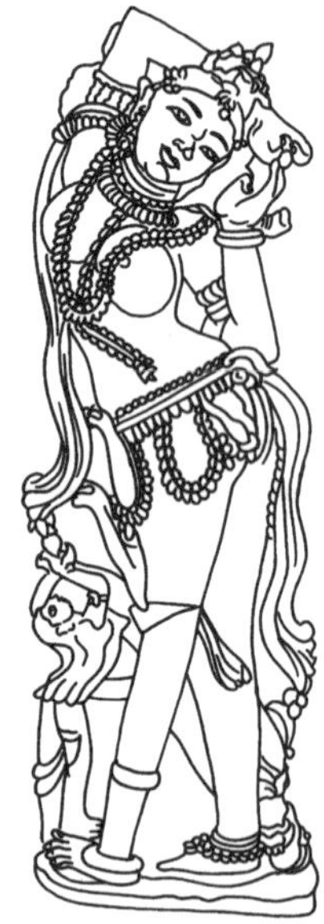

The knots (*granthi*) which obstruct the movement of *kuṇḍalinī* in the *nāḍī*, are three. The principal knots are *brahma-granthi*, *rudra-granthi* and *kṛṣṇa-granthi*[16] or *viṣṇu-granti*. *Kuṇḍalinī* cannot be awakened until the *sādhaka* pierces these knots. The *cakra*s exist in the subtle body and

15. *Śvetāśvatara Upaniṣad*, III.18; *Gorakṣa Śataka*, 13-14.

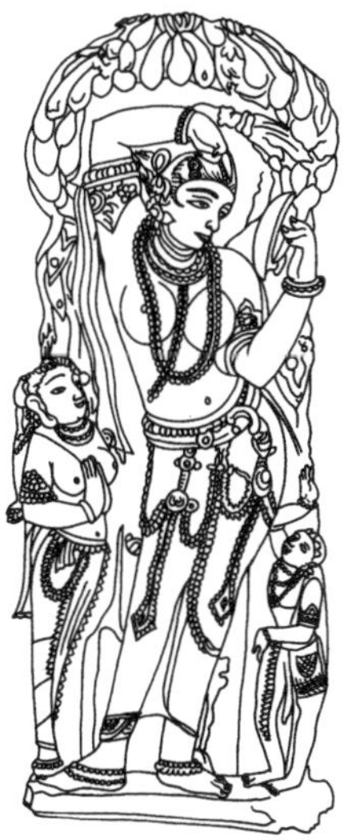

their connection to the physical body is very subtle. The *kuṇḍalinī* is fast asleep in the *mūlādhāra cakra*. Above the *maṇipūra-cakra* is *anāhata*, which means unstruck. It is held in Yoga-Tantra that, when all the senses are shut up and the nerves control the breath, suspended through a yogic process, there arises a spontaneous sound within, which is known as the *anāhata-dhvani* or *anāhata-nāda*. At the *anāhata-cakra*, the *sādhaka* begins to hear spontaneous sound.[17] When *kuṇḍalinī* moves from *anāhata* to *viśuddha-cakra* (*viśuddha* means 'pure') the *sādhaka* gains knowledge of the Ether Elements. The movement continues from *viśuddha* to *ājñā-cakra* (*ājñā* means 'command'). At the *ājñā-cakra* breathing is almost completely stopped, because here the *śūnya*-state (nothingness) begins. In the *śūnya*-state, all names and forms become extinct and only the void remains. When *kuṇḍalinī* moves from *ājñā* to the *sahasrāra*, the final shreds of identity is lost and the *sādhaka* merges himself completely with the universal soul. All differentiation is lost and the result is *nirvikalpa samādhi*, in which nothing is perceived except the universal soul. All fluctuations of the mind disappear.

---

16. Esoterically, Kṛṣṇa is the soul, the *gopīs* are the *nāḍīs*. *Gopī* literally means, secret; naturally, no one else but the *sādhaka* can know what is going on within his body. People say that Kṛṣṇa had 16,000 wives, and of those sixteen thousand, he was quite fond of one hundred. This means that *sādhaka*'s seventy-two thousand *nāḍīs*, sixteen thousand are predominant. Of those sixteen thousand one hundred are quite important and among three *suṣumnā* are quite supreme. Rādhā, the most beloved of the Kṛṣṇa, represents *suṣumnā*. At that time, the *kuṇḍalinī śakti* merges with its Lord in the *sahasrāra*, all the seventy-two thousand *nāḍīs* begin to dance in the cosmic rhythm. Each *nāḍī* vibrates with bliss, thinking that she alone possesses Kṛṣṇa, but, in fact, Kṛṣṇa, being the soul, is everywhere, and dances with all. This is the cosmic dance between Kṛṣṇa and the *gopīs* in the *sādhaka*'s own bodies.
17. Hajari Prasad Dvivedi, *Kabeer* (in Hindi), pp. 46-47.

4

Ulṭā Sādhanā*
(Regressive Process)

WE find that the Nātha *siddhas*[1] called their *sādhanā* as *kāya-sādhanā* with a view to attaining a *kāya siddhi.* The process has been styled as the regressive process or *ulṭā-sādhanā.* The *yoga-sādhanā* of the Nātha *siddhas* in *ulṭā,* firstly in the sense that it involves yogic processes which give upward motion to the whole biological as well as psychological systems which, in their nature, possess a downward tendency, and secondly, in the sense that such yogic practice leads the *siddha* to his original ultimate nature as the immortal being in his perfect (divine) body, back from the ordinary creative process of becoming.[2] The most important

* Hajari Prasad Dvivedi, *Kabeer* (in Hindi), pp. 80 to 94; Nāgendra Nātha Upādhyāya, *Tāntric Bauddha Sādhanā Aur Sāhitya* (Hindi), pp. 3-15; *Haṭha-Yoga-Pradīpikā,* trans. by Pancham Singh.

1. The Nāth cult is a yogic cult and it seems to represent a particular phase of Yoga cult of India. All the great teachers of this cult bear the title of 'Nātha'. So this Yoga-cult is known as Nātha-cult. The traditional belief of Nātha is that Ādi Nātha (Primal Lord) is the first teacher, and all secrets of Yoga proceed from him. This Ādi Nātha is none but Lord Śiva. This cult was never seriously theistic. The Supreme Being was referred to by the epithets *nirañjana* (speckless), *śūnya* (void), *anādi* (that which has no beginning) and Ādi Nātha (Primal Lord). Immortality is recognized as the quintessence of the ultimate nature of Lord Śiva.

   Hajari Prasad Dvivedi, *Nātha Sampradāya* (in Hindi), Allahabad, 1950, pp. 125, 165 and 172; *Kabir* (in Hindi), pp. 52-68.

2. All spiritual endeavours are regressive processes (*ulṭā-sādhanā*) in general sense inasmuch as they give a higher or upward →

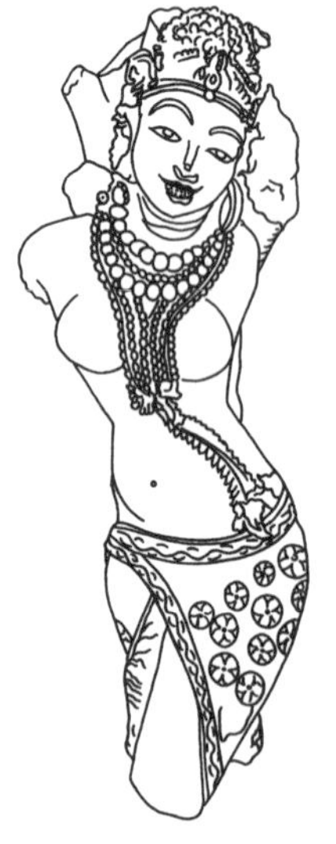

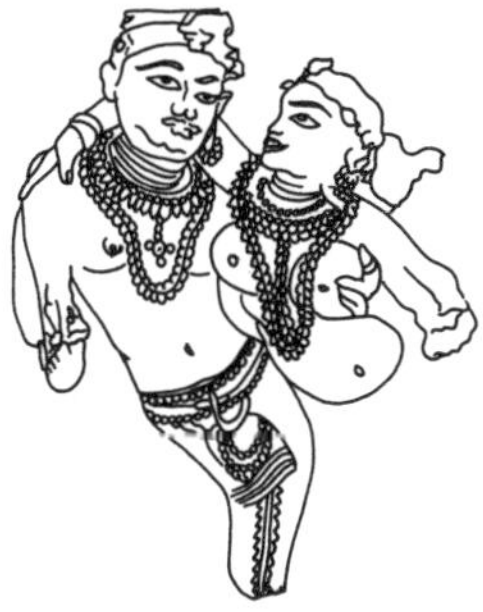

thing is the stress laid on the body as the medium in which truth can be realized. All the Schools of Yoga-Tantra hold that the body is the abode of all truth; it is the epitome of the universe. Attempt has been made in Tantra to identify the universe, completely, with the body. The yogic *sādhanā* is a science of religion, its methodology consists in its analyses of the body and the discovery of all *tattvas* in the nervous system and in the plexus, and thus making the body a perfect medium for realizing the ultimate truth. The adept (*yogin*) believes that the body is the microcosm of the universe; all that which the world is composed of are within the human body. It is by Yoga (Haṭha-Yoga) that one is able to have total control over the body and mind, so they believe in *kāya-sādhanā*. In the *kāya-sādhanā*, Śiva and Śakti reside in the body, the former in the *mahāsukha sthāna* (*sahasrāra*) which is the highest cerebral region, and the latter in the *mūlādhāra*, the lower extremity of the spinal cord.[3] Śiva is the numenal aspect or pure consciousness and perfect rest, and Śakti is the phenomenal aspect of the world of activity, the aspect of change and evolution. The *haṭha-yogī* believes that the region below the navel is the region of Śakti, the domain of *pravṛtti*, activity and change, while the region above the navel is the region of Śiva, the domain of *nivṛtti*. The bliss proceeding from the union of Śiva and Śakti is the highest realization.[4] And this union of

---

tendency to our lower being. It has been said that, when an intense thirst, is felt within for something higher, the mind becomes no more perturbed by desire, and at that state one is said to be in an upward current. It seems that the real significance of the word *pravṛtti* is just the same as the *ulṭā-sādhanā*. It is the process of introversion, reversal of the world of *pravṛtti* to the state of *nivṛtti*.

3. *Śiva Saṁhitā*, 5.151.2; Hajari Prasad Dvivedi, *Nātha Saṁpradāya* (in Hindi), pp. 73 onward.

4. We hear from the time of the *Āraṇyakas* and the Upaniṣads that bliss is the quintessence of Brahman, the Ultimate Being. From bliss proceeds the universe, it is sustained in bliss and it again dissolves in bliss. According to Yoga-Tantra, bliss is the nature

→

Śiva and Śakti symbolizes, in the wider sense, the stoppage of the ordinary process of becoming and retrogression of the whole world process for the attainment of the changeless state of Immortal Being.[5] Further, it is said that the right half of the body is Śiva, and the left half, Śakti (Ardhanārīśvara, united in ones body). Through the nerve *piṅgalā* in the right flows the *apāna vāyu* (wind) which is the stream of Śiva. Likewise, through the nerve *iḍā* flows the *prāṇa-vāyu* which is the stream of Śakti. The *sādhaka,* through the yogic practices, has to bring these two streams into the middle nerve which is *suṣumnā.* If this is achieved, there will be perfect equilibrium of Śiva and Śakti, and the yogic union is supposed to be the cause of *mahāsukha* (great bliss),[6] arising, when one experiences absolute non-duality. If one can realize the truth of the body (*bhāṇda*), one can also realize the truth of the universe (*brahmāṇḍa*).

According to the view of the *yogin,* there are thirty-two *nāḍīs* (nerve channels) within the body. The energy which has its seat below the navel, flows up through three channels. The topmost is called *mahāsukha sthāna* (the place of great bliss). The topmost station is imagined to be a lotus having either sixty-four or thousand petals. Various names are given to the nerve-channels, and among them, *lalanā, rasanā* and *avadhūti* are the most important, for they combine in themselves, at particular stations, the current supplied by the rest.[7] The *avadhūti* is the middle channel and

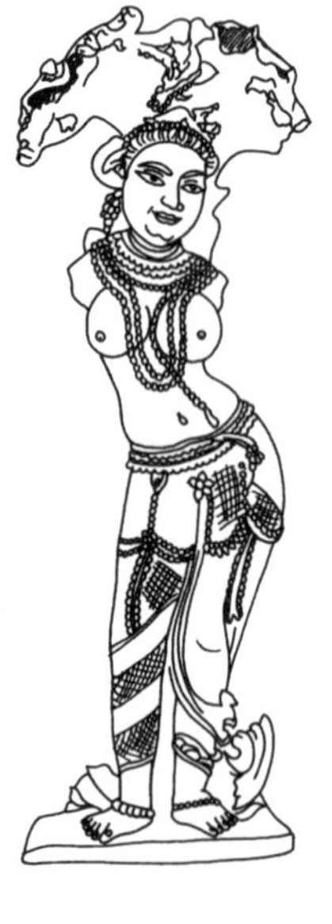

→ of the Absolute, which is conceived both positively and negatively. The Absolute is realized by us when we realized ourself as perfect bliss. The ultimate aim is, therefore, to attain a state of perfect bliss.

Nagendra Natha Upadhyaya, *Bauddha Kāpālika Sādhanā Aur Sāhitya* (in Hindi), Allahabad, 1983, pp. 72 and 121.

5. The view of Māheśvara Siddha.
6. Nagendra Natha Upadhyaya, *Tāntric Bauddha Sādhanā Aur Sāhitya* (in Hindi), p. 140; Haraprasad Shastri, *Advaya Vajra Saṁgraha,* Gayakawada Oriental Series, Baroda, 1928, p. 28.
7. *Bauddha Gāna O Dohā* (in Bengali language), edited by Pandit Hara Prasada Shastri, Calcutta, Bengali year 1323, p. 9.

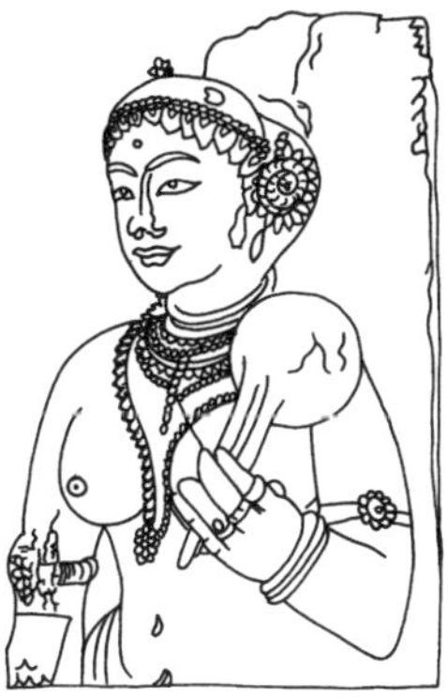

corresponds to *suṣumnā*, while the other two correspond to *iḍā* and *piṅgalā*. There are also a number of stations, compared to the lotuses (wheel = *cakra*)[8] within the body and psychic energy in its upward march has to pass through them. The ultimate goal is the creation of the state of *sahaja*, which is one of great bliss. It is a state which is without beginning and without end, a state which is free from duality. When this state is attained, the objective world disappears from view, and all the aggregates, elements, and senses merge in it. The *sādhaka* then finds himself to be the sole reality, identical with the universe and with Śiva (who is ever free).

It is said by *haṭha-yogīs* that, through the purifying process of *yoga* (the fire of *yoga*), the ordinary body of changes and decay is burnt away.[9] This Yoga School is

8. In the *Ṛgveda*, the word *cakra* is used with reference to Sūrya (Sun) and the Earth and the human body is defined or compared to *cakra*.

   Ṛgveda, 1.16.41; *Atharvaveda*, IX.9.1-2 & IX.9.11; *Kaṭhopaniṣad*, 1.33; Pandit Baladeva Upadhyaya, *Bhāratīya Darśana* (in Hindi), Vārāṇāsī, 1966, pp. 456-57; Nagendra Nath Upadhyaya, *Tāntric Bauddha Sādhanā Aur Sāhitya*, pp. 158 and 60.

9. In the *Siddha Siddhānta-Paddhati* we find that the physical body emerges from the collection of five factors, viz., *karma* (activity), *kāma* (desire), *candra* (the moon), *sūrya* (the sun) and *agni* (fire). Of these, the first two are rather the conditions of the visible body (*piṇḍa*) while the other three are the primary elements out of which the body is made. Of these three, again, the sun and fire are generally held to be the same. Then, the primary elements out of which the visible body is made are reduced to two, viz., the sun and the moon. The moon represents the element of *rasa* or *soma* (i.e., the quintessence in the form of juice) and the sun is the element of fire, and therefore, the body is called the product of *agni* and *soma*. *Rasa* as *soma*, is the food (*upabhogya*) while fire, as the consumer, is the eater *bhoktā* (*Gītā*, 15.13-14), and through the well proportional combination of the consumer and the consumed, the whole creation is sustained. The sun and the moon as *agni* and *soma*, respectively, are manifested in the physical world as the seed of the father and the ovum of the mother, through the combination of which proceeds the visible body, and thus *agni* and *soma* are the two primordial elements of which the whole creation is made.

based on the belief in the two aspects of the Absolute Reality, represented by the sun (Sūrya) and the moon (Candra). The sun stands for the principle of destruction (*kālāgni*) through the process of death and decay, and the moon stands for the principle of immutability.

The main *sādhanā* of *nātha-yogī* had to do with the culturing of the body (*kāya-sādhanā*) implying transubstantiation of the body first into a subtle ethereal body, and then, finally, into an immutable divine body having an eternal existence. The moon, which is the repository of *soma* or *amṛta* (nectar or ambrosia) which gives immortality, is situated just below the *sahasrāra*, the lotus of thousand petals in the cerebrum region facing downwards. The quintessence of the visible body is distilled in the form of *soma* in the moon, this *soma* rejuvenates the body and makes it immortal. In the ordinary course, this *soma* trickles down from the moon above and is dried up by the sun, the fire of destruction situated in the navel plexus; this drying up of the *soma* by the sun leads an ordinary being to decay and death.[10] This *soma* (also known as *mahārasa*, the great juice) must be protected from the sun.

10. In the Yoga-texts the moon and sun represent the two elements underlying physical existence, viz., the element of creation and preservation, and the element of change and destruction. The moon as the principle of non-change and immortality resides in the region of Śiva, and the sun as the principle of change and destruction resides in the region of Śakti. Thus, the moon and the sun are associated with Śiva and Śakti. It is said that *bindu* which is the quintessence of the body is of two kinds — the yellowish white *bindu* and red *bindu*, the former is the nature of semen (*śukra*), while the latter is of the nature of ovum (*mahārajas*). The *bindu* (of white colour to suggest the comparison with seed or semen) is contained in the moon in the upper region, while the red *bindu* (*rakta* or red colour to suggest the comparison with ovum) is contained in the sun in the navel. Generally, the sun is described in the navel, but in the *Gorakṣa Saṁhitā*, Chapter IV, verse 152, and *Kaula-Jñāna-Nirṇaya*, Chapter II, verse 3, it is described in the lowest plexus or *mūlādhāra*; white *bindu* is Śiva and that is the moon, and the latter is Śakti, which is the sun. Therefore, it →

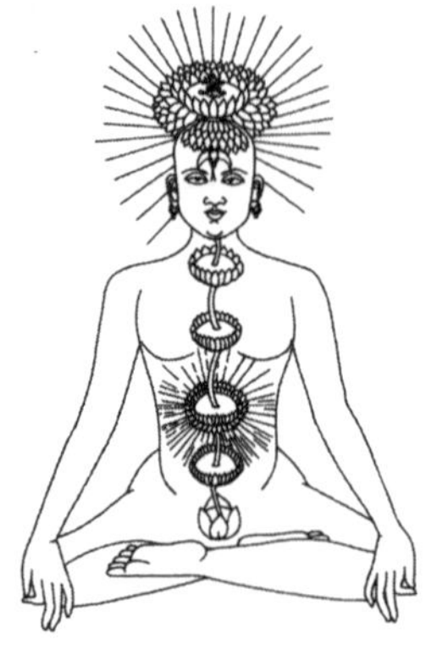

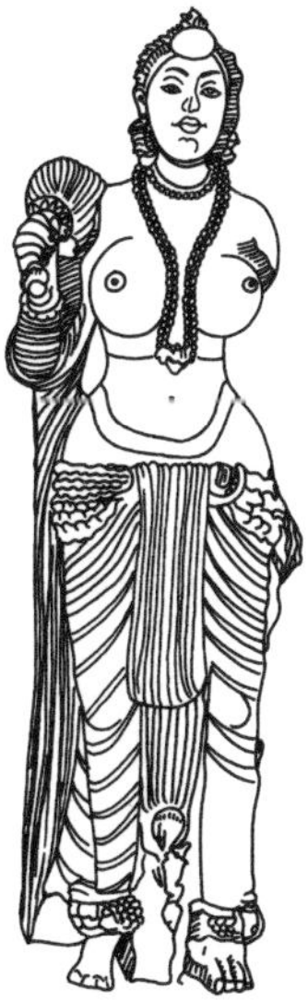

According to the *nātha-yogin*, the Ultimate Reality has two aspects which are symbolized by the sun and the moon; while the sun is *kālāgni*,[11] the principle of death and destruction, the moon is the symbol of unchangeability. The aim of the *nātha-yogin* is to feel within his own self the ideal of non-duality which is possible by the attainment of immortality and the renovation of the body; generally, Śiva represents this non-dual state, and its attainment is possible by connecting the force of the sun and the moon with the body. The essence, which helps the human body to survive, is produced from the *soma*, identified also as the moon, which is the source of the drug of immortality (*amṛta*) and which is found in the *sahasrāra* or the cerebral region of the body. If it is properly utilized, one can attain immortality. But, there is difficulty in that, the *amṛta* dropped from the moon or the *soma* is consumed by the sun which resides in the navel region.[12] However, there is a serpent-like channel within the body having two faces known as *baṅkanāla* or *śaṅkhinī*, and the face from which the *amṛta* is dropped is

→ seems that the conception of the moon and sun have been associated with that of Śiva and Śakti and metaphysically the moon and the sun represent the nature of Śiva and Śakti, respectively.

11. In the *Kaula-Jñāna-Nirṇaya*, Chapter II, this *kālāgni* as Rudra is associated with Śakti, and is said to be seated in the lower region (*mūlādhāra*) within the mouth of *vāḍava*. It is held that these seven lower regions are called *pātāla*, and the seven upper regions are called heaven. Creation is sustained as long as the *kālāgni* remains in the lower regions, but when it turns upward dissolution starts; *Baudha Gāna O Dohā* (in Bengali), edited by Pandit Hara Prasad Shastri, Calcutta, Bengali, year 1323, p. 128; *Siddha-Siddānta Saṁgraha* (in Hindi) edited by Pandit Gopi Natha Kaviraja, Sarasvati Bhavan text 13, Kāśī, 1925, 3/5; Hajari Prasad Dvivedi, *Nātha Sampradāya*, p. 172.

12. The sun is associated with Śakti and the moon with Śiva. Therefore, the moon must be saved from the sun. In the grosser aspect, man must save himself from woman. Charmed and allured by her, man loses vital energy. In Nātha yogic literature, women are regarded as the greatest danger in the path of *yoga sādhanā* and described as the greatest enchantress of the day and consumer of the night.

known as the tenth door (*daśa-dvāra*).[13] This tenth door is the most important in *yoga* and frequently referred to in *yoga* literature.

The door can be closed, and this is possible, and it is achieved only by *kāya-sādhanā* (the disciplining of the body). The *nātha-yogī* believes in three kinds of *śūnya* — *ādi-śūnya*, *madhya-śunya* and *antaḥ-śūnya*. The *śūnya* is to be realized through the *yoga*. By the yogic control of breath, the thirty-two knots in the spinal cord can be loosened, as a result of which the vital winds, *prāṇa* and *apāna* can enter the spinal cord and move as *haṁsa*, the six nerve plexuses — *mūlādhāra*, *svādhiṣṭhāna*, *maṇipūra*, *anāhata*, *viśuddha* and *ājñā*, and on reaching the *sahasrāra* region, assume the nature of *śūnya*. There are seventy-two thousand nerves within the body of which sixty-four can be distinctly located and fifteen utilized for yogic purposes.

The human body, which is called *brahmāṇḍa* (the golden egg or the aura or *Brahman*) is the microcosm. There is nectar rained in its proper place, on the top of the spinal column. With its face downward, it rains nectar, day and night. The ambrosia from the moon has two subtle parts — one of these nourishes the body like water of the heavenly river Gaṅgā, descending as a subtle channel on the left side,

13. *Śvetāśvatara Upaniṣad*, III.18.

It is held in the Yoga-Tantra that the quintessence of the visible body is distilled in the form of *soma* or *amṛta* (nectar) and is reposited in the moon in the *sahasrāra*. There is a carved duct from the moon below the *sahasrāra* up to the hollow in the palatal region; it is well known in Yoga physiology as the *śaṅkhinī*. This is the *baṅknāla* (i.e., curved duct) frequently mentioned in the vernaculars through which the *mahārasa* (i.e., *somarasa*) passes. This curved duct *śaṅkhinī* is described in the *Gorakṣa-Vijaya* as the serpent with mouths at both ends. The mouth of this *saṅkhinī*, through which the *soma* or the *amṛta* pours down from the moon is called the *daśam-dvāra* or tenth door of the body as distinguished from the other nine ordinary doors. This tenth door is the most important in Yoga; through this tenth door nectar trickles down from the moon. Ordinary people know nothing of its secret.

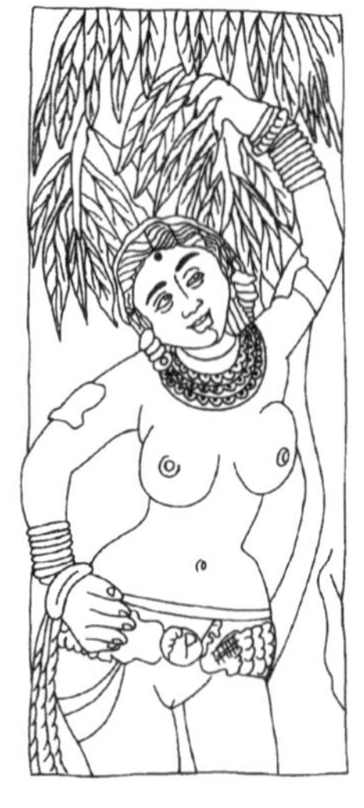

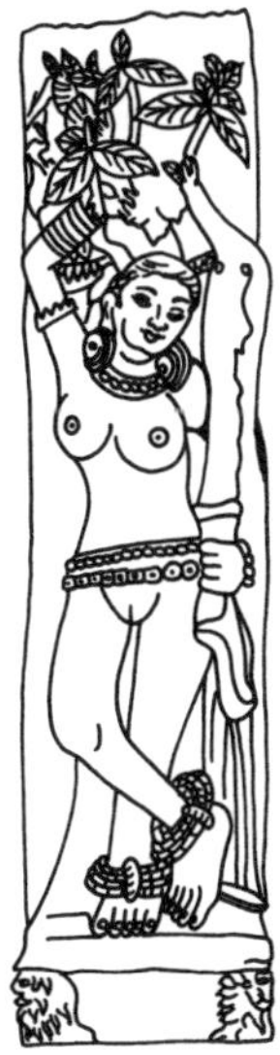

while the other ray of ambrosia, brilliant as the milk enters the central nerve of spinal column in order to maintain and recreate the moon in its proper place on top of the central great axis. At the lower region of the great axis of Meru is the sun, located within the body itself. From the inner sun situated at the navel, a subtle channel emanates to the right side of the body and carries the solar fluid upward by the power of its rays. The *Haṭha-Yoga-Pradīpikā* speaks of these two nerves as day and night. The *Sammohana-tantra* says that the left nerve is the moon because of its mild nature, whereas the nerve in the right is called sun because of its fierce nature. The left nerve is said to carry the seed and the right, the ovum, the seed is said to be Śiva — it is moon, and the blood is the Śakti; it is the sun. The nerve in the left is *ālī* and the right is *kālī* which represent the vowels and the consonants.

Esoteric teaching of the *yogin* (*nātha* and *haṭha-yogī*) declares that if one truly wishes to advance spiritually, one must work consciously to activate the subtle body. Through the basic ingredient and raw energies which exist in every-one, they must be focused and channelled, consciously. The emotion and mind should be brought to bear on the conscious evocation of an all-powerful subtle body which can then serve as a source of strength, intelligence, and transcendence. This is one of the most important secrets of the Yoga tradition.

5

Yogic Sādhanā of Sahajīya

A very nice exposition of this *sādhanā* is found in Vaiṣṇava and Buddhist Sahajīya and Sufism in the process of divine love.

This *yoga* is more psychological than physical or physiological. Sufism[1] as well as Vaiṣṇavaism is a cult of devotion,

---

1. The Sūfīs recognized and described the human body as the house of the temple of the Dear One. They say, about the people going on pilgrimage, that, in vain, they are searching the Beloved in temples and mosques and other places. 'The Man of the house is dwelling in the house, have you become mad by searching Him outside?' It is your own fault that you are roaming about for ever.

   The Sūfīs have often described this body as the 'place of the king,' the various plexuses have been described as the various lotus-ponds, and the six lotus-ponds (i.e., the six plexuses excluding the highest one, the *sahasrāra*) are again associated with the six seasons. The idea is this king dallies in different seasons, in different ponds, specially suited to the different seasons. So the one Ultimate Truth resides and functions differently in the different plexuses. They also talk about *anhada-nāda*, this word generally stands for *anāhata-dhvani*, which is all-pervading and eternal. In the process of becoming the Being, the first stage is the *śakti* (power) and the next stage is sound, the cosmic vibration from which evolves the visible world. It is the cosmic music and first music. For listening to this *nāda*, the *sādhaka* must withdraw his senses from outward objects, the mystery of sound (*anhada-nāda*) becomes unfolded to the *sādhaka*, and in tune with the cosmic rhythm, which arrests all the states and processes of mind and draws the *sādhaka* near to the Supreme. To listen to it and to which mode of sound (*nāda*) the *sādhaka* would hear depends on his *sādhanā*. All rivers go to the Ocean. In the *sādhanā* of *nāda* that ocean is the ocean of *bhāva* (emotion). The rivers are the *nāḍīs* and the

→

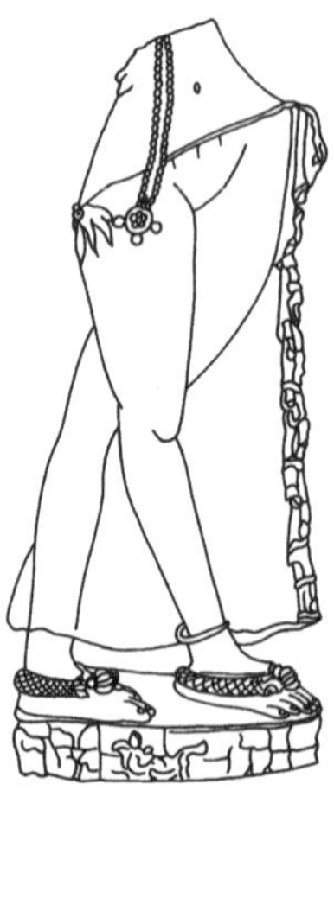

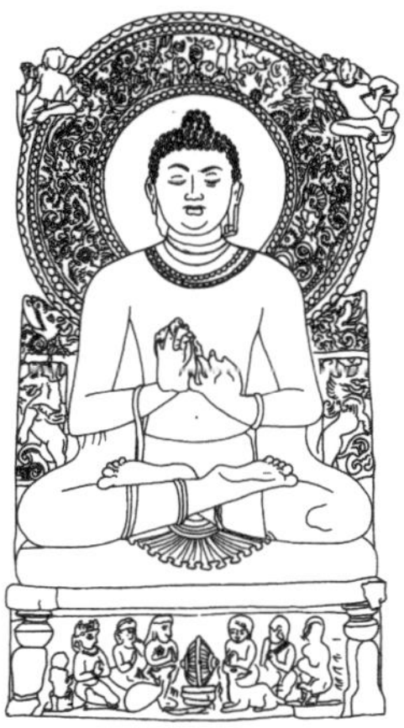

dedication with love. Here, love was conceived of as *sahaja*. This *sahaja* is divided into two parts as lover and beloved or enjoyer and the enjoyed; this division of the one into two is for self-realization. In terms of Vaiṣṇava Sahajīyas, the *sahaja* manifests itself in two currents — love (*rasa*), the exciting cause of love and support of love (*rati*) and are represented by Kṛṣṇa and Rādhā. It is held that man and woman on earth are but physical representations of *rasa* and *rati* or Kṛṣṇa and Rādhā in the corporal form and represent the *rūpa* (form) or external manifestation of Kṛṣṇa and Rādhā, who reside, so to speak, in every man and woman as the *svarūpa* or the true spiritual self. The *sādhanā* consists, first, in the realization of the *svarūpa* in *rūpa* and after this realization the pair (lover and the beloved) should unite in love; the realization of infinite bliss that follows from such a union is the highest spiritual gain. But this bliss of *sukha* is not misunderstood as a gross sex pleasure. It is the subtlest and the highest state of becoming that could only be reached by experiencing distinct stages or moment of bliss in an ascending order. This union is the union of personal ego, which is known as female with the male (Absolute), this is the cosmic union of universal dualities.

There is no denial of the fact that when we are deeply absorbed in any intense emotion (human love), we transcend our ordinary physical, biological and psychological existence, and even it may be admitted that such states of transcendental emotion may be transformed beyond recognition into the state of arrest. In a unique flow of intensely blissful realization, uninterrupted by the notions of subjectivity and objectivity, there dawns an

---

→ land is the human body or the *sādhaka*'s body. First the *sādhaka* follows the river into the sea and the sea will flood the rivers, which will overflow their banks with overwhelming divine passion, which is known as *bhāva-samādhi* which can lead to *nirvikalpa samādhi*.

infinite oneness in the mind, which is said to be the state of unity of emotion (*samarasa*).[2]

It is stated in Yoga philosophy that, when the states and processes of the mind are arrested, the *yogin* attains his 'own true nature' (*svarūpa*). The Vaiṣṇava Sahajīya also states that, where all the subjective and objective disturbances of the mind are absolutely lost in the supreme realization of bliss, we attain our true self, which is *sahaja*. This final state of Yoga is called *sahaja* state or *sahaja samādhi* or *śūnya-samādhi*. This state of *sahaja* is closely associated with the idea of *advaya* or *yuganaddha* which is the idea of *samarasa* or the sameness or oneness of emotion. In a deeper sense, the state of *sahaja*, is the state of perfect equilibrium, which transcends all our perceptual knowledge with positive and negative attributes. All the subjective and objective disturbances of mind are absolutely lost in a supreme realization of bliss and in that state we attain our true self, which is *sahaja*. To judge this state of *sahaja* as a pure state of *samādhi*, a *sādhaka* practises *yoga* in the plane of mind (*citta-bhūmi*). In that state of perfect quietude the *sādhaka* becomes one with the whole universe and realizes a non-dual existence. In such a state 'He himself is Rasa and

2. *Samarasa* is closely associated with the idea of *advaya* and *yuganaddha* is the idea of *samarasa* or oneness of emotion. In deeper sense *samarasa* means the realization of the oneness of the universe amidst all its diversities, — it is the realization of one truth as the flow of a unique emotion of all-pervading bliss. There is no sense of duality or difference anywhere; in such a state everything — whether lowest, or the middle or the best — should be realized as the same. The self should be realized as neither something static, nor something dynamic. Through transcendental meditation on the underlying oneness of the cosmic principle, everything should be viewed as of the same character and function. All the entities come out of trascendental knowledge of the form of *samarasa* — they are all equal and non-dual in nature. When through the yogic process one enters into the state of supreme bliss (*mahāsukha*), the whole world becomes the form of a unique emotion in the nature of *mahāsukha*, and through this unique emotion of bliss, the whole world, as static and dynamic, becomes one.

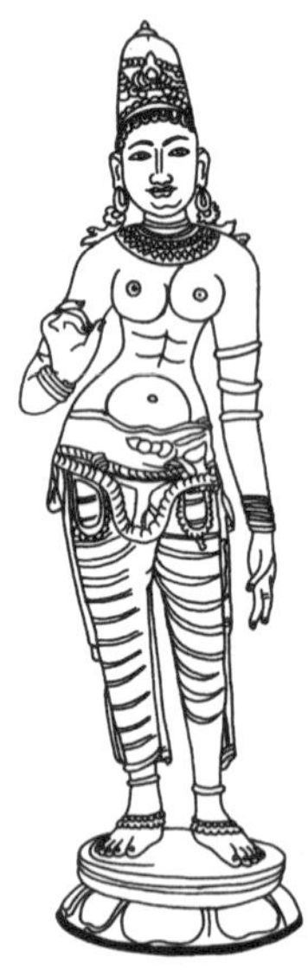

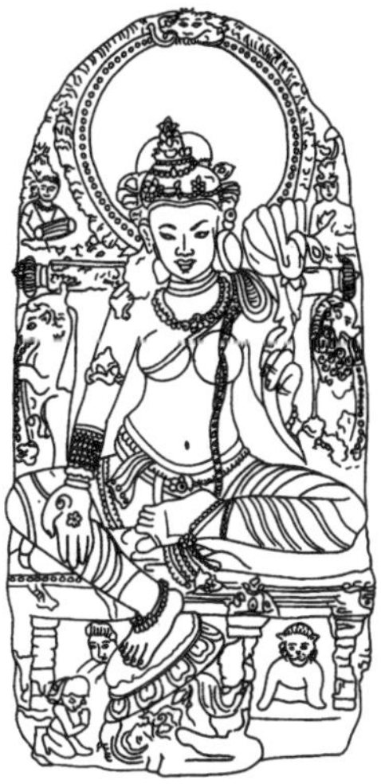

himself is Rati, himself is Rādhā, himself is Kṛṣṇa; he is, at once, the meditation, the meditator and the divinity (meditated upon).'[3]

3. As, when embraced by the dear woman, one knows neither anything external nor internal, so also a man, when deeply embraced by the inner self, knows neither aything external nor internal. *Bṛhadāraṇyaka Upanisad* IV. 3.2.1.

santo, sahaja samādhi bhalī
sāi tai milan bhayā jā dinatai, sūrat na anla cali

— *Kabeer-bānī, pada* 41

Hajari Prasad Dvivedi, *Kabeer*, p. 262.

6

Yogic Sādhanā of Buddhists

THE development of Tantrism effected a radical change in the outlook and character of the Indian religion, which aimed at the salvation of all by the spirit of universal love for all mankind. Actually, the fundamental principles of Yoga-Tantra were conceived by great minds with the best intentions, but the way, advised for salvation, was very dangerous to the ordinary people. Most of them fell victims to temptation and perished on the way before they could reach the land of bliss.

The period under review/witnessed not only the decadence of Buddhism but also the appearance of a new phase of the religion in which original, ethical and philosophical principles were superimposed in such a way that an esoteric yogic system evolved, combined with endless rituals and form of worship, that it could hardly be called Buddhism, any longer. However, it must be admitted that this new type of yogic *sādhanā* did confer on the adept some superhuman powers and also led many to the realization of high spiritual states. This new phase of Tāntric-Yoga in Buddhism envisaged something very deep and subtle to be realized only by those who were initiated into the secrets by their teachers.

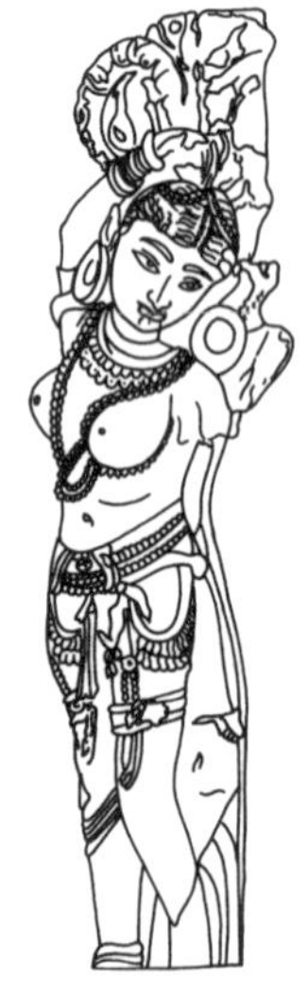

The Buddha found enlightenment and out of his infinite compassion taught the way for salvation which he had discovered. The world is a place of suffering, if for no other reason than for the reason that its joys are transient and all lives end in decay and death. All creatures are suffering in

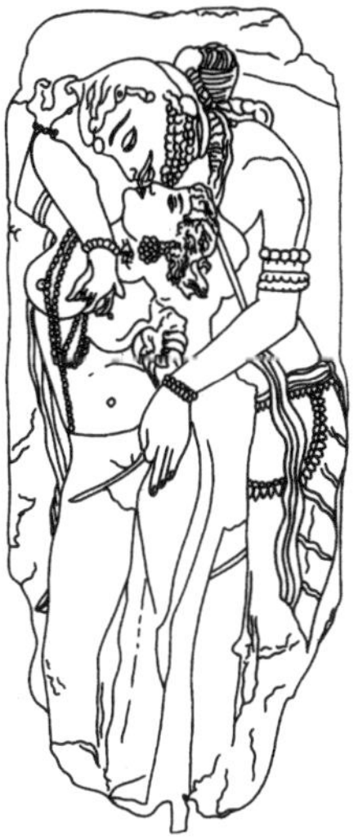

an endless cycle. He said that physical and mental constituents are kept going by desire. It is desire alone which leads to rebirth. Gnosis is to realize this and act, accordingly. So people should eschew desire and attain salvation. All living beings are equally entitled to respect and love. Salvation consists in a state of blissful calm so long as this life lasts, and no rebirth, when it comes to an end.

Buddha took it for granted that all that is contained in the world is impermanent, and therefore, full of misery. He promulgated the noble Eightfold Path which may give freedom from the miseries of birth and death. *Nirvāṇa* is like the extinguishing of a lamp. As the lamp is extinguished when there is no more oil, so man gets *nirvāṇa* when he has no more suffering (*kleśa*). This explanation of *nirvāṇa* is as given in Hīnayāna. Nāgārjuna, the founder of the Mādhyamika system of philosophy explained the condition of mind in *nirvāṇa* as *śūnya* and described it as a condition about which neither existence nor non-existence neither a combination of the two nor a negation of the two can be predicated. The followers of Yogācāra School were not satisfied with this explanation of *śūnya* which, as described by Mādhyamika, is an indescribable condition. They wanted to have a positive element in *śūnya*; and that positive element is *vijñāna* of which the individual is composed.[1]

According to the Mahāyāna conception, *śūnyatā* or perfect wisdom and *karuṇā* or universal compassion, generate in one's mind the *bodhicitta*, a state in which one is free from all worldliness.[2] The *bodhicitta* next proceeds on an

1. The Yogācāra theory of *vijñāna* or consciousness being, akin to Tāntric belief of superiority of spirit to the matter, paved the way for *sādhanā* and *siddhi*; by such *siddhi* one attains supernatural power. Such practices are traced to Guhyasamāja, assigned to Asaṅga (third century AD).

2. *Bodhicitta* means blissful state of mind or enlightenment. When the *bodhicitta* mingles with *śūnya* or the infinite spirit, in the highest state of meditation, the mind is filled with innumerable

→

upward march, through ten different stages (*bhūmis*), and when the last stage is reached, one becomes a perfect *bodhisattva*.[3] Buddhism interprets the whole thing in a different way. Here *śūnyatā* is identified with *prajñā*, the female principle, and *karuṇā* with *upāya*, the male, and it is held that the inner union of the two produces supreme bliss. Since the human body is the abode of Buddha, and also the epitome of the universe, liberation must come through the action of the body alone (*kāya-sādhanā*) and this can even lead one to the realization of the ultimate reality. From the metaphysical point of view, *prajñā* is the passive spectator, while *upāya* or *karuṇā* is the active agent that stirs up waves of mentation in *prajñā*. This idea seems to be closely akin to the popular Sāṁkhya view and thus, metaphysical significance of *prajñā* and *upāya* has a close bearing on the conception of Śakti and Śiva.

Mahāyāna Buddhism was subdivided into two distinct schools, the Mantrayāna and Pāramitāyāna. The Mantrayāna seems to be the introductory stage from which other offshoots like Vajrayāna, Kālacakrayāna and Sahajayāna, etc., arose in later times. The Vajrayāna conception of *bodhicitta* appears to be the same as advocated in Yogācāra, the idea of which can be gained by a reference to the *Tattva-Saṁgraha*. The *boddhicitta* is like a continuous stream of consciousness which changes every moment, the consciousness of the previous moment giving rise to or causing the consciousness of the succeeding moment. The chain of

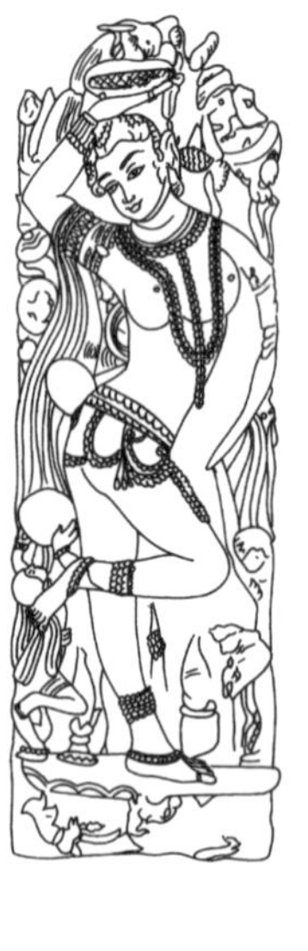

→ visions and scenes, then the *sādhaka* visualizes the germs — syllables, which gradually assume the shape of deities, first indistinct, and then, changing into perfect glorious and living form, the embodiment of *śūnya*.

3. S.B. Dasgupta, *Introduction to Tantric Buddhism*, pp. 91-93. He is also called the *mahāsattva* as he is full of the bliss of infinite knowledge, and he is always engaged in the right method of religious observance (*samaya*). He is called the *samaya-sattva* — as he is eternally associated with disciplinary practices for the attainment of wisdom, he is called *bodhisattva*, and as he is associated with perfect wisdom he is called *jñāna-sattva*.

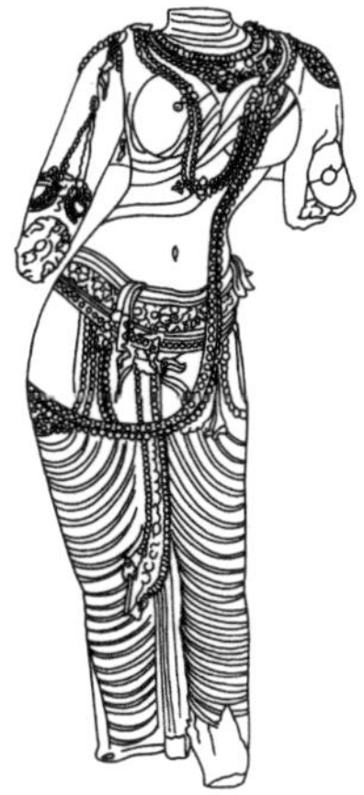

momentary consciousness which is, without beginning or an end, operating in unison with the all powerful force leads it either to degradation or to emancipation according to the action done which is good or bad. In the eye of a Vajrayānist, the external world has much the same significance as it appears in Yogācāra. They hold that external objects have no greater reality than dream, and their reality cannot be proved by reason.

Within the fold of Vajrayāna there arose a school known as Kālacakrayāna. It concerns itself with the yoga-tantra and anuttara-yoga-tantra and incorporates the doctrines of the Sahajayāna also. *Kāla* means the ultimate immutable knowledge (*prajñā*) or the state of *śūnyatā*, while the *cakra* means the cycle of the world process, or the body of the *sādhaka* containing the potency of existence of the universe, which is just the principle of *upāya*. Therefore, *kālacakra*[4] implies the absolutely unified principle of *prajñā* and *upāya*, and that is the *bodhicitta*. One distinctive feature is the stress on time which is the common meaning of the term *kāla*. Time, with all its divisions and subdivisions (moment, hour, day, night, week, fortnight, month and year) dwells within one's body, in which lies the whole universe with all its animate and inanimate objects. And time with its divisions is caused by, or is the production of, the vital wind (*vāyus*) that remains diffused throughout the entire nervous system of one's body. One can control the vital wind in the nerves

4. The word *kālacakra* means the wheel of time or the circle of time. In another word *kāla* means time, death and destruction. The *kālacakra* is the wheel of destruction and Kālacakrayāna means the vehicle for protection from the wheel of destruction. In the sixth chapter of *Tantrāloka* of Abhinavagupta, he has discussed the theory of *kālacakra* and has devoted his attention to the exposition of the doctrine of *kāla* (time) and the processes of keeping oneself above the influence of time. Every syllable of the word *kālacakra* is said to be pregnant with a meaning. The syllable *ka* indicates unruffled casuality in which there should be the final absorption as is indicated by the syllable *la*. *Ca* indicates unsteady mind, and *kra* means the series of events or the process.

by yogic practices, and thereby put oneself above all influence of the whirls of time which is the root cause of all miseries including decay and destruction.[5]

The Sahajayāna School is an offshoot of Vajrayāna. The exponents of the Sahaja School put the whole emphasis on their protest against the formalities of life and religion. For they adopted human nature itself as the best appliance for realizing the truth. Hence, one must proceed through the natural way, which lies not in discarding the inborn propensities of human beings and total annihilation of the passions, but in sublimating the same. The Sahajīyas would never prescribe any unnatural strain on human nature but would take human nature itself as the best help for realizing the truth.[6] It is for this reason that this path has always been described as the easiest and most natural (*sahaja*). The real origin of this cult lies more in outside Buddhism than inside it. The Buddhist *sahaja* cult, notwithstanding the Buddhist tone and colour which it assumes; is essentially an esoteric yogic cult. Side by side, with the commonly known theological speculations and religious practices there had been flowing in India an important undercurrent of esoteric yogic practices from pretty old times. These esoteric practices, when associated with the theological speculation of Śaiva and Śākta, have given rise to the Śaiva and Śākta

5. One's own body in which the whole world is manifest, has a resemblance to the doctrines of Sahajayāna and Nāthism and this makes it probable that the Kālacakrayāna is embodied in the teaching of Vajrayāna, Sahajayāna and Nāthism.

6. In the Anuśāsana-parva of the *Mahābhārata*, where Bhīṣma (Bhīṣma-Pitāmaha) describes to Yudhiṣṭhira the really sacred places of pilgrimage, we find that the mind, with the transparent water of purity and truth, when associated with the lake of patience, is the best of all places of pilgrimage. He whose whole body is washed with water cannot be considered to be the really cleansed one. One, who has controlled all his senses, is the really 'clean one'. He is pure within as well as without. To dive into the water of bliss of Brahma-knowledge in the lake of the pure heart, is the best of all the bathings, and he alone, the wise recognize, to be a real pilgrim.

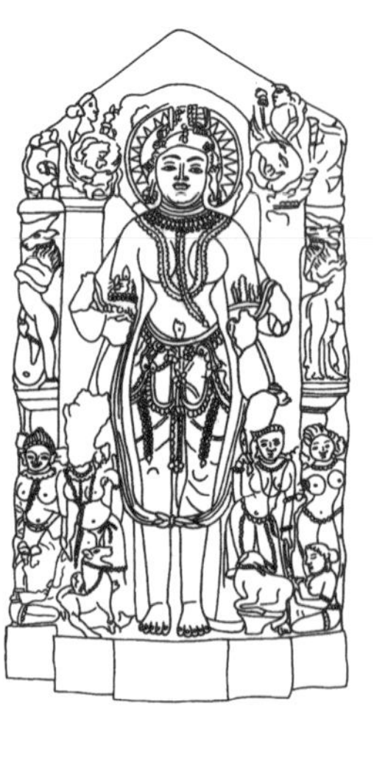

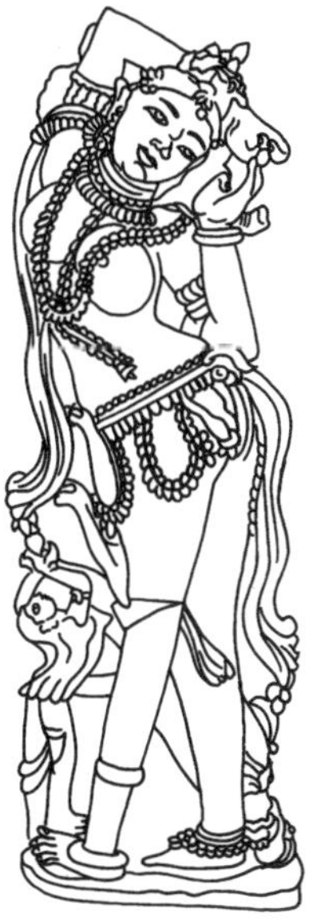

Tantrism, and again, when associated with speculations of Bengal Vaiṣṇavism, the same esoteric practices have been responsible for the growth of the esoteric Vaiṣṇavite cult, known as the Vaiṣṇava Sahajīya that never prescribes any unnatural strain on human nature. The Sahajīyas were averse to the method of knowing the truth through discursive method and were not in favour of religious formalities. The Buddhist Sahajīyas and the *nāth-yogin* believe in *bindu-siddhi* or yogic control of semen (*vīrya*).

According to the Tāntric view, the act of creation is due to union of the two principles. These are known as *prajñā* and *upāya* or *śūnya* and *karuṇā*. This is also known as *lalanā* and *rasanā*, respectively.[7] The union of *prajñā* and *upāya* is *yuganaddha* or *samarasa*. One who can unite these two principles in oneself can have the highest knowledge and supreme bliss and become free from the fetters of birth and death. This is known as the *mahāsukha* (greatest pleasure) or *nirvāṇa* and real manifestation of *bodhicitta*. In the Buddhist yoga-tantra the element of *nirvāṇa* is described as incessant bliss (*sukhamaya*). It is the abode of both enjoyment as well as liberation. It is called *mahāsukha*, where there is no change or decrease. It is the seed of all substance, it is the ultimate stage of those who have attained perfection, it is the highest place of the *Buddha* (perfect enlightenment). *Mahāsukha* is something which has neither existence nor annihilation, it

7. *Prajñā* and *upāya* are also known as *lalanā* and *rasanā*, which are the names of the two nerves, *iḍā* and *piṅgalā* in the Hindu Tāntric nerve-system. That in which two nerves commingle is called the *avadhūti*. That is known as the *suṣumnā* nerve in the Hindu Tantra and this nerve is regarded as the way to attain *nirvāṇa*. It is stated that *lalanā* is of the nature of *prajñā* and *rasanā* of *upāya* and *avadhūti* stay in the middle as the abode of *mahāsukha*. The nerves in the right and left in the microcosm of the body represent the principle of duality. Their separate function which binds one to the world of sufferings must, therefore, be checked by the *yogin* and these two nerves must unite with the middle nerve and function conjointly. The middle nerve is, therefore, the middle path which leads to the non-dual state of *sahaja*.

has neither a beginning nor any middle, nor any end; this transcendental supreme bliss is neither the not-self nor the self.

The *sukha* is not possible at all with the body, without the body none would ever be able to seek the *saukhya*. So, great importance is laid on the human body which is believed to be the abode of truth and also the medium of realizing the truth. Through the union of *prajñā* and *upāya* the great element is produced in the form of bliss, which yields *paramānanda;* after the cessation of *paramānanda* is produced *virāmānanda*, and supreme bliss that follows *virāmānanda* is of indescribable nature. It is bereft of all the senses, it is the ultimate stage of liberation of the *sādhaka*s, the pure transcendental non-substantial *bodhicitta*. The bliss that is produced through some cause, itself destroys the cause of *saṁsāra*. The nature of *mahāsukha* cannot be realized through the theories of all other false constructions. Through the purification of *prajñā* and *upāya*, it is revealed that *mahāsukha* is the one non-dual knowledge. When *prajñā* and *upāya* are combined together in oneness, the non-dual knowledge is produced which is *mahāsukha* or *sahaja* or the innate nature of self and the world, around.

This new type of yogic *sādhanā* developed a theology of its own, which is different from the philosophy of canonical Buddhism. According to these esoteric Buddhists, *bodhicitta* is the highest truth, it is absolute. It is the innate nature of the self and the world. This *bodhicitta* is explained as a unified state of *śūnyatā* (void) and *karuṇā* (universal compassion). *Karuṇā* is a strong emotion of compassion, it is the dynamic principle that leads one to an active life for liberation not only of one's self but also of others; it is, therefore, the active principle and is called *upāya* (the means). *Prajñā*, as pure consciousness (*vijñapti-mātratā*) or pure wisdom, represents the domain of *nivṛtti*, while *upāya*, as the active principle, represents the domain of *pravṛtti*. If we examine the practices of Buddhism, we shall find that

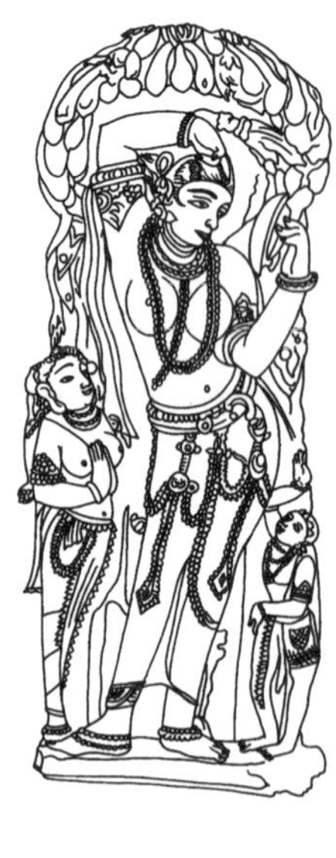

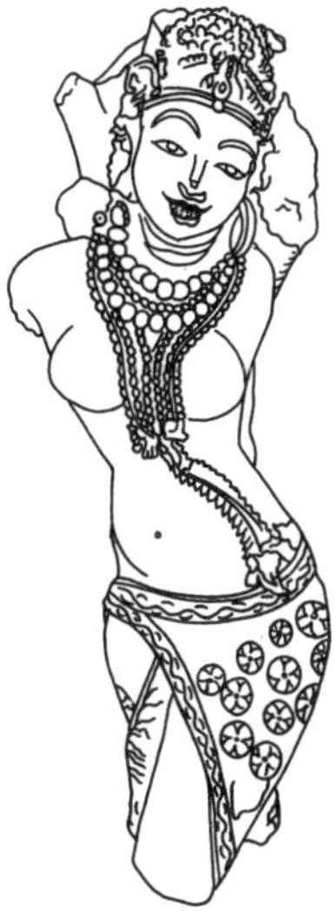

the final aim in all such cases was the attainment of an infinitely blissful state of *samādhi*, through the absorbing intense emotion of love or love-pleasure. In a unique flow of intensely blissful realization, uninterrupted by the notions of subjectivity and objectivity, there is an infinite oneness in the mind, which is said to be the state of unity of emotion (*samarasa*); when all the subjective and objective disturbances of the mind are absolutely lost in a supreme realization of bliss, we attain our true self, which is *samādhi* or *bhāva samādhi* or *sahaja-samādhi.*

The *sādhanā,* involving the physical and psychological union of *prajñā* and *upāya,* leads to the inner union of the two, and through this yogic union is produced supreme bliss (*mahāsukha*),[8] which, according to Buddhist yoga-tantra, is the very nature of the absolute. One realizes the absolute only when one realizes one's own self as perfect bliss. The ultimate end is, therefore, to attain this state of perfect bliss. In our ordinary life, we do feel like experiences, intense pleasure in our sex-experiences, but, between the sex-pleasure and perfect bliss, which constitutes the ultimate nature of our self, there is an abysmal difference. The experiences of sex-pleasure is extremely transitory and defiled in character as they only fasten us to a lower plane of life. But the sexo-yogic *sādhanā,* is a *sādhanā* which is calculated to be capable of transmitting; even gross sex-pleasure into the realization of infinite bliss in which all the activities of the mind are absolutely lost, and in which the self and the world around are lost in an all-pervading oneness.[9]

---

8. The character of *mahāsukha* is described in *Jñānasiddhi,* Chapter VII; See two Vajrayāna works, G.O.S. N. XIIV, p. 57; this new idea was known as the *mahāsukhavāda,* and the form of Buddhism which was based on this *mahāsukhavāda* was known as Vajrayāna.

9. The exponents of Yoga have admitted to the fact that it may be possible to attain a state of arrest even through some strong sensation or intense love-emotion but this kind of arrest of →

The *bodhicitta* is no more the state of mind in which there reigns only strong determination to attain perfect wisdom (*bodhi*) but it signifies the production of an extremely blissful state of mind through the yogic union of the two. This is further elaborated by the identification of different philosophical concepts with various parts of the nervous system of the human body and the conception of the attainment of the final bliss as a physical process.

According to esoteric Buddhism, the body is the abode of truth and, at the same time, the best medium for realizing the truth. With this belief, it located four plexuses (lotuses) in different parts of the body along the spinal column. The first is *nirmāṇa-cakra* situated in the naval region, representing the *nirmāṇa-kāya* or the principle of material trans-formation or created body, also known as *rūpa-kāya;* this body is generally for guidance of common worldly men and beings. One assumes an earthly form which is subject to all human frailties. The second is the *dharma-cakra* situated in the cardiac region, representing the *dharma-kāya*, or the principle of non-dual cosmic existence, the universal principle, which has no form, is infinite and external without appearance or disappearance. The third is the *saṁbhoga-cakra* situated near the neck, representing the *saṁbhoga-kāya* or the principle of the body of bliss. Above all these, and transcending all these, is the plexus (lotus) in the head, which is the seat of absolute truth. An additional nervous-cycle is *uṣṇīśa-kamala* in the central region which is the symbol of the Buddha, *vajra-kāya* or *sahaja-kāya* and which corresponds to the Śākta concept of *sahasrāra*. The

→ mind is very transitory and, as such, falls far short of the final state of *samādhi*. *Samādhi* of *yoga* proper does not mean a temporary arrest of mind.

In this state, there is the excess of the *tamas* (i.e., the gross material stuff) and under the sway of the *tamas* mind falls asleep or swoons as it were. It may be called momentary steadiness. There is possibility to replace this to an ordinary active state at any moment.

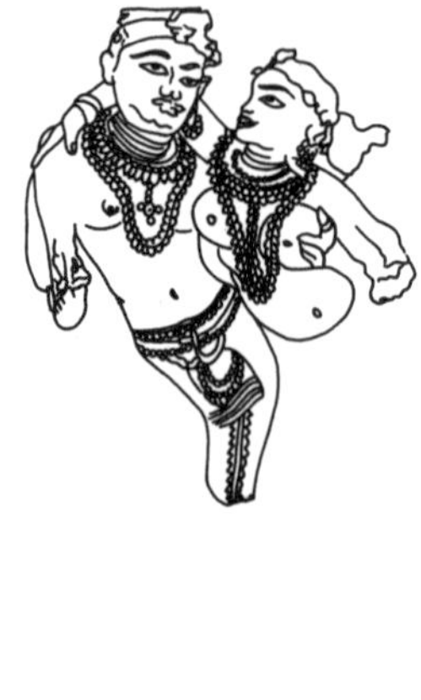

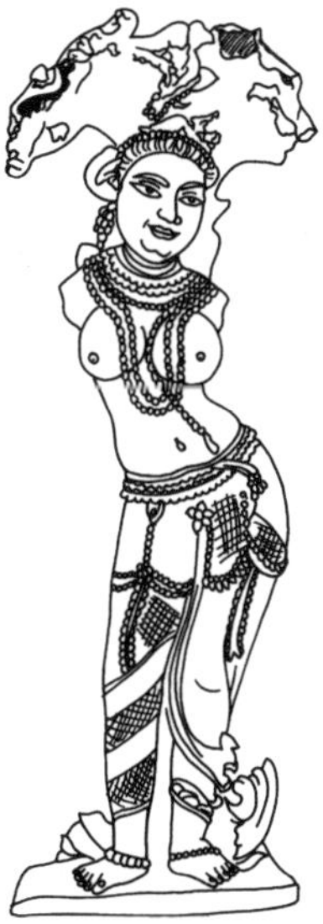

cosmic energy (conceived as a feminine principle) remains as a fire force in the *nirmāṇa-cakra* and here, associated with all gross principles of defilement, she acts as the principle of phenomenalism. She must be roused and dissociated from all principles of defilement and given an upward motion, so as to reach the *uṣṇīśa-kamala*, which is the region of perfect purity.[10] Again the important nerve on the left side of the body, called moon or the river Gaṅgā, represents *prajñā*, the women, and the nerve on the right side, called sun or the river Yamunā, represents *upāya*, the Lord. The left and the right should be controlled and commingled in such a way that all the functions (including the flow of the vital current *prāṇa* and *apāna* in the two nerves) may be completely unified in the middle path, called *avadhūti*. (*Avadhūti* has been explained in Buddhist texts as that which, through its effulgent nature, destroys all sin.) Such a perfect unification, resulting, ultimately, in the realization of infinite bliss (*mahāsukha*), is the quintessence of the *boddhicitta*. *Prajñā* (the goddess) manifests herself in every woman and every man is the embodiment of *upāya*, the Lord.

In the actual *sādhanā*, the man and the woman must, first of all, transcend their corporal existence and realize their true self as *upāya* and *prajñā*, respectively. With such realization they should unite and control the sex act in such a way that the downward motion of seed may be arrested and an upward motion is given to it till it reaches the

---

10. In Yoga-Tantra, the semen is called *bodhicitta*. The fall of the semen is considered a great sin. The semen must not be emitted, for, otherwise, the *yogin* falls under the Law of Time and Death. For checking the flow of semen, the *sādhaka* practices coitus reservations by taking recourse to Haṭha-Yoga or the psycho-physical technique. The semen instead of flowing downward is led by *yoga* to the highest centre of the bodoy or the *uṣṇīśa kamala* of Buddhist yoga-tantra.

    Nagendra Natha Upadhyaya, *Tāntric Bauddha Sādhanā aur Sāhitya* (in Hindi), pp. 315; *Haṭha-Yoga-Pradīpikā*, by Pancham Singh, pp. 83-88; T.N. Mishra, *Buddhist Tantra and Buddhist Art*, p. 30.

highest plexus and remains there motionless. This motionless state of the seed in the highest plexus conduces to infinite bliss and tranquillity. The realization of the highest bliss is the realization of the highest truth. *Prajñopāya* (*prajñā* and *upāya*) is, therefore, equivalent to *mahāsukha* (supreme bliss) and entirely auspicious (*sāmantabhadra*). The state of perfection is neither duality nor non-duality. Wisdom conceived as the female is to be combined in one's own self for the purpose of liberation which is perfect enlightenment through the practical experience of the female principle. *Prajñā* or wisdom is linked with a state of intense emotion called *sukha* (bliss) or *mahāsukha* (great bliss) which is conducive to complete enlightenment. The highest state of the union of the two (this union is the union of the personal ego, which is known as female with the male 'Absolute,' this is cosmic union of universal dualities or union of the individual with the infinite.) is that of supreme love and it is the real *sahaja mahāsukha*.[11]

The union of *prajñā* and *upāya,* through the principle of *yuganaddha* for the purpose of the non-dual state,[12]

11. This supreme process of *yoga* is eternal. It originates from our passion. Our passions are part and parcel of our nature and our nature is never transgressible. It is, therefore, wise to transform these passions in the yogic process for realizing the truth. If the *sahaja* can once be realized, everything can be attained. It is the realization of one truth as the flow of a unique emotion of all-pervading bliss, when, through the yogic process, one enters into the state of supreme bliss (*mahāsukha*). The whole world becomes the form of a unique emotion in the form of *mahāsukha* and through this unique emotion of bliss, the whole world, as static and dynamic, becomes one.

12. The idea of *yuganaddha* is that the final state is where all kinds of dualities are absorbed in a principle of non-duality. This principle was adopted by the Sahajīyas in their process of *yoga.* The nerves in the right and the left in the microcosm of the body represent the principles of duality; their separate function which binds one to the world of suffering, must, therefore, be checked by the *yogin* and they must unite with the middle →

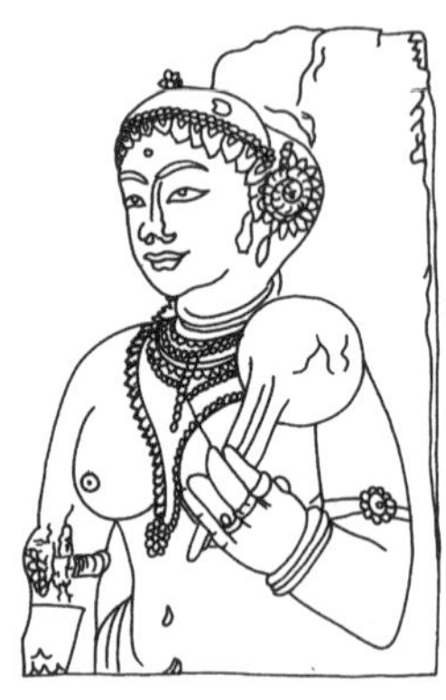

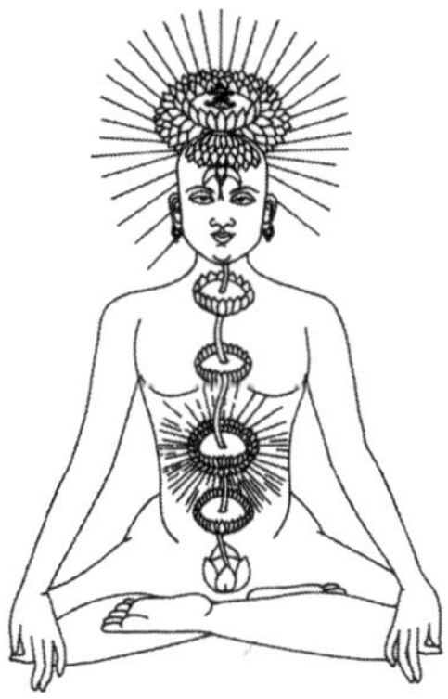

symbolized by the physical union of the *sādhaka* and his partner, brings in succession *rāga* (emotion) and *mahārāga* (intense emotion, evidently transcendental, resulting from a genuine feeling of compassion); *samarasa* (oneness of a motion) in which there is no cognition of *prajñā* and *upāya*, and finally, the *mahāsukha* or great bliss which is or the nature of the absolute unity of *prajñā* and *upāya*, the non-dual quintessence of all the entities without which perfect wisdom is never possible.

The final aim in all such cases was the attainment of an infinitely blissful state of arrest (*samādhi*) either purely through a psycho-physiological process of *yoga* or through the absorbing emotion of love, strictly disciplined and intensified through the practice of *yoga*. Intense human love or pleasure, thus transformed beyond recognition, has the capacity to produce a supreme state of arrest. In a unique flow of intensely blissful realization, uninterrupted by the notions of subjectivity and objectivity, there dawns an infinite oneness in the mind, which is said to be the state of unity of emotion (*samarasa*). All the subjective and objective disturbances of the mind are absolutely lost in a supreme realization of bliss and, in that state, we attain our true self, which is *sahaja*. It is the abode of both incessant bliss (*sukhamaya*) as well as liberation. It is called *mahāsukha*, where there is no change or decrease. It is the seed of all substances; it is the ultimate stage of those who have attained perfection; it is the highest place of *sukha*, where all kinds of duality vanish in a unique realization of the supreme bliss.

This bliss is not to be misunderstood as gross sex-pleasure. It is the subtlest and the highest state of becoming that could only be reached by experiencing a distinct stage

---

→ nerve and function there conjointly. This middle nerve is, therefore, the middle path which leads to the non-dual state of *sahaja*.

(momentary of bliss in an ascending order). It demarcates the *cakra* or the centre of consciousness at different planes or levels of anthropomorphic personality. The *cakra* along with their particular 'flavour' of joys transform the individual personality, stage by stage, into cosmic existence or selfless immortality.

In Yoga-Tantra, we find that the world proceeds from the bliss which is the cessation of all duality and is the nature of ultimate reality. It has been said that bliss (*ānanda*) is to be known as *Brahman*, from bliss proceeds all the objects, through bliss they live, and in bliss do they return and merge.[13] We find an echo of the same truth in the utterances of the Sahajīyas, who say that all beings are born in *sahaja*; they live in *sahaja* and again return to *sahaja*. The *sahaja* is the *rasa*, the supreme emotion of love, the quintessence in everybody. It is the primordial emotion, it is the desire and from this desire proceeds everything. There is sometimes the tendency of explaining the two stages of *sahaja* (i.e., *rasa* and *rati*) under the imagery of the seed and ovum and the cosmos as following from their union, just as it is explained in the texts of the Sahajīya Schools. Both the self and the non-self, being thus the product of *sahaja*, are homogeneous in their ultimate nature, and it is, therefore, stated that the realization of the nature of the self, through the culture of love, leads also to the realization of the ultimate nature of the non-self.

A dominant feature of this school is its stress on the middle path, avoiding the opposite extremes of views. The final aim is that, all kinds of duality are absorbed in a principle of non-duality. The nerves in the right and the left in the body represent the principle of duality; and they must be united with the middle nerve and function jointly. The middle nerve is, therefore, the middle path which leads to the state of *sahaja*. Therefore, the flow of *bodhicitta* must

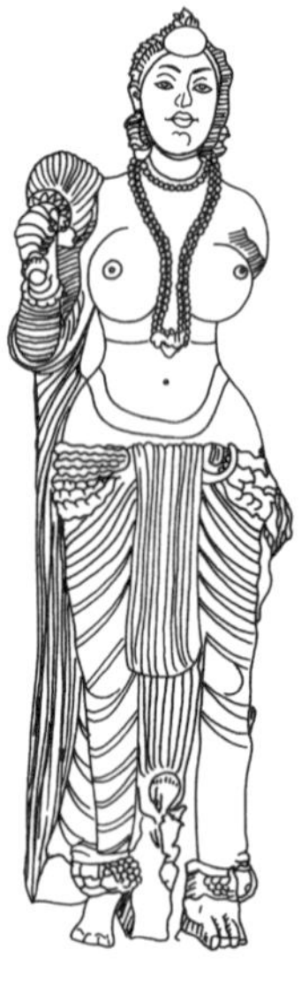

13. *Taittirīyopaniṣad*, III.6.

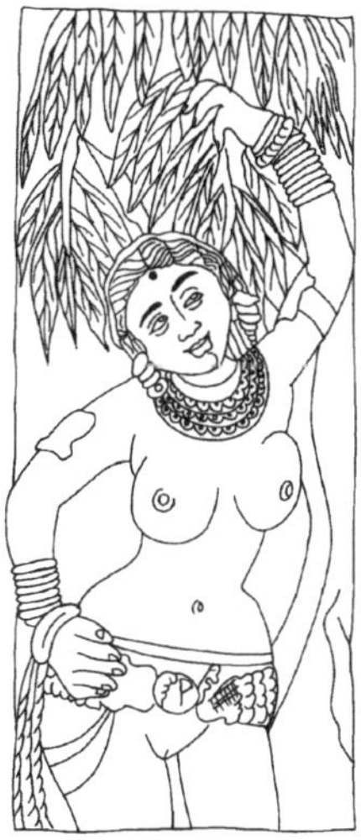

be regulated along the middle nerve, and this is the most important, and, at the same time, the most difficult part of *sādhanā*, and it is for this reason that we find repeated warnings to the novice to take practical suggestions from a preceptor, at this stage. If the flow of *bodhicitta* moves either left or right, the whole thing is spoiled. The *apāna vāyu* (wind) has always a downward motion; the *prāṇa* an upward motion; therefore, the *yogin* should arrest the course of both the *prāṇa* and *apāna*, and, then, make them flow through the middle nerve and, with this flow of vital wind within the middle nerve, the *bodhi* will also flow upward and reach the *uṣṇīśa-kamala*, and thereby, *mahāsukha* will be produced. The *bodhicitta* should then be made steady by making steady the breath, and this stage of *yoga* is the ultimate stage for the *yogin*. In this production of the *bodhicitta*, four stages associated with the four centres (*cakra*) are distinctly marked, and on the basis of the four stages, we find mention of four *mudrā*s (viz., *karma-mudrā, dharma-mudrā, mahā-mudrā* and *samaya-mudrā*), which are the four stages of Yoga. There are four mental states called the four moments (viz., *vicitra, vipāka, vimarda* and *vilakṣaṇa*)[14] and four kinds of bliss — *ānanda, paramānanda, virāmānanda* and *sahajānanda*.[15]

14. *Vicitra* is the moment when the realization of pleasure is attended with various kinds of emotions resulting from physical union; *vipāka* is the moment when bliss matures to knowledge; *vimarda* is a higher moment when the realization of the bliss is attended with the consciousness of the ego as the realizer of the bliss; *vilakṣaṇa* is the moment when the realization transcends all these three and the realization of the bliss is free from any emotion of attachment or detachment. In the *vicitra* moment there is the realization of *ānanda*, in *vipāka, paramānanda*, in *vimarda, virāmānanda* and in the *vilakṣaṇa, sahajānanda*. — *Hevajra Tantra*

15. About the nature of these four kinds of bliss, the *Hevajra Tantra* says that *ānanda* is the pleasure of passion which disturbs the mind; *ānanda* means ordinary transient pleasure; *paramānanda* is the realization of full bliss or more intense pleasure; the next stage is the stage of *virāmānanda*, the detachment of the →

This theory of moments and four kinds of bliss is very important from the *yoga* point of view; for the lay *yogin* who will not be able to distinguish between the one moment from the other and one kind of bliss form the other, may take even gross sensuality to be *sahaja*-bliss (*mahāsukha*); but that is practically adopting the path to hell. It is for this reason that the four moments and four kinds of bliss must be very clearly distinguished; a perfect knowledge of the bliss follows only from perfect knowledge of the moments. This *sahaja-ānanda* (great-bliss) is the Absolute of the *yogin,* connected with the yogic practice of the Sahajīya. The concept of the *sahaja-sundarī* (the female force) should not be confused with the woman of flesh and blood, associated with the actual yogic practices. She is but an internal force of the nature of *śūnyatā* (vacuity) or *nirātmā* (essencelessness) and the great bliss residing in different pleasures in different stages of yogic practice. In the *Sādhanamālā*, we find that *mahā-mudrā* resides in the navel, and she is produced of *mahāsukha*, and for intense search, she is described as of the nature of fire. She is the nature of the first vowel, she is taken to be the wisdom by the Bauddhas,

→ worldly pleasure, and *sahajānanda* is the final bliss. In the *Sekoddiśa ṭīkā* we find that even in the stage of *virāmānanda*, the *sādhaka* retains his consciousness of egohood, i.e., the realization of the bliss in this state is associated with some sort of self-consciousness but this self-consciousness is totally lost in the stage of *sahajānanda*, when the knower and the knowable are lost in the oneness of the perfect bliss. Of the sixteen digits of the moon the first five represent *ānanda*, up to the tenth is *paramānanda*, up to the fifteenth is *virāmānanda* and the sixteenth represents *sahajānanda*. Again, corresponding to the four stages, viz., the stage of wakefulness (*jāgrata*), dream (*svapna*), deep sleep (*suṣupti*), and the fourth and final state (*turīya*), we have four elements, viz., body (*kāya*), speech (*vāk*), mind (*citta*) and knowledge (*jñāna*); we have four kinds of bliss in the each of these states and thus the actual number of bliss becomes sixteen in all.

Nagendra Natha Upadhyaya, *Tāntric Bauddha Sādhanā aur Sāhitya* (in Hindi), Kāśī, Saṁvata, 2015, pp. 3-18; T.N. Mishra, *Buddhist Tantra and Buddhist Art*, pp. 48-49.

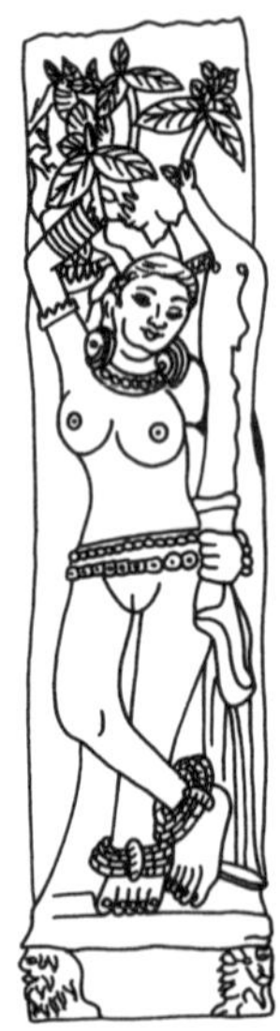

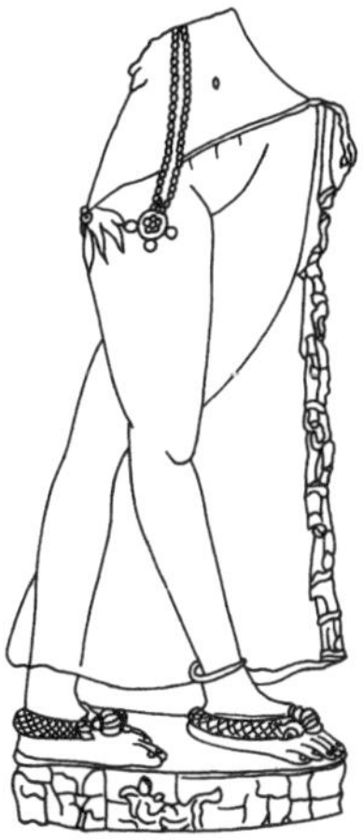

she remains pervading the three elements (*tri-dhātu*), and is never perceived by lay people (*pṛthag-jana*).[16]

It is clear that the production of *bodhicitta* and its upward march through the different *kāya*s to the *uṣṇīśa-kamala* to be transformed into *mahāsukha* is closely associated with the question of raising the Śakti from the lowest pole of phenomenalism to the highest pole of absolute truth. When Śakti reaches the *sahaja-kāya*, she becomes *śūnyatā* herself, and our perfect *citta* becomes Lord Vajrasattva; real *mahāsukha* follows only when this *śūnyatā* is united in the *sahaja-kāya* with the Vajrasattva.

The *sādhaka* body, with its physical structure and biological process, represents the manifestation of the same energy which is at play in the structure and processes of the vast cosmos. The *sādhaka* should concentrate his attention on himself and realize the truth within, with the clear conviction that the truth that is realized within is the truth that pervades the universe, without. The different kinds of energy that we find working in nature are different expressions of one great energy. This is known as correlation of forces.

As a man versed in the science of poison knows poison as poison and then swallows some quantity of it and yet he never falls swooning thereby. On the other hand, he gets cured of diseases. So also is the case with an expert *yogin*, who attains liberation through enjoyment. The *citta* or mind being the ultimate ground of all creation, the nature of *citta* will determine the nature of all appearances in the form of action; and so, all actions done with pure mind cannot but be pure even if sex-passion is evolved in them. All the notions of right and wrong are created by the *citta*, and it is through the *citta* again that they are all destroyed. It should be remembered that whenever *citta* clings to the object of

16. *Sādhanamālā*, vol. II, p. 448 (Gaikwada Oriental Series).

desire, the ultimate nature of the self can be realized through the worldly objects, only then, the ultimate nature of the world is realized as the vacuity through the instructions of the preceptor. In such a state there seems no difference between the world and the vacuity as there is no difference between the water of river and its waves. Profound and secret are the ways of this cult. Who can say anything against this cult. Who can hear this voice? Who is really engaged in this path, nobody knows. This path is just like an underground tunnel through which the water flows incessantly, freely, to attain salvation

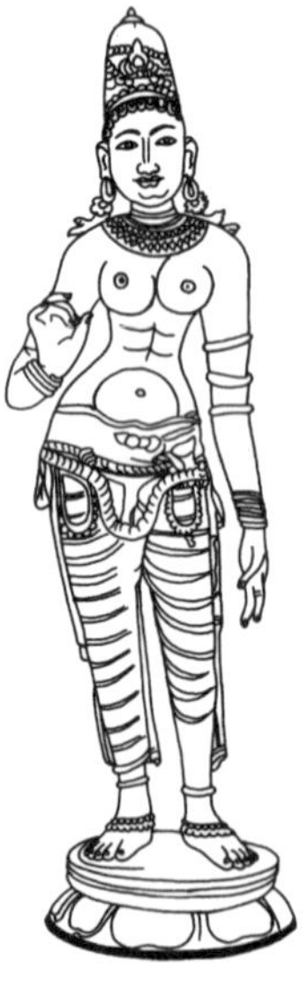

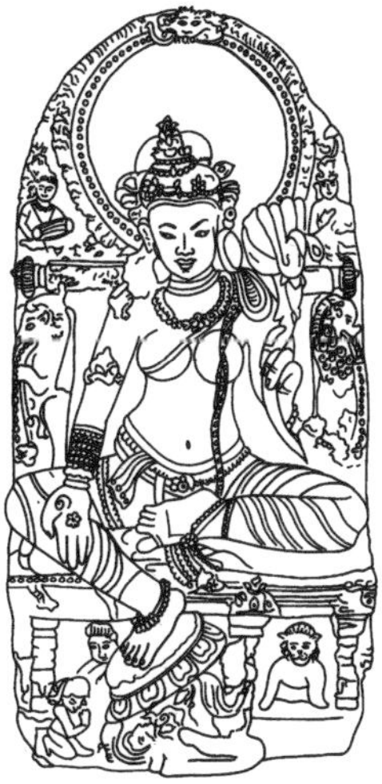

7

Religious Cult and Sensuousness in Art

INDIAN art depicts life as interpreted by religion and philosophy. Art, in all periods of development, was closely associated with rhythm of life, including the life of gods and all living being on earth. The Indian tradition, however, interprets the living world as manifestation of the God. The symbol of art voices the same truth and, so, do our philosophy and myths. The purpose of Indian art has been as such, to communicate the great truths to mankind through architectural, sculptural and pictorial reconstruction of the power that maintains stars in their courses. Every Indian religious structure and art form is regarded as a replica of an unseen celestial brilliance. This may also be described both as theological and traditional; tradition means a kind of healthy discipline conditioned by beliefs and prescriptions, which embrace the whole of a civilization in all its modes and trends.

The image or icon or any visible deity has been the medium through which a devotee could transfer his one-souled devotion to his god. The deities are a product of psychic excercises of the most subtle character and visualized by the worshipper in the course of intense meditation. These psychic exercises are called *sādhanā*. The act of *sādhanā* has a special bearing on the history and evolution of icons. The Indian religious thought, the omnipresent god, the creator of the universe, are supposed to reside in everything, and as much of his presence is felt in the loving heart of a devotee as in stocks and stones. To a *sādhaka*, who realizes the presence of the supreme *Brahman* within himself, there is hardly any need for a temple or a divine image for worship. The images of the gods and goddesses are representations meant for those who cannot realize or comprehend the divine spirit in their hearts. The thoughts of thinkers made manifest and concretized by various means such as speech, pictorical and sculptural representations, signs and symbols, that helped in evolving divine images. In its metaphysical essence, the formless undergoes a definite mode of cosmic operation. It arises from certain movement of life-force that animates all matter, and by a process of expansion and growth or of condensation and construction which causes it to crystallize in uncertain shapes. These, as their outer circumscription, show the nature of formation (*dhyāna-rūpa*). Lines, forms and colours are not accidental but are direct manifestations of these inner forces related to the spiritual reality. All these means have been utilized to depict divinity at the level of the common man in order to lift him up, gradually, to the sublime height of true realization.

India is a land of many religious faiths and even within the same faith, there have been many sects and sub-sects, often in sharp differences with one another, irrespective of beliefs and tenets. All the Indian religions are known to have adopted common norms for the expression of their thoughts and beliefs through art. Religious differences have hardly been able to divert this norm from its logical course. The norms remain the same for all religions irrespective of subjects depicted. The difference lies only in iconographic contents. The *bhakti* (devotion) gives a significant impetus to the construction of images and houses of gods. Emotional attachment with gods was considered a road to salvation (*mokṣa*), the easiest one, and a path open to all. Devotion popularized image-worship, as meditation of the unmanifested Absolute was considered a difficult process.

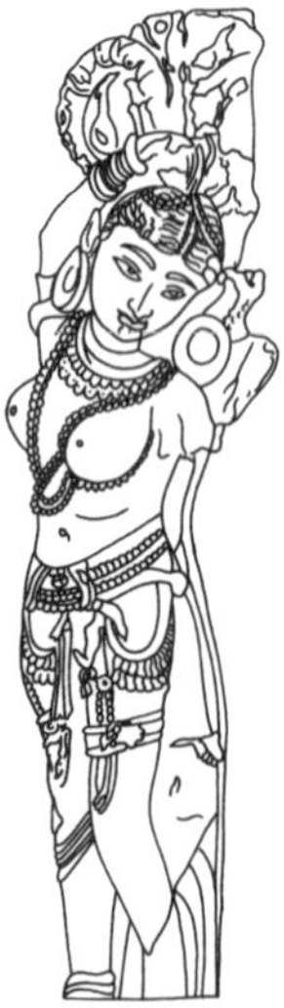

The origin of image-worship in India can be traced back to very early times and the circumstances behind such a

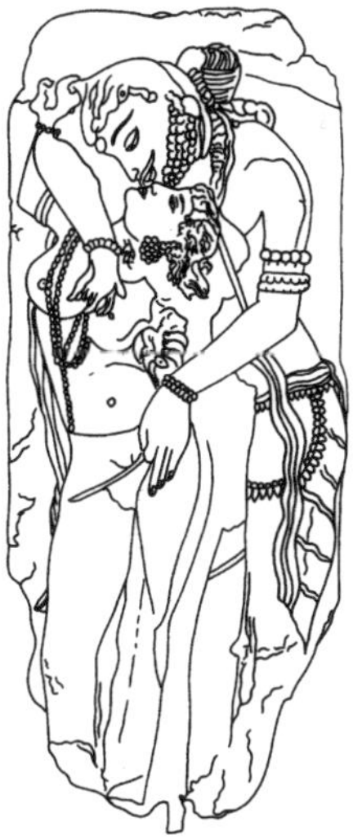

development are not exactly known. The image was probably not unknown to the Vedic peoples but the religion of the Vedas knew no idol-worship The Jainas denied the idea of the Supreme Being. They recognized the practice of worshipping the image of their *tīrthaṅkara*s. The history of the image-worship in the Buddhist tradition is traced back from the first century BC and it is revealed that the liberal Mahāsāṁghikas and, then, the Mahāyānists paved the way for devotees to go for the idols of the Buddha for offering their devotion, probably to satisfy the religious emotions of lay-disciples. The Buddha is not a proper name, but an attribute of one who recognized as having attained wisdom (*bodhi*), that cuts the darkness of ignorance and radiates/ illumines. The figure of *bodhisattva* (who requires certain *pāramitā*s to qualify himself for the attainment of Buddhahood) was the first to be introduced. This was, probably, due to the fact that the Master (Buddha) was basically a teacher (*guru*), and not a saviour god, and those who were orthodox were anxious to avoid any form of worship and took care of Buddha's relics in reverence. But the said convention shortly disappeared. The mortal and the historical Buddha, transformed into an idealized abstraction and he began to be deified. A teacher, thus, was turned into the Lord. The *bhakti* (devotion) or the cult of *bhakti* denotes primarily the loving adoration of some persons by their followers; secondarily, the affectionate and mystic devotion for some personal deity who is the object of worship. There was the belief on one person (Buddha) as the spiritual being, the faith that his power is sufficient to secure salvation and the goodwill prevailed, and the conception of the nexus binds together *tathāgata* and his worshippers. That *bhakti* and the ritual of worship were already prevailing during the post-Buddha period could be proved in the worship and the prayer offered to the relics (*stūpa*), and symbols that underwent transformation and introduced iconographic types of Buddha with the Indian conception of a great man (*mahāpuruṣa lakṣaṇas*). Another concept of Buddhism that finds its reflection in the iconography has been the concept of the three bodies of Buddha. This three-fold division was of philosophical nature and was designated as *dharma-kāya* (word of Buddha), *saṁbhoga-kāya* (body of bliss) and *nirmāṇa-kāya* (numenal body). A further development was the creation of mystical *dhyānī* Buddhas for the four directions and one for the centre of the world; and therefore, these ideas show that they included the worship of the five *dhyānī* Buddhas.[1]

1. These *dhyānī* Buddhas represent the five cosmic elements of which the world is composed of. They are described as the progenitors of the five *kula*s or the families of gods and goddesses. It is in this way that the Buddhists built a well-classified pantheon with its multiplicity of gods and goddesses and these were represented in art. They were required to show their origin by holding on to their heads the miniature figure of their parental *dhyānī* Buddha. These five *dhyānī* Buddhas are endowed with five different body colours in their *sādhanā*s. White is prescribed for Vairocana. It symbolizes delusion, pacification, purity, the element of water, the aggregate of form perceptions, and goodness. The east is indicated by white maleness, and wisdom of discrimination. It also stands for compassion and perfection of *nirvāṇa*. Ratna-sambhava is yellow, that denotes pride, prosperity and affluence. The south, the element of earth stands for the aggregate of sensations, the wisdom of equality. Akṣobhya is blue-bodied and represents hatred, destruction, killing. The element of space or air represents unchangeability, firmness of mind, the wisdom of *dharmadhātu* and the aggregate of consciousness. Amitābha's red body signifies passion, hatred, subjugation and empowerment. The west, the element of fire represents the aggregate of sensations and perceptions. He symbolizes a female and represents compassion (*karuṇā*) also. Red is the colour of Vajravārāhī as a sign of her devotion to the service of all sentient beings. The thought of enlightenment (*bodhicitta*) represents the union of *prajñā* (insight) and *upāya* (means) of red and white colours, respectively and this union leads to a great bliss (*mahā-sukha*). The green colour of Amoghasiddhi symbolizes envy, the multitude, the element of air, the north, the concept of consciousness and accomplishment of wisdom. Green is the combination of white (pacifying), yellow (affluence) and blue (destruction). The goddess Tārā who covers a whole range of such functions is depicted as green. T.N. Mishra, *Buddhist Tantra and Buddhist Art*, New Delhi, 2000, pp. 70 and 82-83.

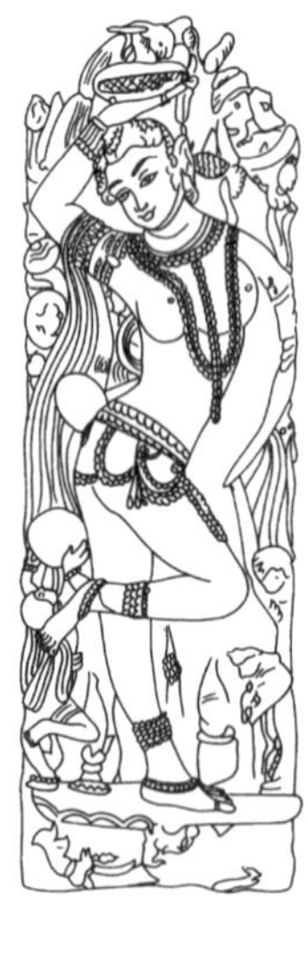

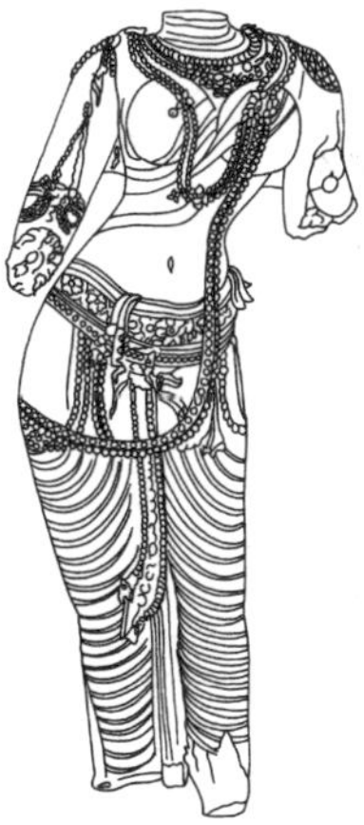

The final phase of Buddhism received inspiration from Tāntric religion which essentially meant devotion paid to the female energy or Śakti, which, in its grosser aspects, encouraged sexual practices as a means to salvation. The imagination on the part of the sculptors and also the product of their chisels were very greatly influenced by the spirit of the age in which they flourished as well as by the situation in which they worked.

The art of sculpture and painting attained a state of perfection in ancient India that could stand comparison with what was attained in other countries. The Indian artist was not wanting in originality and vigour in the handling of his subjects. He tried to remain true to the nature, and in the representation of the birds and animals, he remained often unsurpassed. Throughout the ages, Indian art evinces a consistent growth, each succeeding phase starting with the heritage of the preceding one and leading the style to their natural and logical fulfilment. Religious urge has been behind the full efflorescence of art styles. In early period of the history of Indian art, the imagination of the artist was not tied down by any religious prescription, which, however, became the bane of art, in later times. One of the characteristic features of Indian art and architecture is the quality it derives by using motifs, rich in symbolism, and mythical imagery. An early factor that brought about visible changes in natural and progressive state of Indian art was introduction of Tāntric ideas in the worship of Hindu as well as Buddhist deities.

In the following lines an attempt is being made to study the influence of Tantrism and related impact of sensualism in art. To begin with, one of the characteristic features of Indian art and architecture has been the quality it derives by using motifs rich in symbolism and mythical imagery. *Mithunas*, for instances, which appeared in early Indian terracottas and on the *dvāraśākhās* of the Gupta temples, were imageries appeared as decorative appendages to

Indian architecture, when translated into stone. We may also note that very few specimens of Indian art have offered such a fruitful source of comment and controversy as have erotic sculptures of Koṇārka and Khajurāho laid bare. Here we have generic couples trying to convey some kind of masonic symbolism, the meaning of which we shall endeavour to discover.

The presence of erotic portrayals on the mass of religious structures and temples, has often perturbed strikingly and disturbed the feelings of the religious-minded people. The *mithuna* seems to have an obsessation in the subconscious minds of the Indian people so as to find a prominent expression in their religious thinking and architecture. The motif that had such an overwhelming place on the sacred monuments of a vast civilization is likely to have manifold cultural bearings. There might have been more than one strand of tradition behind such an assuming theme. It occurs and reoccurs as an essential element in the well-defined sculptural planning of the Hindu temple through the ages. There can hardly be a place more sanctified in purpose than a shrine of god for people who built it. This very fact of the frank portrayal of sensuousness and sex in religious art is usually taken, at once, as conflicting and damaging in the psyche of the people. But was it so? This we have to examine carefully to find out an answer.

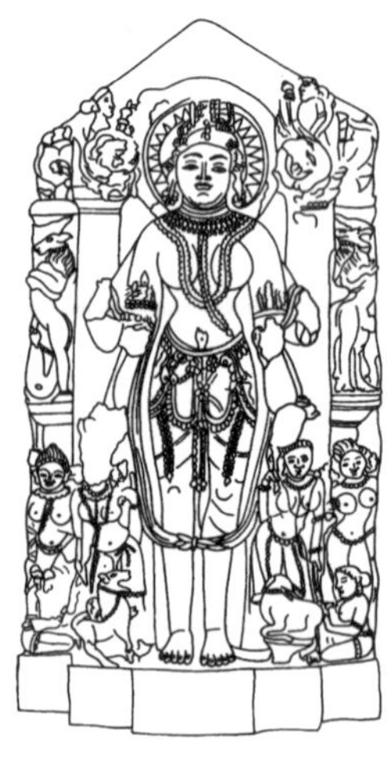

The time has come and situations demand a review afresh of the depictions of lust sensualities and careless abandon of sex on the religious structures and look for proper interpretations of the themes and compositions of the early and medieval art. A reference may be made here to the cult of Śiva that goes back to a very early time; some trace it even to the pre-Vedic period as Śiva reportedly represented as Paśupati on a seal and his phallic emblem, the *Śiva-liṅga* was found in the remains of the Indus Valley Civilization. Whatever may be the origin, Śiva is said to

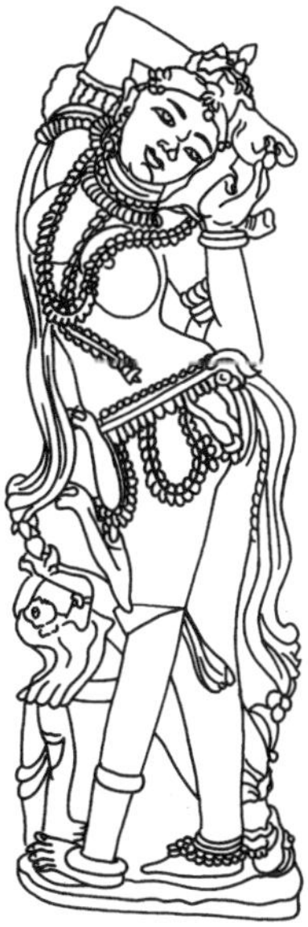

have attained his characteristics out of the concept of Vedic Rudra and thereafter, gradually rose to the present-day prominence. It appears that from the very early times, certain mystic practices were attached with Pāśūpata religion a saint tenet.[2] When non-eligible persons began to adopt this cult, considerable deterioration had set in and the system itself fell into disrepute. But it is to be remembered that any mystic cult can be distorted and can become vitiated by left handed practices (*vāmācāra*). In initial stage of Śaiva worship both human as well as phallic forms of the god were at first enshrined in the main sanctum of the Śaiva temple.[3] It became a general custom afterwards to place *Śiva-liṅga*s only in it and use them as the principal object of worship, the human figures of Śiva being distributed in relief in various parts of the temple walls.

Archaeological materials from the Indus Valley also point to the existence of a fertility cult in proto-historic India. The discovery of numerous phallic stones and ring stones, the figure of a male ithyphallic horned god (probably the prototype of Śiva) and the figure of a Mother Goddess are ample evidences to indicate the prevalence of

---

2. This system has three basic categories — *paśu* (individual soul), *pati* (Lord Śiva) and *pāśa* (bond). Śiva who is *niṣkala* and *nirākāra* (undifferentiated and formless) manifests in form (*ākāra*) to help the aspirant (devotee) in *pūjā* (worship) and *dhyāna* (meditation). Man is microcosm and ontologically divine, but because of *pāśa*s which conceal the active powers of the soul, he does not know this oneness with *pati* (Lord) and identifies himself with *mala*s (taints) of *āṇava* (egoism), *karma* (deeds) and *māyā* (immersion in the material world).

3. According to Śaiva Siddhānta system, when Para-Śiva wills for creation, a thousand part of his self emerges out of him as Parā-Śakti. From her, in turn, Ādi-Śakti and from the latter Icchā-Śakti (will power) form and in turn Jñāna-Śakti (knowledge) and then comes Kriyā-Śakti (activity). From these five Śaktis emerge the five aspects of Sadā-Śiva, viz., Īśāna, Tatpuruṣa, Aghora, Vāmadeva and Sadyojāta. These forms are connected with the five activities (*pañca-kriyā*); they preside over the five elements, viz., ether, air, fire, water and earth.

the said cult.[4] However, no representation of the avid sexual act has been reported either in art or among the ritual materials of the Indus civilization. The earliest depiction of the sexual act among the objects excavated so far in India is found on a pot of the chalcolithic period at Dāimābād.[5] Another early representation of sex has been noted in the Kapgallu cave in Mysore.[6] Significant materials on the possible connection of the depiction of erotic couples *vis-a-vis* fertility cults, began to appear in the historical period.[7] The secular subjects drawn from everyday life were introduced in the art of historic terracottas and in stone. The fertility cult was accepted in religious theme and were given an artistic treatment in such a way that it turned out into an art-motif. The process of secularization and sensualization of ritual or cultic objects is clearly noticeable in the ivory figure of Śrī, found at Ṭer, that has been

4. John Marshall, *Mohenjo-daro and the Indus Civilization*, London, 1930, pp. 5-55 and 59.
5. *Indian Archaeology — A Review*, 1958-59, fig. 7.
6. D.H. Gordon, *Pre-historic Background of Indian Culture*, Bombay, p. 116.
7. *Indian Archaeology — A Review*, 1962-63, pp. 5-6.

   Motichand, *Lalit Kala*, No. 8, pp. 8-9.

   Yakṣī and tree, a motif seen frequently, in railing of the Buddhist *stūpa* at Bharhut (185-72 BC), is a symbolism that goes back to a period in Indian history when trees were regarded as objects of worship and which is associated with old fertility festivals when youth and maidens gathered the flowers of the *śāla* tree. There are many legends relating to the power of women and *yakṣī* to bring trees into immediate flowering by embracing the trunk or touching it with their feet which may be interpreted as symbolically of the soul's union with divinity.

   At Sāñcī (first century BC), the *yakṣī*-figures show a marked sculptural advance. One of the figures, on the north gateway, is a drastic and dramatically effective adaptation of the women and tree motifs. 'A sense of vitality is communicated both from the iconographical and aesthetic point of view in the presentation of the tree motifs. In the frankness of their erotic statements, the Sāñcī *yakṣīs* are a perfect illustration of the union of the spiritual and the sensual which runs like a thread through all the religious art in India.

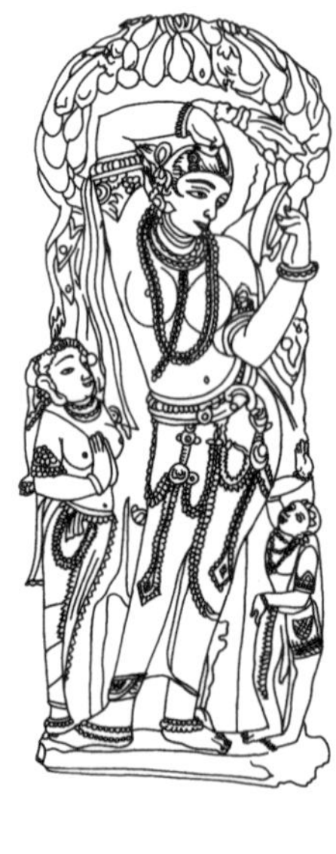

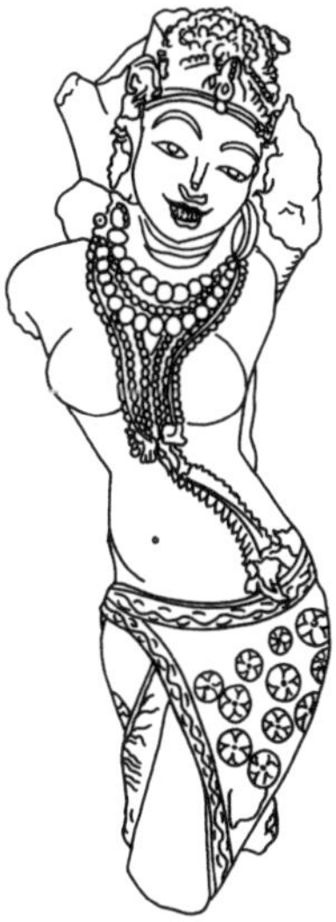

assigned to the second century AD. Śrī was the goddess of abundance, fertility, blissful prosperity, luck and beauty. Her fertility aspects are revealed in *Śrī Sūkta*, a *khila* or in the appendix of the *Ṛgveda*. The cults of fertility (specially, the cults of Goddess Śrī) have a direct bearing on the depiction of *maithunas* in religious art. When the ancient customs of ritual meant for the community, the fertility and virility came in the face of evolved sexo-moral propensity in the society and found their way to art representations in the service of religion.

All important religious sects of the country — Hindu, Jaina and Buddhist — presented sensuous and erotic motifs in their art. Sensuous representation in art was a pan-Indian cultural feature. It implies a common cultural substratum which influenced religious sects, all over India. This common substratum is seen in those beliefs and practices which show the primal connection between sex and religion. Far from being suppressed, sex played an important part in the religious life of early communities and civilizations. It was realized and was felt necessary to experiment in art before conventionalizing the aspects in texts like the *śilpa*-canons. Forms, once accepted in art, have a tendency to become conventionalized and assume the character of motifs. In the culture of India which glorifies traditional values, the processes of conventionalizing become a major factor leading to persistence and inertia in the use of motifs.

The religious structures were the means to express the above-mentioned philosophy and motifs. The subjects drawn from everyday life were introduced in the religious architecture also. It must be remembered that every work of Indian architecture — Hindu, Jaina and Buddhist — must, first and foremost, be regarded from the point of view of its metaphysical aspect, that is, as a kind of replica of some unseen region of which the metaphysical factor determined the plan and elevation. Thus, the temple is the house and body of the deity; its fabric, the very substance of the divinity. Ritual and dedication contributed to the selection and laying of every piece of material of which the temple was built, since this fabric itself was the mystic equivalent of the body of *puruṣa*. The temple is in more ways than one to be thought of as heaven on earth and, traditionally, ascribed to divinity. Hindu, Jainas and Buddhists all used the same style with slight modifications of structure to meet their ritualistic needs and, as if, to lead the worshipper towards the centre of spiritual union with the divine. The sculptural decoration of the temple points the way to that desired union; this is the meaning implicit in the multiple representations in the frieze of *maithuna*s of men and women in erotic embrace, which is the ultimate union of the soul with the divine.

However, secular and religious sculpture reflects an ambivalence that is characteristic of all Indian mythology, literature and art and seemingly appears as a celebration of the sensuous even though the intent is spiritual. The gods and goddesses are spiritual entities but their forms are often sensuous, if not erotic; youthfulness is also regarded as an essential feature, and indeed, this is true of all Indian gods and goddesses. The glorification of youth and sensuousness remained pivotal in all religious sculptures (*sada ṣoḍaśa vārsikim*). Perhaps, the semi-nude forms of the female are desirable and seen more to celebrate life than to renounce it. The frank eroticisms of some images, particularly *yakṣī*s (celestial nymphs) and *mithuna* (lovers in dalliance), play a pervasive role in embellishing the temples.[8] It may be noted that an architect of ancient temple did not like the *maithuna*s to mean only human couple; sexual pairs of all kinds of beings were in his mind; but this symbol was generalized, in most cases, and were accommodated in all the three religions — Hindu, Jaina or Buddhist. From the very earliest times, the *mithuna*s have

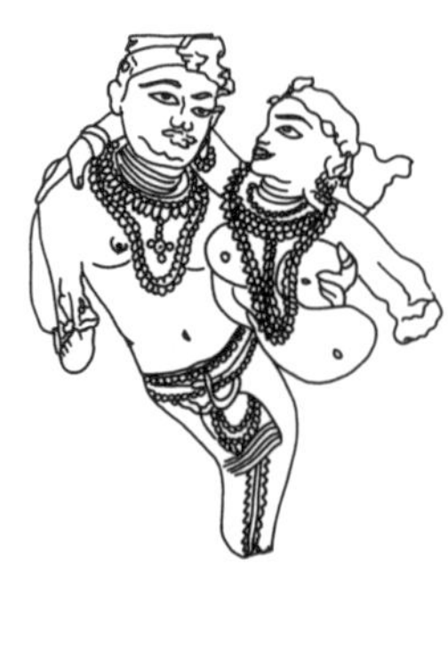

8. P. Pal, *The Sensuous Immortals*, London.

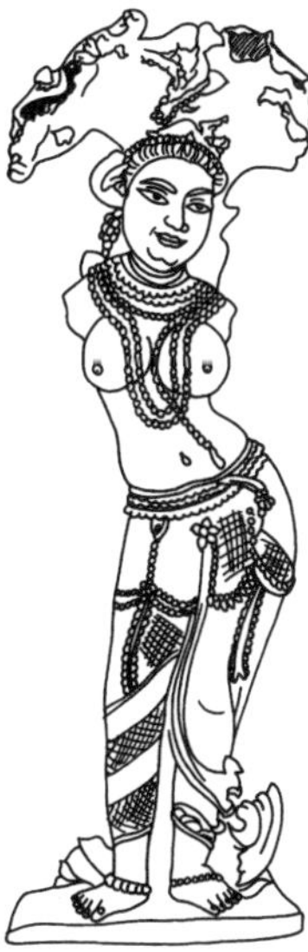

been appropriated by Buddhist builders at Sāñcī, Bharhut, Kārle, Kānheri and Nāsik. Their presence in numerous Hindu temples did not make it peculiarly a Hindu (brāhmaṇa) conception, either. The temples of Rājpūtāna offer numerous evidences of their use by Jaina builders.

The documentation of secularization and sensualization is clearly noticeable in *stūpa* architecture and, in particular, in the reliefs adorning *stūpa*s at Amarāvatī and Nāgārjuna-koṇḍa. But the Āndhra School emphasizes depiction of scenes in the life of the Buddha prior to his enlightenment, specially, his life before abandoning *saṁsāra*, his stay in harem, the luxurious life he led in the court, etc. The depictions are more sensuous than religious. The art was hardly religious at all, and far less Buddhistic. It does not speak of nor aim at suggesting the Buddhist ideal of renunciation or *nirvāṇa* or discipline or strict ethical virtues including avoidance of woman. Rather, it is frankly naturalistic and essentially sensuous. The disciplined body and conquered mind happen to have been the characteristics of the art of the Gupta period. The relief-sculptures of Amarāvatī and, particularly, of Nāgārjunakoṇḍa revealed all the dramatist personae as seemingly engaged in enjoying their life, for the last time, before entering into a stage of detachment and discipline. The treatment rendered in art is, no doubt, artistic and poetic. But we must remember that such amorous figures were motifs all placed just next to the Buddhist scenes. There must have been something in social climate of the time that encouraged the use of erotic motifs as a form of embellishment in religious art. The idea was to indicate the impermanence of physical beauty and the futilities of worldly attachments. The quest was for the ultimate truth, ultimate beauty.

In the paintings of Ajantā and Bāgh, the figures involved in dance and music and festivals of love are seemingly dark aboriginals, specially in the large dance panel on the facade of the Bāgh caves. The rhythmic splendour of many other scenes in both the cave complexes derives its sap that runs through nature. The thrills of burning passion are seen everywhere on the walls to inspire human emotion and feelings. The feelings of youth burst in the act of love with abandon. All the *Jātaka* myths become blurred in the fresh freedom of prevalence of youthful pleasure-loving couples. In the art expression at this place, one finds a complete statement of indivisible union of the sacred and secular art. In the Ajantā wall paintings, one feels a definite departure from the art of early Buddhism, where emphasis was more on symbolic expressions, keeping, thereby, one away from the world of reality. Ajantā paintings laid bare a kind of religious romanticism imbued with lyric quality, a reflection encompassing every aspect of life as such in the spiritual sense, and as an aspect of the divine. Sensuous physical beauty became an emblem of spiritual beauty. Hence, it reminded that life had become an art, but the ultimate goal of it was never forgotten.

The art of India and the religion and culture absorbed several foreign traits from certain central Asian nomadic tribes including the Śakas and the Kuṣāṇas who reached India in the first century BC and ruled over the northern part of India, including Pāṭaliputra. The depiction of the erotic motifs in Indian art during this period was considerably influenced by the socio-cultural milieu of the period. The secular and sensual interests largely affected their portrayal through this social mutation. Yet some of its earlier aspects were retained. Erotic themes of this period visibly received more romantic touches in their depictions. Sensual and worldly interests were clearly betrayed in full bodied and enticing figures of *yakṣīs* or female figures on the railings of Mathurā. An important development during the early third century AD was traced in the representation of the couples and other erotic themes on the doors and the entrances of the monuments. The available *maithuna* motifs of the period underwent major changes including the

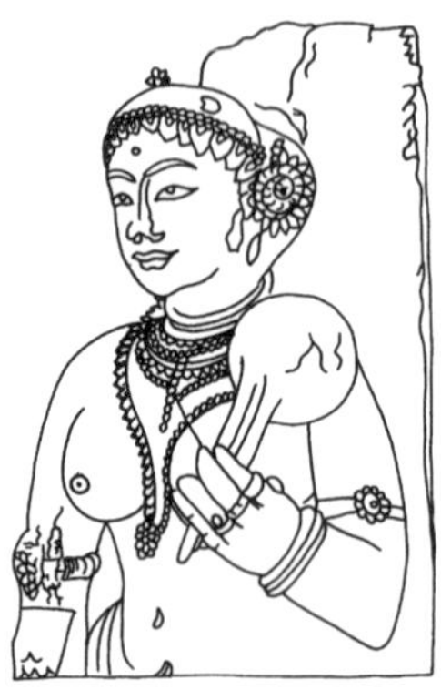

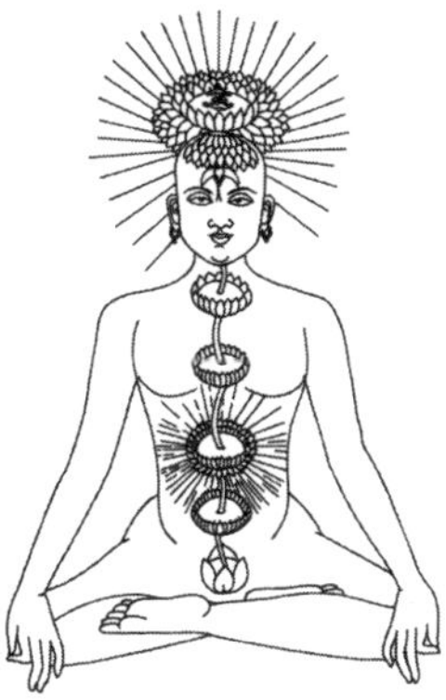

deeper sensualization of the motifs, as such. The profuse use of the *maithuna* motif in art with the increasing number and with greater sense of depth in sculptures paved the way for an advancement in the artist's understanding of human figures. The increasing interest in the depiction of avidly sensuous forms suggests that, by this time, *maithuna* motif became a socially acceptable form of decoration and reflected the cosmopolitan culture of urban Mathurā.

The consequent urban development in the early centuries of the era seems to have encouraged a taste for offering more voluptuousness in art. Erotic depictions were permitted in religious art because it was considered auspicious. The Indian aesthetic traditions have close relationship between the visual and performing arts, particularly dance and drama. The literature of Bāṇa gives us a picture of life of *nāgaraka*s who met occasionally for cultural discussions (*goṣṭhī*s); this kind of gathering gave further opportunities for various artistic pursuits. The lovely girls in the poems of Kālidāsa were endowed with the secret of the sensual mystery and the secret of all life. The profuse carvings of erotic scenes that begin in the Gupta and post-Gupta temples were not only to excite the sensual feelings of the onlooker but to initiate, at the same time, of the divine presence in these very situations where we are most likely to forget them. It is this social climate that possibly encouraged Vātsyāyana to compile his *Kāmasūtra* (the masterly textbook on love, into the four-fold Hindu scheme of life). The period also witnessed the plays of Bhāṣa and Śūdraka, who flourished at the time. Undoubtedly, there is much individualistic activities in the poetries and paintings of the period and in the rich, expansive feudal empire where the world becomes a kind of kaleidoscope, which reveals the loveliest flowers in its turnings, and one finds wonder and delight in contemplating the haunting, tender beauties. The habitual preachings of generation after generation of learned men left a substratum of metaphysical awareness that informs even in the mundane literature and art of what is called the period, classical Renaissance in India, which coincided with the Gupta period in about the fourth century. So, complete, is the hold of this transcendentalism that what was then called *kalā* (art) is throughout reflective, at one remove or another, of this philosophy of the life process. From the fifth century AD and onwards there was a change in the political scenario which influenced the socio-economic pattern of life. Another significant development was the rise of Tantrism. Magical beliefs and practices acquired great importance under Tāntric cults. From the fifth century onwards we get inscriptional evidences of Tāntric worship. Belief in Tantra became a significant factor in influencing the erotic art of the period.

Certain temples are found relieved of erotic figures, but do they show the influence of any kind of regional style? The depiction of erotic motifs in art has had a long tradition from the remote past. Conventions and the relationship of Tantrism to sexual depiction have to be viewed in the historical perspective. The *mithuna* (amorous couple) has been traditionally accepted in Indian art as an auspicious symbol since the historical period. In the so-called Daśā-vatāra temple at Deograh, built at about fifth century AD, *mithunas* were found carved on the plinth. This seems to suggest the flexibility in the placement of erotic motifs. In the sixth century AD the depiction of *mithunas* was introduced, for the first time, in the temple architecture of Aihole, Paṭṭadakala, Bādāmī and Mahākūṭeśvara. Their presence was on the door point and their inclusion was along with other auspicious decorations. Seemingly, such depictions in the *dvāraśākhā* appear to have had a magico-religious function. These sculptures in highly amorous poses indicate that priests and devotees, at this time, did not object to their presence on the religious edifices. By this time, the temples were recognized as important socio-

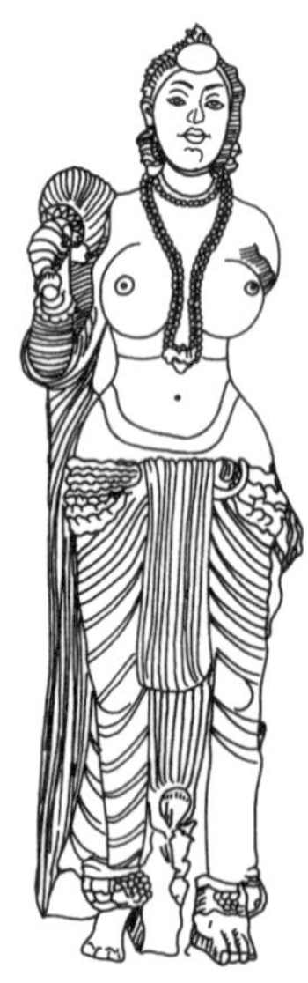

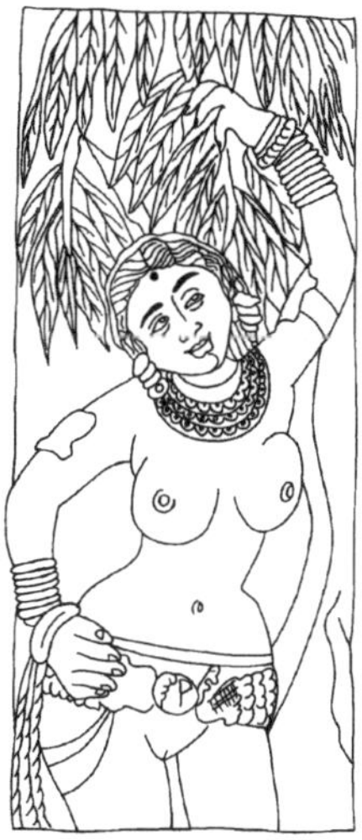

religious centres. It also provided opportunities for development of arts. The cave of Bādāmī profusely laid bare the presence of a sizeable number of erotic motifs. Sensuous compositions with poetic touches are clearly seen in the bas-reliefs over all the pillars and pilasters, in the rear wall of the varandahs as well as in the *maṇḍapa*, lintels and ceilings, etc. Erotic motifs can also be seen in the Buddhist cave-arts at Ajantā and Ellorā. Ajantā paintings offered a sort of religious romanticism imbued with lyric quality, a reflection encompassing every aspect of life, as such, in the spiritual sense, and as an aspect, the divine. But even in this splendrous art, which exalts all human emotions and feelings, we are made to feel the evanescence of the phenomenal world. Sensuous physical beauty became an emblem of spiritual beauty. The juxtaposition of a nude figure and a *mithuna* scene in an inconspicuous corner of the Paraśurāmeśvara temple of Bhuvaneśvara in Orissa possibly points to its magico-religious association. The other temples having *mithuna* depictions and exhibiting apparent Tāntric impact are the temples of Bhuvaneśvara, Kailāśanātha temple of Ellorā and the Someśvara temple of Mukhaliṅgam. But the depiction of *maithuna* was not acceptable at all. The period reveals a contrast in the treatment of *mithuna* and *maithuna* themes; the former was accepted as a convention, and the latter had to make way due to the *śilpa* rules.

The temple architecture from eighth to ninth century onwards provided opportunities for the exhibition of artistic talents and the power of wealth. The temple architecture and the icon of the god and the related art became chief concern for the artists and their patrons. Superstition and belief in magic held sway over such people and, at the same time, the regional outlook influenced the cultural pursuits. The atmosphere, around the medieval temples, was a breeding ground for luxurious living and degenerated sexual practices. The institution of *devadāsīs* also vitiated the atmosphere of the temple. The temple services of *devadāsīs* became popular in the religious life of the medieval temples and the services included devotional dance, drama and music. References of such activities are replete in the writings of Patañjali, Bāṇa, Kālidāsa, Bhavabhūti, Daṇḍin and many others. In the embrace of his beloved, a man forgets the whole world — everything both within and without — and enjoys greatest joy, *ānanda*.[9] Bliss Incarnate, is beyond reach, except to the most selfless seeker. Our human happiness gives but a glimpse of the boundless joy in store for us, provided we recognize our true self for the briefest moment.[10] With that characteristic genius for elaborating the highest sanctions, the Hindus, accepted a view of God, in which not only is human sexual pleasure exalted as the joy nearest to the realization of God, but everything in life becomes divine.[11] The medieval temples are to be viewed against the aristocratic and affluent backgrounds, a view which is far from the ideals of Upaniṣadic asceticism.

From the third century BC to the seventh century AD the Indian art had a common denominator; but from the eighth century onwards the regional spirit in art gradually asserted itself. Curiously enough, in spite of the passage of time, the classical tradition of Indian art was still being maintained in places. The erotic motif has experienced such regional variations. The attitude towards erotic realization in art appeared different in each region. The place was allotted to the erotic motifs on the temples in accordance

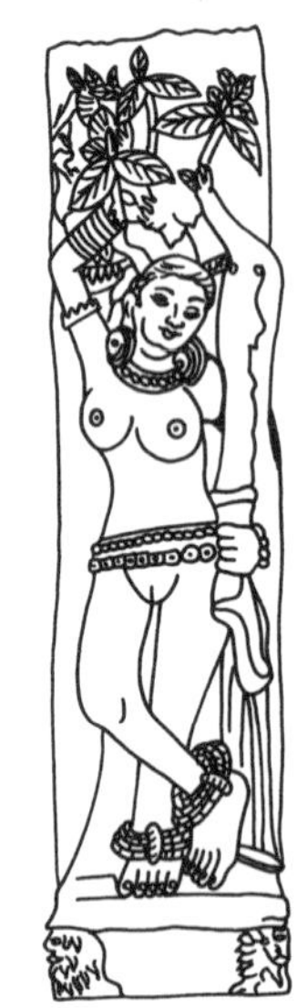

9. The difference between the two states of experiencing *ānanda* may be just of the height and duration; on the two extremes of attainment, the one is gross and transitory, while the other, subtle and everlasting.
10. *Bṛhadāraṇyaka Upaniṣad*, IV.3.21.
11. *Ibid.*, IV.3.32; *Taittirīya Upaniṣad*, II.8.

    Paul Deussen, *The Philosophy of the Upaniṣad* (reprint), New Delhi, 1979, p. 143.

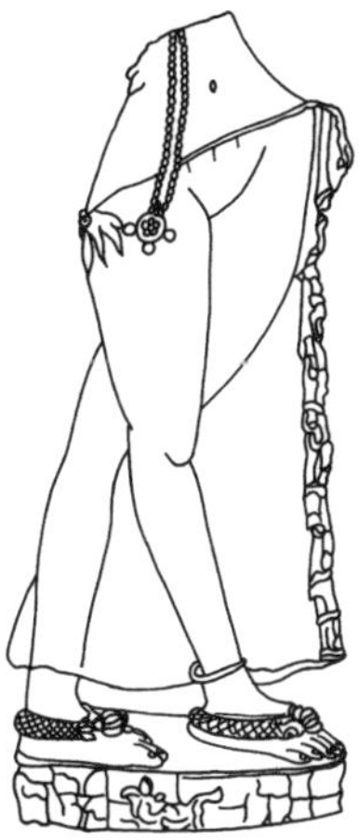

with the architectural canons of the region. But the sectarian feelings had not been the determining factor in the treatment of erotic motifs on the temples. The sexual representation is seen in the Hindu temples of all sects — even the rare shrine of Brhmā in Gujarat has the representation of coital couples. Jaina and Buddhist shrines of the mediaeval period, likewise, are also not found free from erotic compositions. It can, thus, be concluded that, in general, the nature of sexual representation was not determined to any significant extent either in theme or in form by the kind of religious sect to which the temple belonged. For instance, there is nothing Śaiva, Śākta or Vaṣṇava in the treatment accorded to the erotic motifs on the temples. The Pārśvanātha temple of Khajurāho and Ratnāgiri in Orissa are among a few Tāntric Jaina and Buddhist shrines that deal in sexual scenes. Eroticism, as an auspicious motif, appears to have been accepted in the art of the period. The presence of such compositions seems to fulfil some particular functions; they probably suggest the prevalence of some strong belief and are not necessarily connected with any religious sect. More likely, that these have been associated with a religious substratum common to all the regions.

A temple is the abode of divine principle including its physical and spiritual aspects along with all its antecedents and consequents. That the appropriation of amotary representations on the temple exterior was intended to keep the individual, as he discovered his unfulfilled desires a way from his actual entry (spiritual) to the inner sanctuary. According to the belief, the erotic portrayal on the temple walls was intended to protect the monument against natural calamities.[12] It certainly had a considerable appeal to the masses. Every religious expression has its own magic and

12. T.P. Bhattacharya, *The Canons of Indian Art*, Calcutta, 1963, p. 232.

this can hardly be denied in the case of amotary sculptures since they are believed to have protected the walls of the edifice through the centuries.

There is yet another explanation for the sexual motifs. Such motifs are based primarily on the philosophical concept of the Upaniṣads, according to which, the erotic motifs convey the non-dual state of the highest Reality. But this explanation is inadequate as it fails to account for the existence of numerous sculptures, depicting gross sexuality. Another view may be that erotic figures are an expression of *kāma* (sex) the third *puruṣārtha* in the fourfold Hindu scheme of life.[13] But *kāma* is only subservient to *dharma;* it is not an end itself. Unrestrained gratification of sexual urges was never prescribed in religious texts.

Many religious and philosophical movements contributed their different hues to the multi-coloured canvas of the ancient culture of India. The ultimate aim of life is to attain release (*mokṣa*) and art is one such means to attain this aim. So much ado has been made about the frank eroticism of the sculptures of the religious shrines that, perhaps, now is the time for a valid observation. A creative sensuousness has always been regarded as an important source of energy, of vital urge in life, as much in religious and spiritual quest as in the quest for expression; and the *maithuna* idea of this

13. *Dharma, artha, kāma* and *mokṣa* are the four *puruṣārtha*s. Man could attain perfect happiness by serving them. *Dharma,* the practice of social righteousness, *artha,* the pursuit of prosperity, *kāma,* the pursuit of pleasure (*ānanda*) and *mokṣa* (liberation) were all considered complementary as well as exclusive of each other. The sanction established by the Hindu religion seemed to show deep insight into the practical issues involved. And, though sexual pleasure was considered the symbol of Supreme Bliss, the seekers for liberation achieve their aim through detachment which can only come after attachment.

Indian art is so intimately associated with the Indian religion and philosophy that it is difficult to appreciate it fully unless one has some knowledge of the ideals that governed the Indian mind.

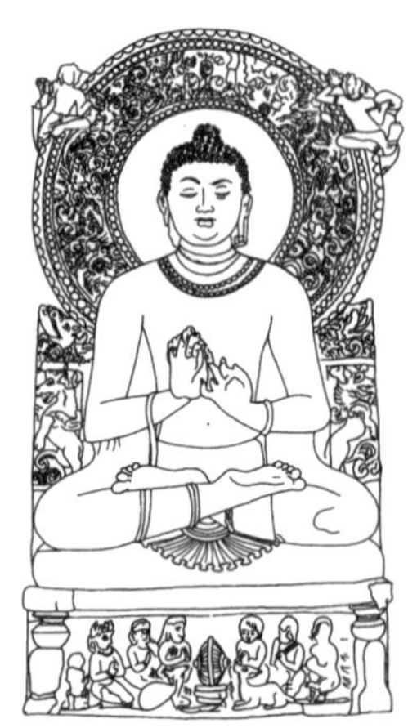

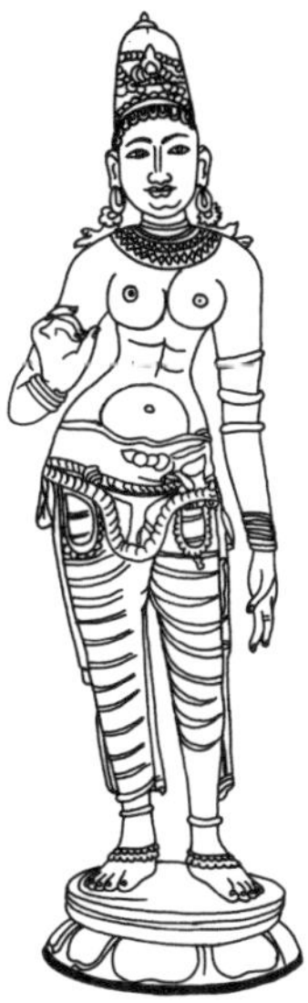

sādhanā finds most creative expression. Indeed, it was accepted as a normal and essential expressions of life, without any shame or secrecy, attached to it, as indicated by the temples of Purī and Koṇārka, where admittedly the eroticism is not only in the sensuous suggestiveness but the sexual act included in a wide variety of poses and attitudes. Perhaps, the artist got the inspiration from Vātsyāyana's *Kāma-Sūtra* which appears to have influenced the art of the period and no creative imagination had remained unaffected by the tenderness brought to the human relations. Certainly, the odour and sweat of sex is made sacred, and no shame is attached to it. The habitual preachings, generation after generation, of learned men left a substratum of metaphysical awareness which offers Immortality in that realm where there are joys and delights, enjoyment combined with felicity and extreme fulfilment of the desire of *kāma*.[14] This blissful condition comes to be epitomized in the word *ānanda* and in the Upaniṣads the essence of all human knowledge is comprehended under this concept, identified with the Ultimate Reality.

The depiction of couples on terracotta art are considered by some as the representative of the ritualistic pair in fertility rites. The portrayal of couples on stone-monuments indicates an auspicious relation. In the early medieval period, the depiction of erotic pairs was attributed with a magico-religious significance. After the ninth century AD the general acceptance of sexual motifs indicates the prevalence of some beliefs in favour of being socially accepted. The portrayal of ascetics in sexual acts in that period seems to be far from the principle of the yogic ideal of *mokṣa* (for attaining *sahaja* state).[15] These scenes may have

14. *Ṛgveda*, IX.113.11.
15. The Tāntric ideologies, basically, believed in the motif of the individual soul as male with reference to the universal soul as female; in the Tantra, this was not only theoretical but had a →

Tāntric association but public display of such practices contradicts the basic tenets of Tantrism which was of a highly secretive in nature. Tāntric orgies of *cakrapūjā* would very probably correspond where many pairs participate in a simultaneous orgy. The basic undercurrents behind sexual depiction were, in all probabilities, magico-religious beliefs and practices associated with sex, as found in fertility rites, in general, and Tantrism, in particular. Erotic sculptures are influenced not by any philosophical symbolism but by those religious beliefs and practices which reflect the primal connection between sex and religion.

In the medieval period, nearly all religious cults were influenced by Tantrism and every god was given a female consort, known as Śakti or *prajñā*. They addressed a goddess by a general term of 'Bhagavatī'.[16] Tāntric

---

cardinal application in actual practice. According to Tāntric philosophy, the pleasures of the flesh are indeed exemplary and, indeed, different from the joys of the Soul. It is not for infatuated pleasure that one has to satisfy one's desires but it is the only way to control and employ the 'desires' to their highest capacity for reaching the Ultimate Pleasure or *sahaja*-bliss. The sexual union is not a mere symbol stating the great truth but it is the path or vehicle itself, the union being employed to reach the quintessence of all the union. The bliss (*sukha*) is not misunderstood as a gross sex-pleasure. It is the subtlest and the highest state of becoming that could only be reached by experiencing a distinct stage or moment of bliss in an ascending order.

16. The evolution of the religious system, known as Śaktism, which glorifies the goddess as the prime source of all energies, is the development of the Neolithic period. Originally, the goddess was a symbol of fertility in predominantly agricultural societies. This aspect of fecundity and abundance has reminded basic to the Indian concept of the goddess, whether Hindu, Jaina or Buddhist and accounts for much of the voluptuousness of the female forms both divine and human, in Indian sculpture. The Śākta religion seems to have been profoundly influenced by the Sāṁkhya philosophical system. While Vedānta advocates monism, Sāṁkhya deals in dualist theory stating that both the manifest and unmanifest worlds were created by *prakṛti* for the sake of *puruṣa*. *Prakṛti* is regarded as →

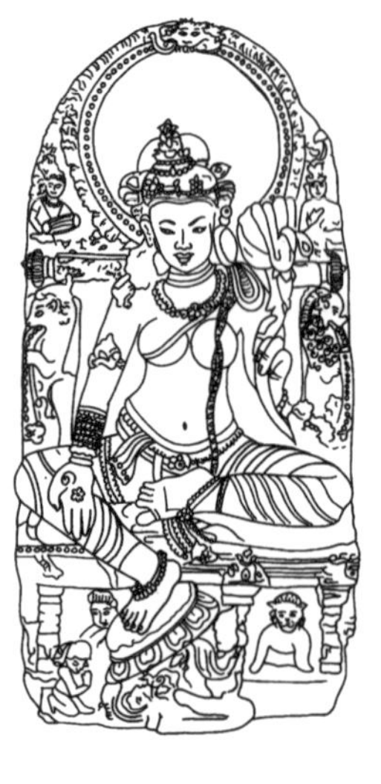

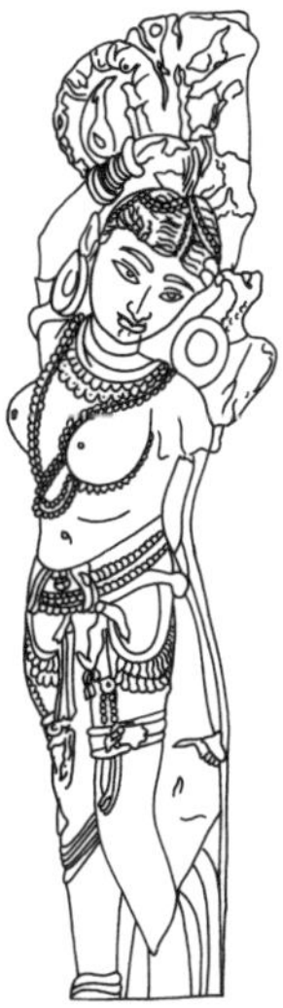

literature and belief give impetus to the worship of gods with their consorts which is also found reflected in medieval iconography. Temples of Bhuvaneśvara, Khajurāho, Kadwana, Nāgdā, Belūr, Halebiḍ, Somanāthpura and Ambarnāth have representations of deities in pairs and, at times, in amorous attitudes along with their Śaktis. Female and male genitals, known as *yoni* and *liṅgam* in India are worshipped and considered that such a worship would grant power and grace to its devotees. In India, Pāśupatas enshrined *liṅga*s to commemorate the dead teacher. The *nāthapanthī*s bury their deads instead of following the Hindu practice of cremation and represent the symbol of *yoni-liṅga*[17] on their graves. The body of a *yogī* who has attained liberation is identified with Śiva and hence, the symbol of the latter represented on the grave. The Pāśupatas, the Kālāmukhas and the Śaiva Siddhāntins were given the highest position in the temple organization, in many places of India.

→ the active principle, while *puruṣa* is a passive spectator. Since the word *puruṣa* means 'man' and *prakṛti* is equated with the nature or woman, as the embodiment of all energy (*śakti*) she is the source of all creation. In Buddhism, she is the symbol of knowledge or wisdom. *Prajñā* personifies passive and inert and is activated by the male, who symbolizes *karuṇā* or compassion in Mahāyāna and *upāya* or the method in Vajrayāna Buddhism. It is as a result of the union between the active male *upāya* and the passive female *prajñā* that ultimate enlightenment (*bodhicitta*) is realized. In art, this idea is often expressed by the sexual embrace of a god and the goddess (*yuganaddha* or *yāb-yum*).

17. In term of *yoga*, it symbolically represents the process of unification of the two breaths, *prāṇa* and *apāna*, *piṅgalā* and *iḍā*, the opposites Sun-Moon, into the Central *nāḍī suṣumnā*. It is believed that by this process of combining the polar opposites and unifying them in the *suṣumnā*, the *yogī* can transcend the human condition and go beyond the phenomenal world and pass into that non-conditioned and timeless state in which 'there is neither day or night.'

18. Buddhism of the Pāla and Sena periods represent that

Tantrism was a powerful religious movement which emerged out of the coalescence between primitive magic and highly evolved spiritual ideals. Tāntric practices are older than the written scriptures on the subject. Their systematic introduction into Hinduism, Jainism and Buddhism took place in about the fifth century AD. The period from seventh to twelfth centuries were the peak periods of the Tāntric cults of Hindus, Jainas and Buddhists. Buddhist Tantrism was prevalent in Orissa, Bengal and Bihar. The Hindu shrines of Bhubaneśvara show the amalgamation of Pāśupata, Śākta and Buddhist Tāntrics influence in their relieved iconography. Images of the time of Pāla-Sena period show evident Tāntrics influences.[18] The monasteries of Nālandā, Pahārpur and Ratnāgiri were centres of Buddhist Tantrism. The cult of *yoginī* in about the ninth and tenth century AD became reasonably popular.

The erotic figures on temples represent Tāntric *sādhaka* in the non-dual state of divine bliss? We know that this

---

outgrowth of Mahāyāna which is described as Tantrism, an assimilation of the elements of Hindu religion into Buddhism, such as the concept of Śakti or female energy of *bodhisattva* and reliance on magic spell and rituals. The worship of mystical *dhyānī* Buddhas and the creator, Ādi-Buddha, a Buddhist Brahmā, completely replaced any devotion to the person of the melted Buddha. This phase of Buddhism is described as the Vajrayāna; this was popularized in art, during the eighth and ninth centuries. On the principle of Tāntric Śaivism and Vaiṣṇavism, these new interpretations suited the prevailing environment and hardly disturbed the form and structures of art in any degree. No doubt, Tantrism contributed to the evolution of multiplicity of iconographic types of form but were all summarized within the form and structure of contemporary norms. India presents the scene of a cultural milieu in which all the divergent elements have been brought together to form a common pattern. The prevailing art-stages have mediated among the above sects and denominations in order to bring them all over with the existing norms for the purpose of artistic expression of their ideas and thoughts.

T.N. Mishra, *Buddhist Tantra and Buddhist Art*, New Delhi, 2000, p. 78 (fn).

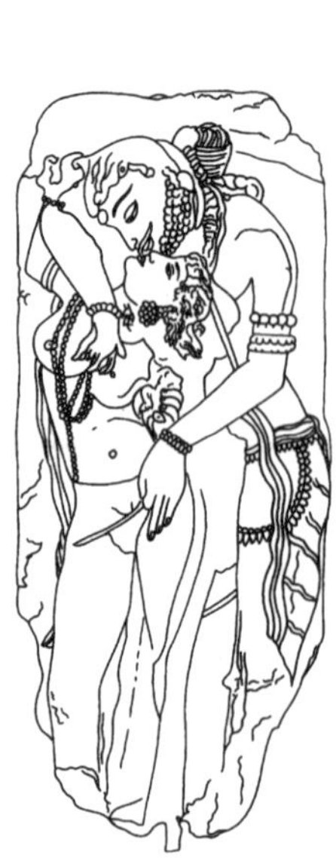

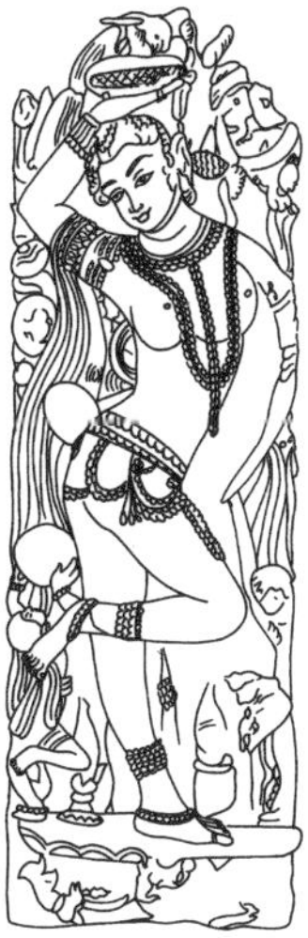

sādhanā was not meant for pleasure but was undertaken as a ritual act and, in this light, only a few sculptures were found relieved according to Haṭha-yogic discipline. Moreover, the male figures are often shown with protruding stomachs or disproportionate bodies which indicate that they were not adept in Yoga or Haṭha-Yoga.[19] The eternal bliss of the non-dual state is rarely reflected in the sculptural depictions. Only a handful sculptures of Orissa and Khajurāho present lovers in a state of bliss. The esoteric rites (*vidhis*) of Pāśupata, (who influenced many *aghorī* Tāntric sects), are considered relevant in explaining certain erotic depictions on temples by the famous iconographists. But it is wondered that the Tāntric esoteric doctrines were ever exposed to the general public! The initiatied persons were not to expose their practices in front of the common people. Only specially initiated persons (and that too, *vīra* type not *paśus*) had the privilege of practising the ritual of sex. Tāntric literature advocates strict secrecy of the rituals. The true Tāntric art is functionally related to the *upāsanā* and *sādhanā* to attain the non-dual *sahaja* state. The theory of the *maṇḍala* or mystic circle, *yantras* or mystic diagrams aided the *sādhanā* to reach his spiritual goal. Such art is non-decorative, it is cultic. The Tāntric shrines of India are, therefore, not associated merely with erotic display.

Tantrism was the major factor in bringing about the spiritual transformation in the depiction of *mithuna*. The change in the depiction was due to social permissiveness and due to the influence of Tantra. Ritualistic sex gradually acquired a hedonistic tinge. The Tāntric concept of *maithuna*

19. *Yoga* has played an important role in the formulation of the imagery of the gods and goddesses and is common to Hinduism, Jainism and Buddhism. All the Jaina *tīrthaṅkaras* always represented as ideal *yogīs*, engaged in meditation, whether seated or standing. More significantly, since *yoga* is considered the best means of attaining control over both body and mind, the relaxed body of a perfect *yogī* provided the sculptor with the ideal form for his gods.

never allows the easy attainment of *mokṣa;* instead of the rigorous path of asceticism, this method was introduced to achieve salvation.[20] The sexual representations in religious art, basicallly, lies in the idea of fertility rites, seen the world-over. The central idea is that religious and secular aspects of sex were operative behind erotic depiction in temples and the interest in sex as *bhoga,* which was cultivated for its own sake rather than for religious purposes. This is also found in literary works including poems dealing with religious themes which were endowed with sensuality and a worldly consciousness that is seen in temple scupltures where there is nothing spiritual in expression or association. However, the attributes of prosperity, fruitfulness and fertility are still associated with erotic motifs. The cultic function was associated and then superseded by aesthetic and sensual feelings.

Feudal social conditions were the right soil for the development of Tāntric religion and Tāntric art. The feudal atmosphere fastened interest in superstitions and supernatural beliefs. Belief in the magical power of sex reinforced in this atmosphere. It is mainly the rapid spread of Tāntric elements and crystallization of feudal tendencies that provided suitable soil for this outburst. It appears that the serious intent of Tāntric practices was lost, and religious practices were reduced to pleasurable activities. The erotic sculpture is not Tāntric art but art as influenced by Tantrism and sensualized without being functionally related to Tāntric *sādhanā.*

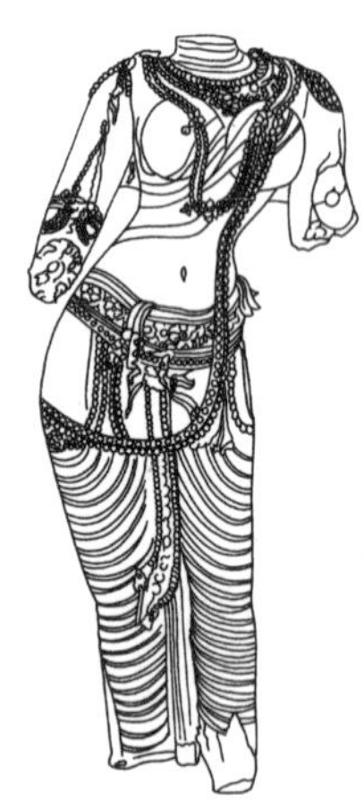

20. What kind of *sādhanā* may transform gross sense-pleasure into the boundless serenity of perfect bliss? In our ordinary life, we have the experience of the most intense pleasure in our sex-experience. Wide is the difference between this sex-pleasure and perfect bliss which is the ultimate nature of the self and not self; yet the distinction can be wholly removed by a total change of the perspectives and processes. The sex-yogic *sādhanā* of Tantra is a *sādhanā* for transforming this sex-pleasure into a realization of infinite bliss in which the self and the world around are lost in an all-pervading oneness.

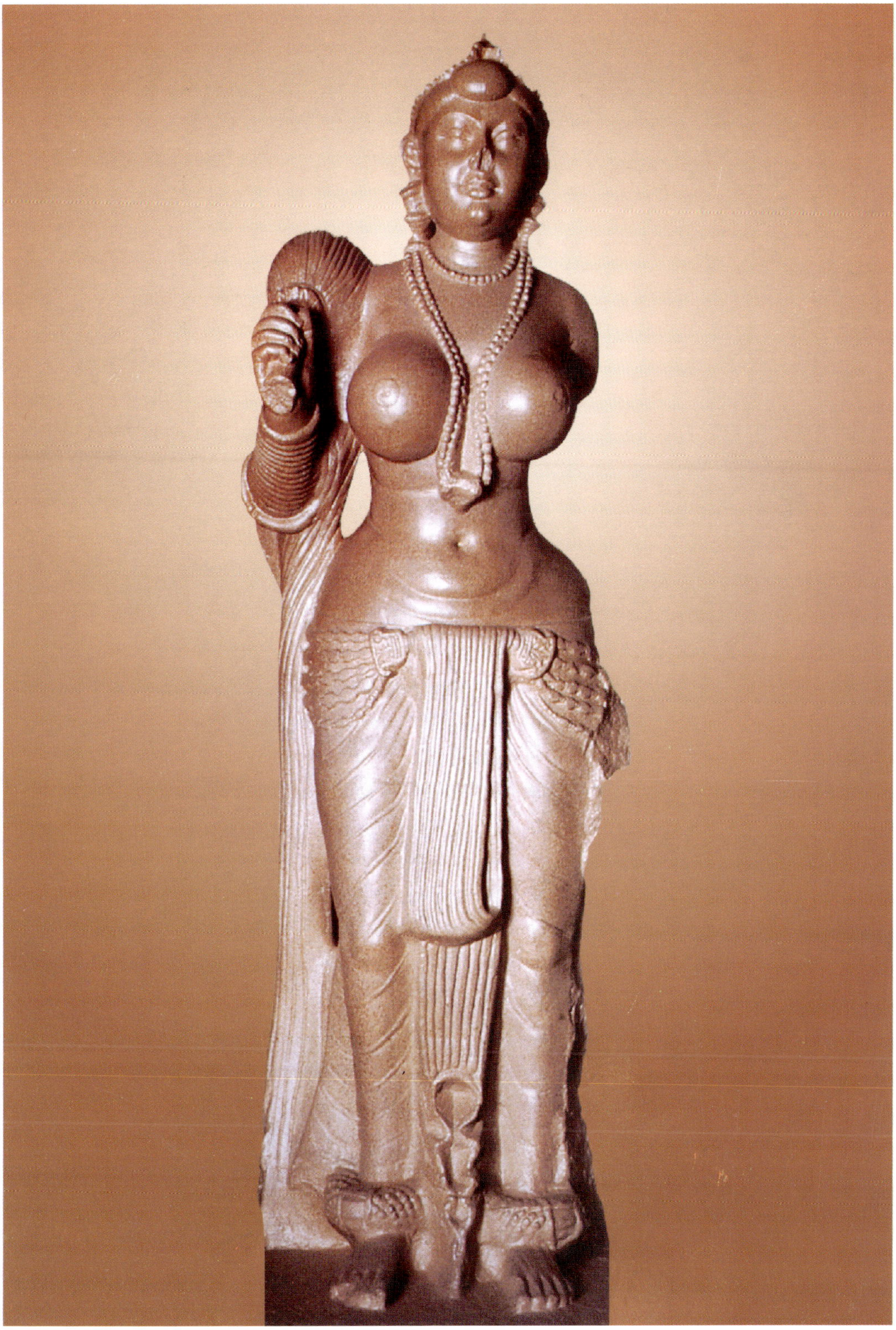

1. Didaraganja, *yakṣī*, sandstone, third century BC.

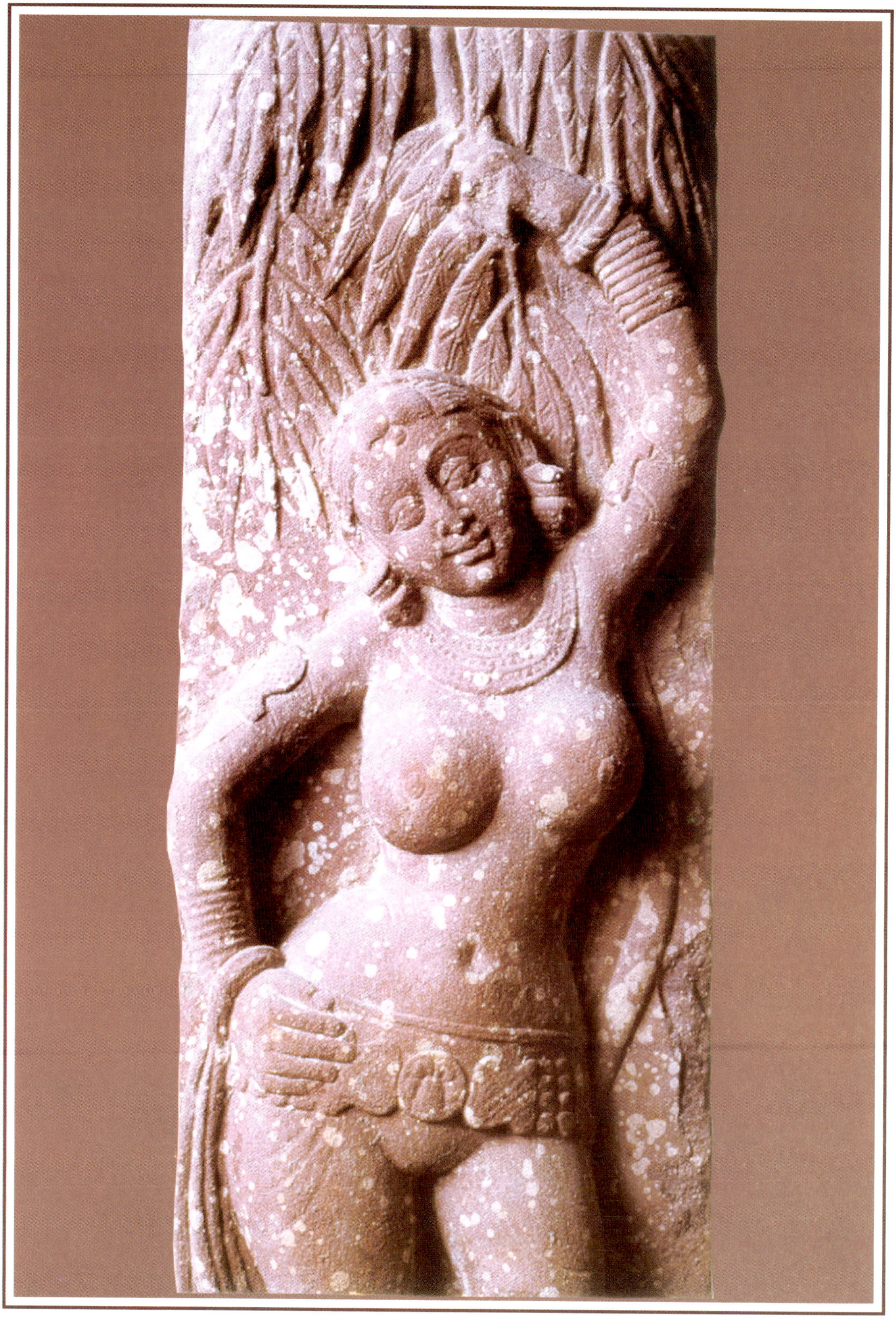

2. *Yakṣī* under tree, red sandstone, second century AD.

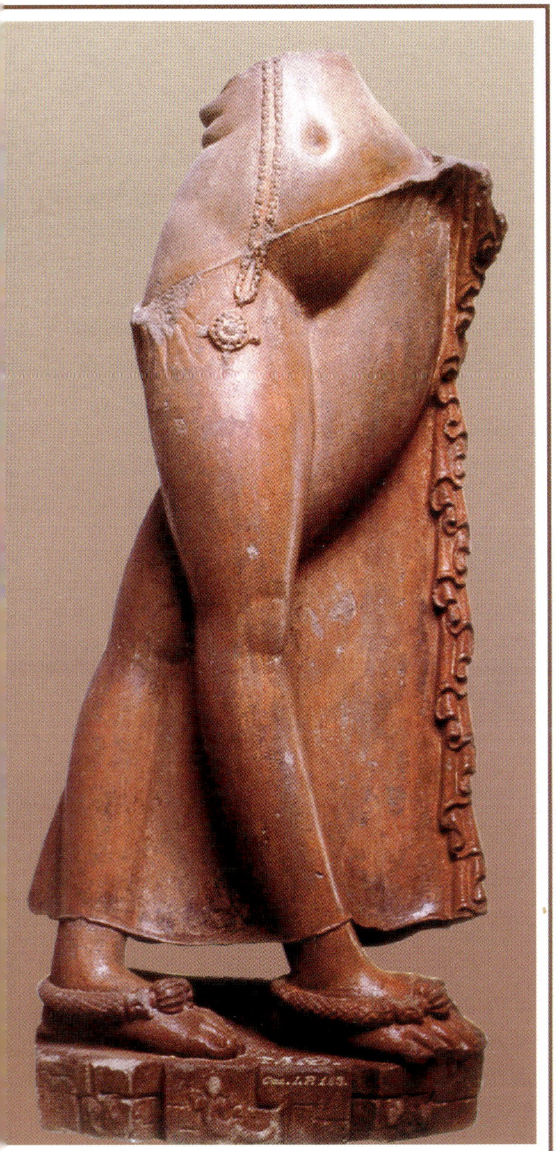

3. Woman and Scorpion, red sandstone, fifth century AD.

4. Attendant (female figure), red sandstone.

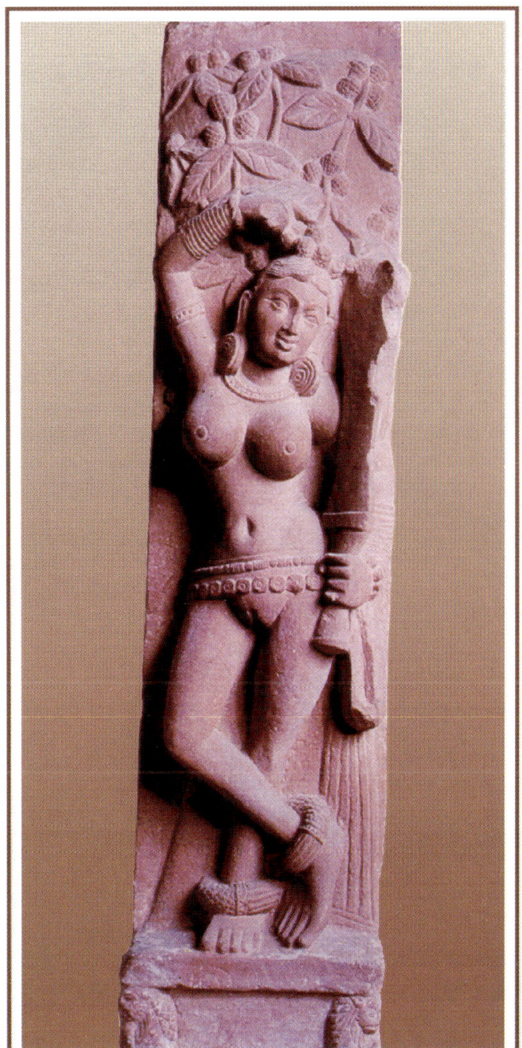

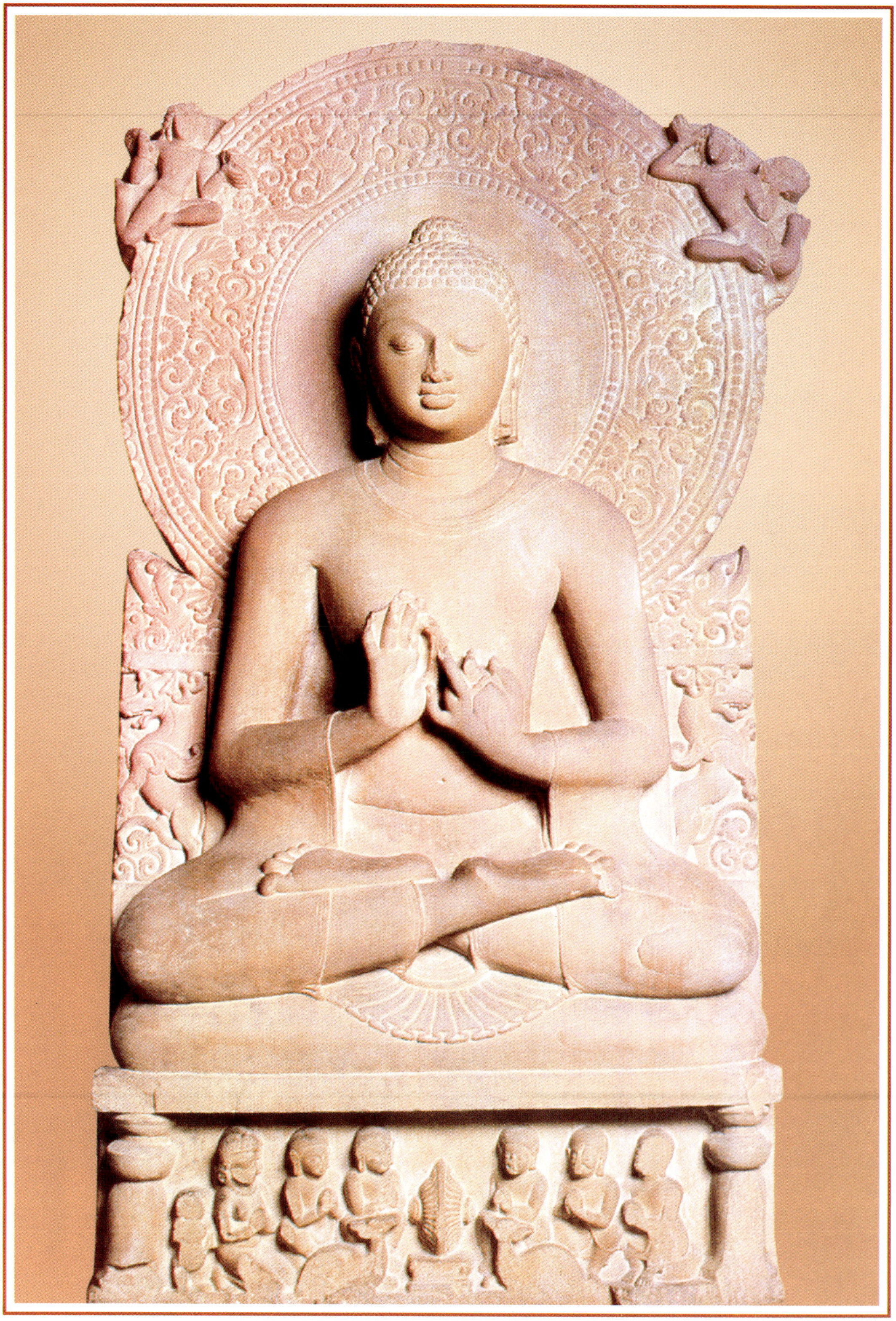

5. Buddha, sandstone, fifth century AD.

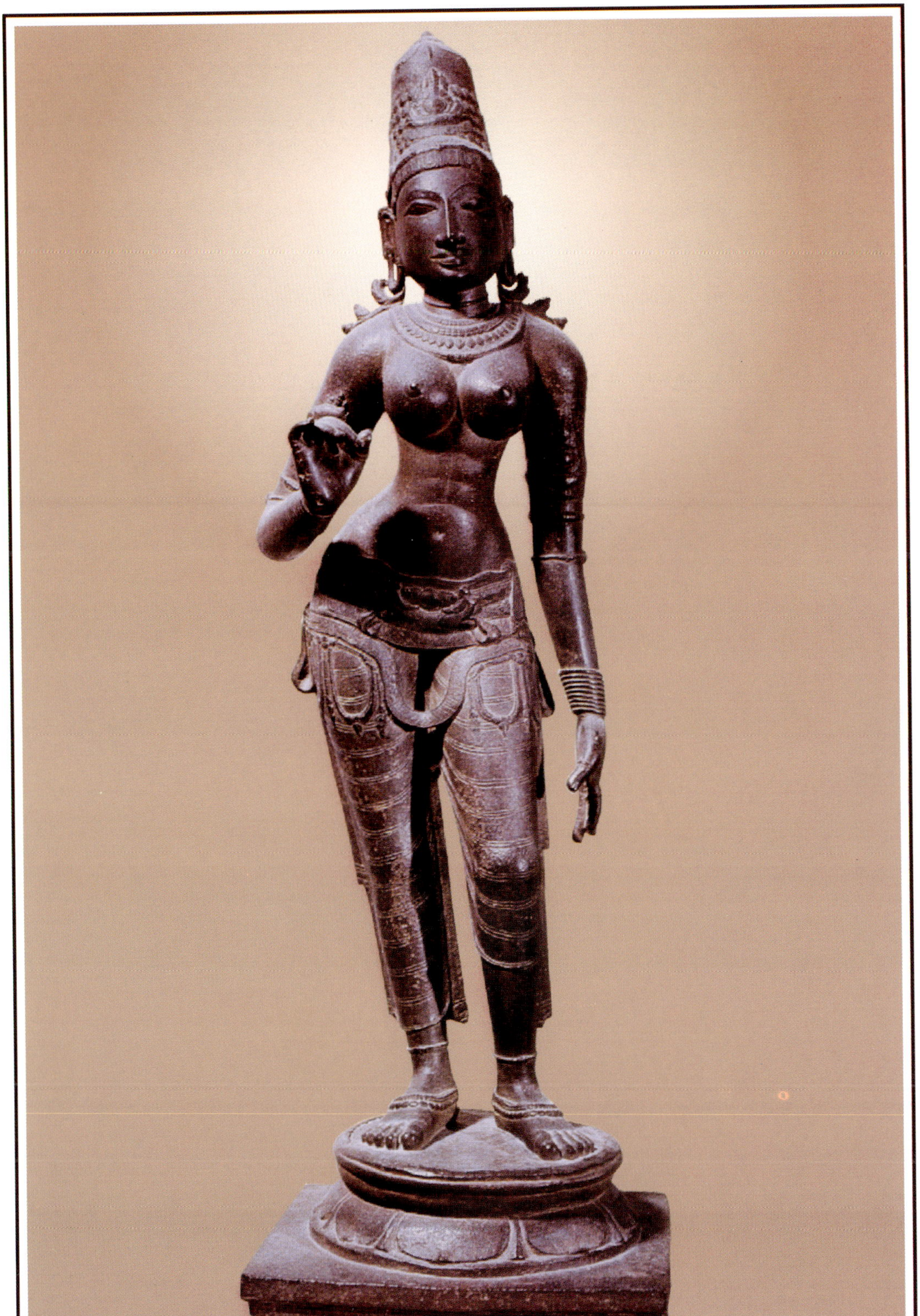

6. Pārvatī, bronze, tenth century AD.

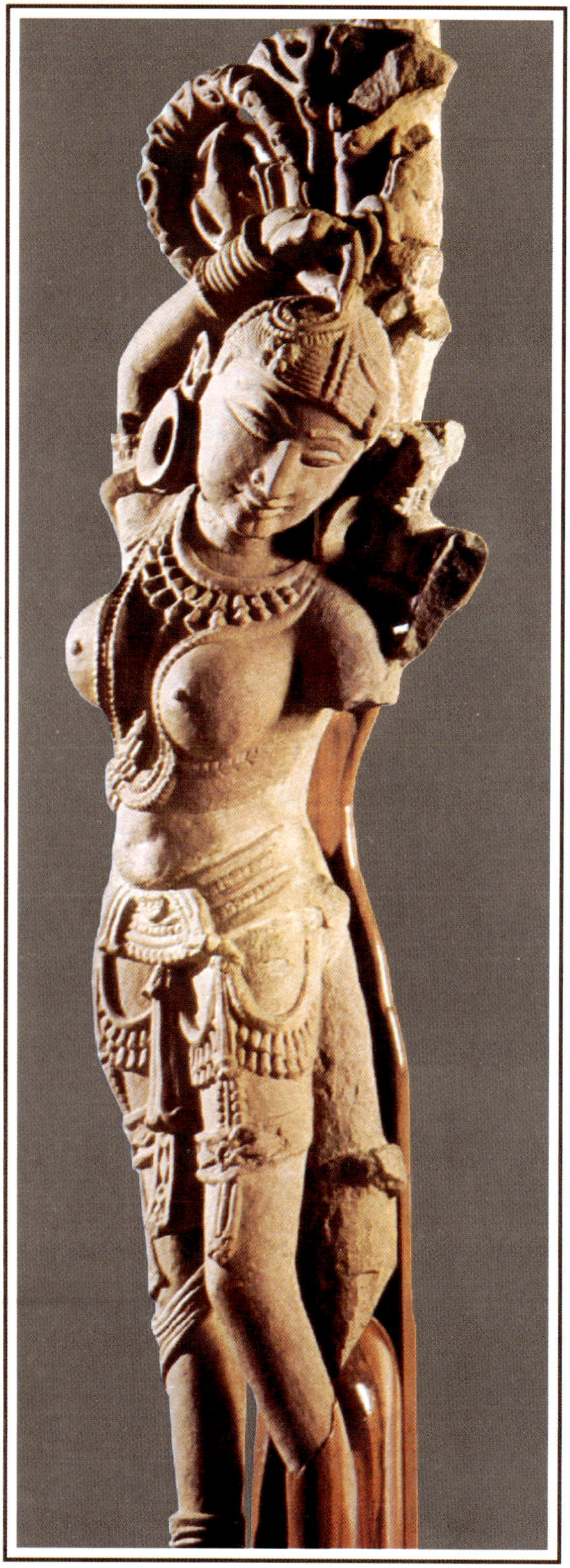

7. A Celestial Female, sandstone, twelfth century AD.

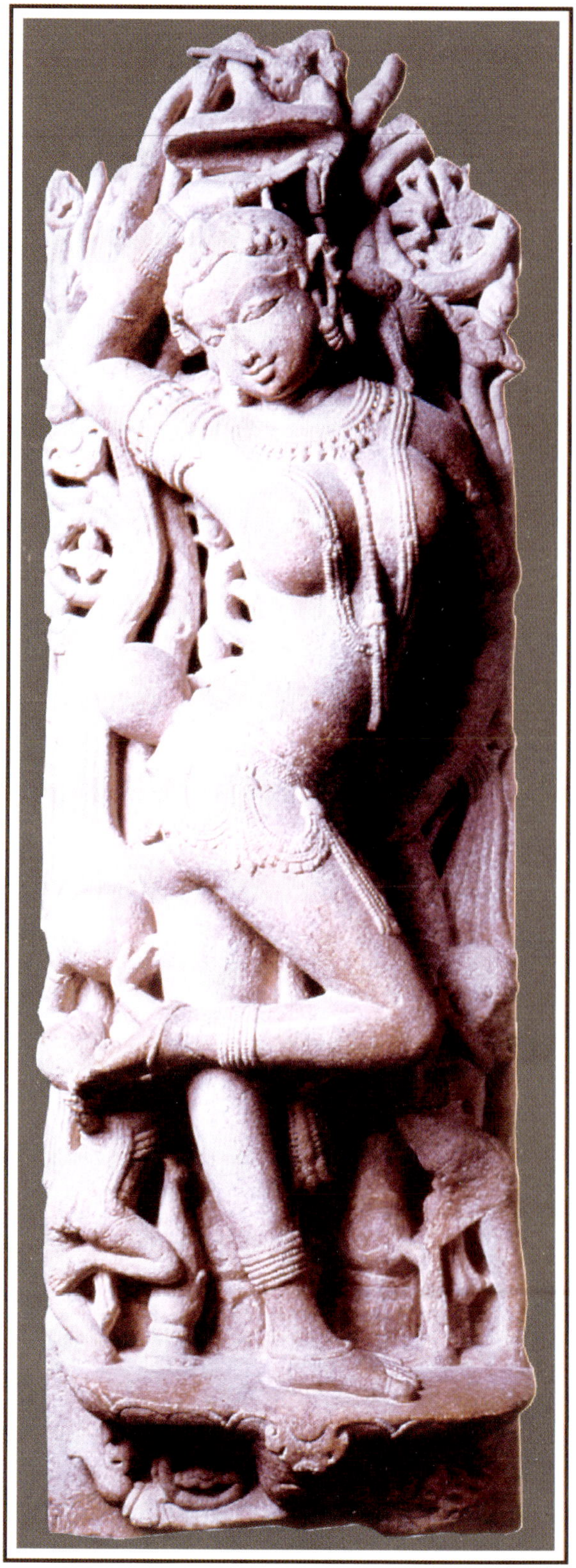

8. The Maiden, perhaps, marble, eleventh century AD.

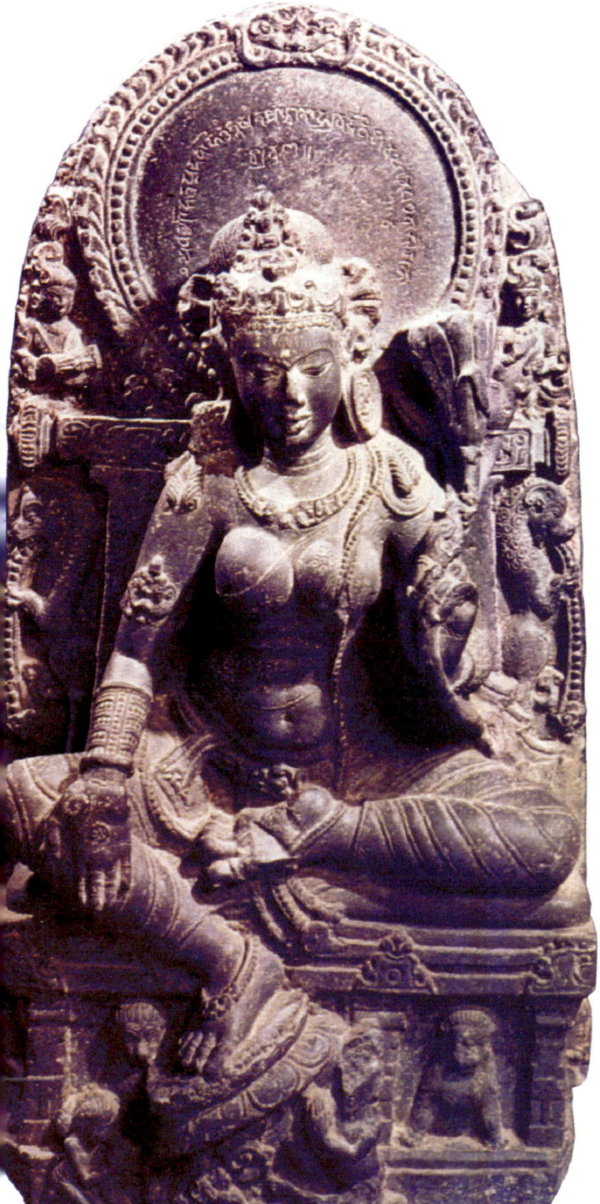

9. Buddhist goddess (Tārā), black stone, tenth century AD.

10. Lovers (*Mithuna*) sandstone, eleventh century AD.

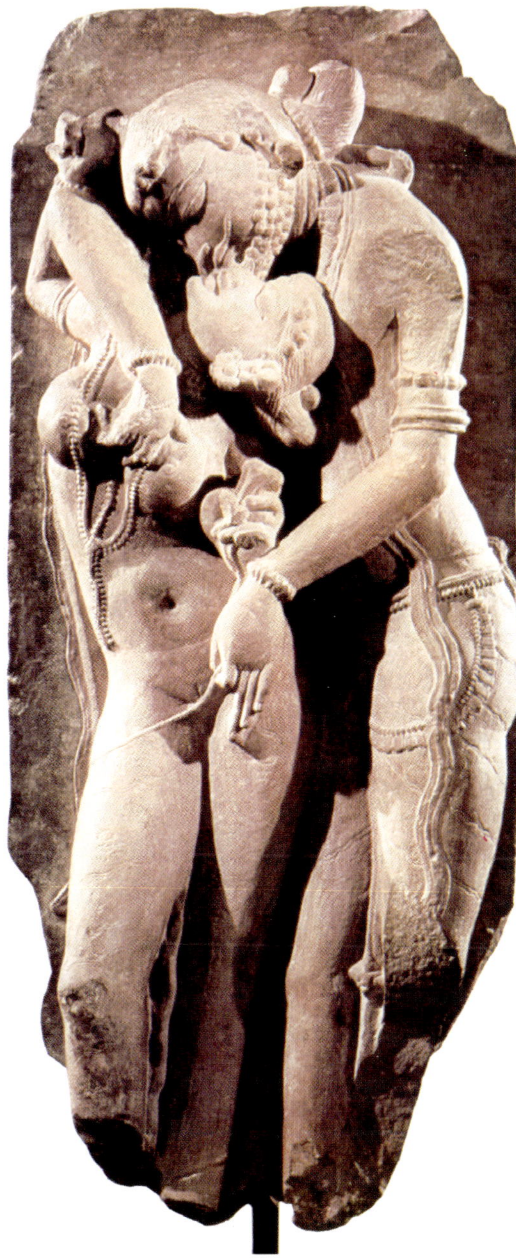

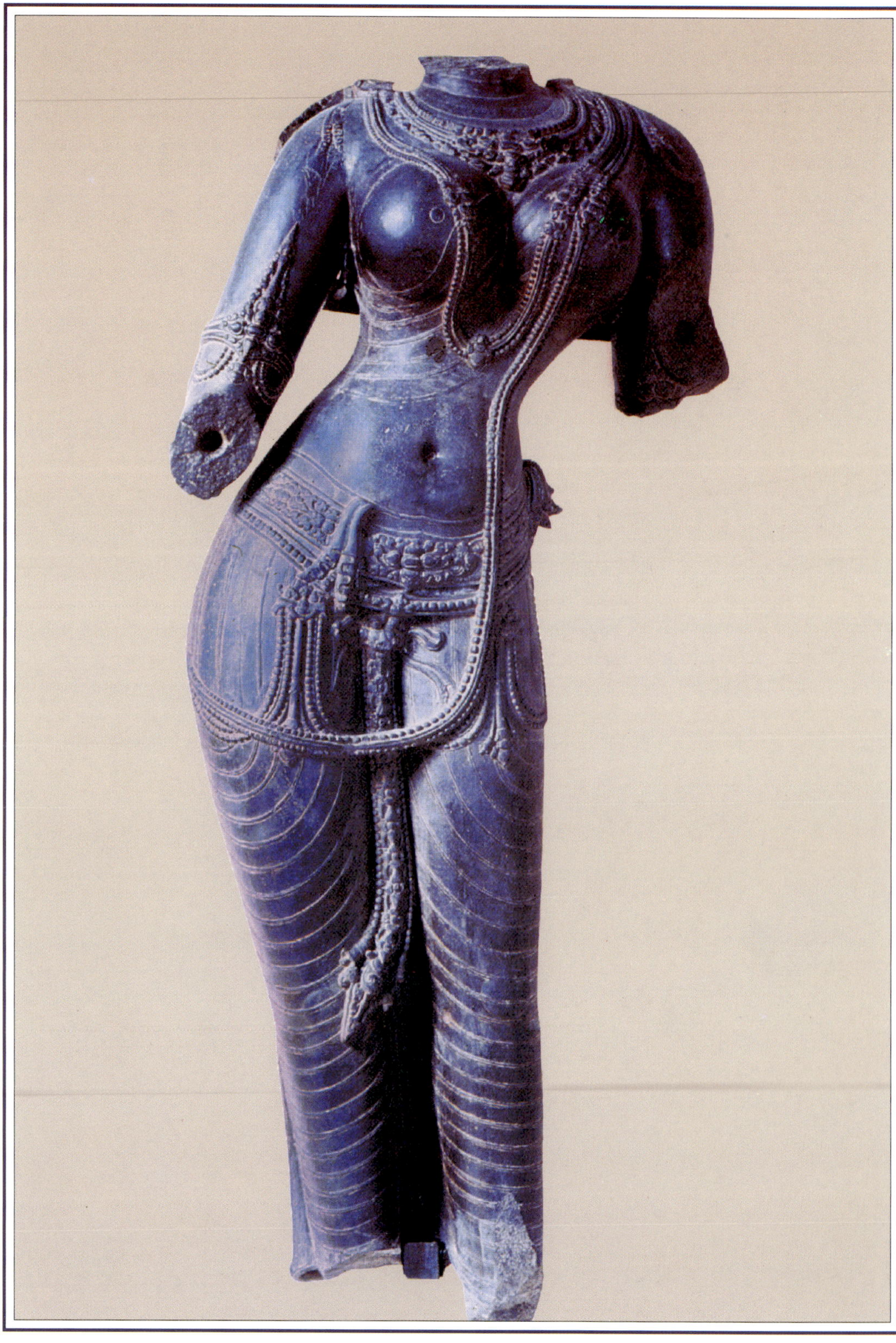

11. Tārā, black stone, eleventh century AD.

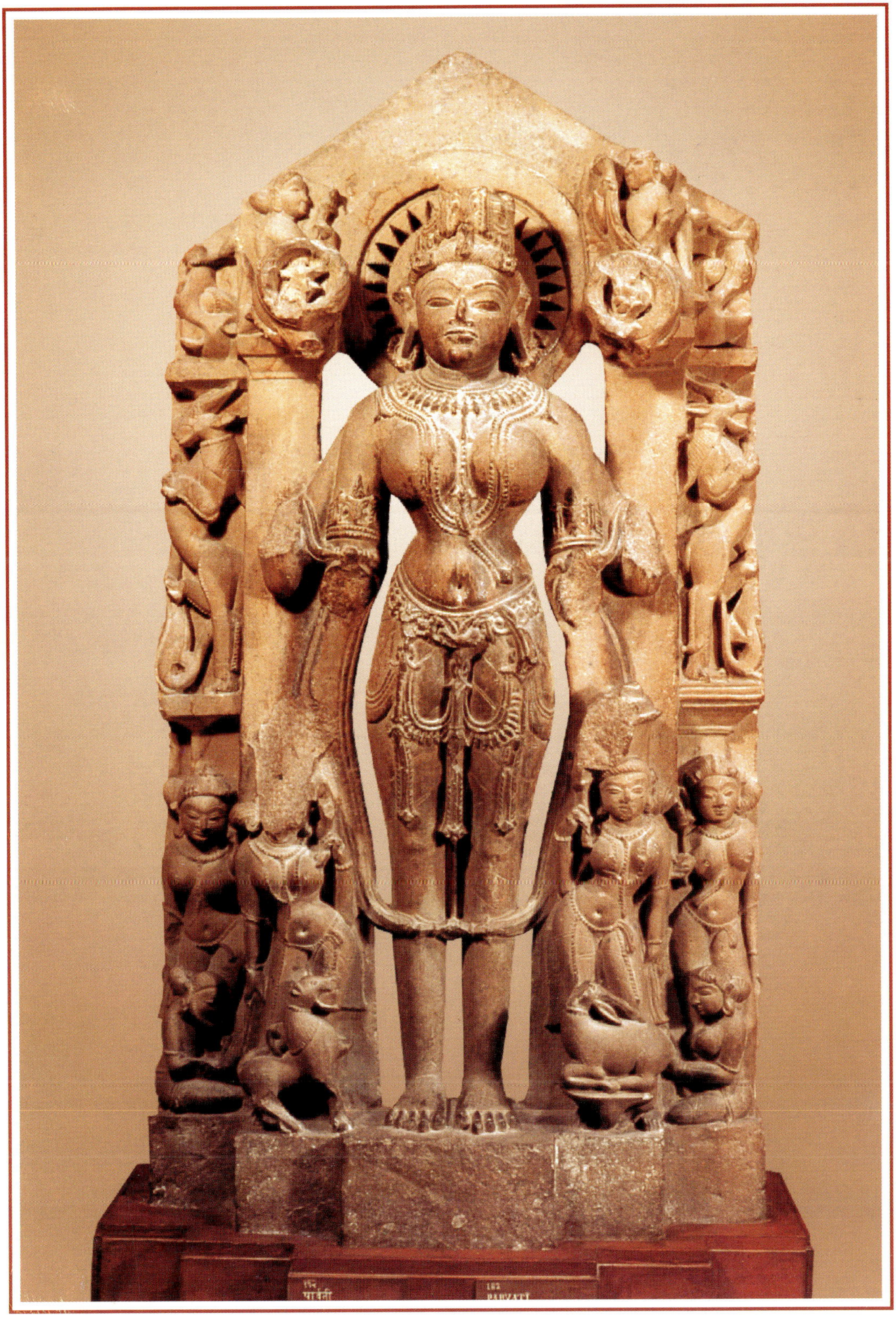

12. Pārvatī, sandstone, eleventh century AD.

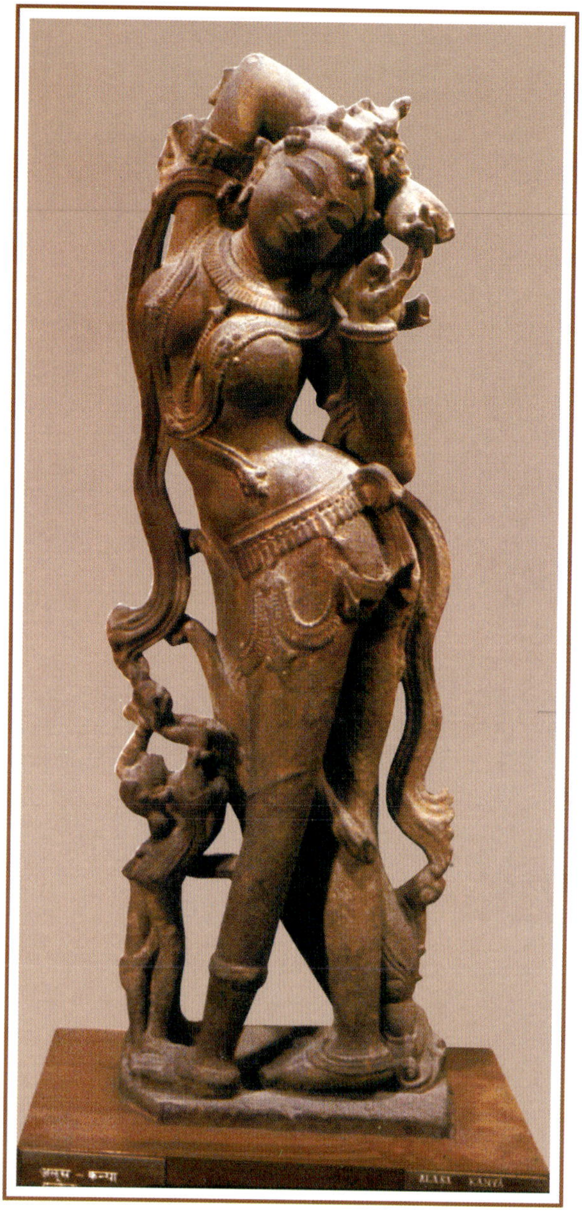

13. *Alasa Kanyā*, sandstone, eleventh century AD.

14. A *yakṣī*, sandstone, eleventh century AD.

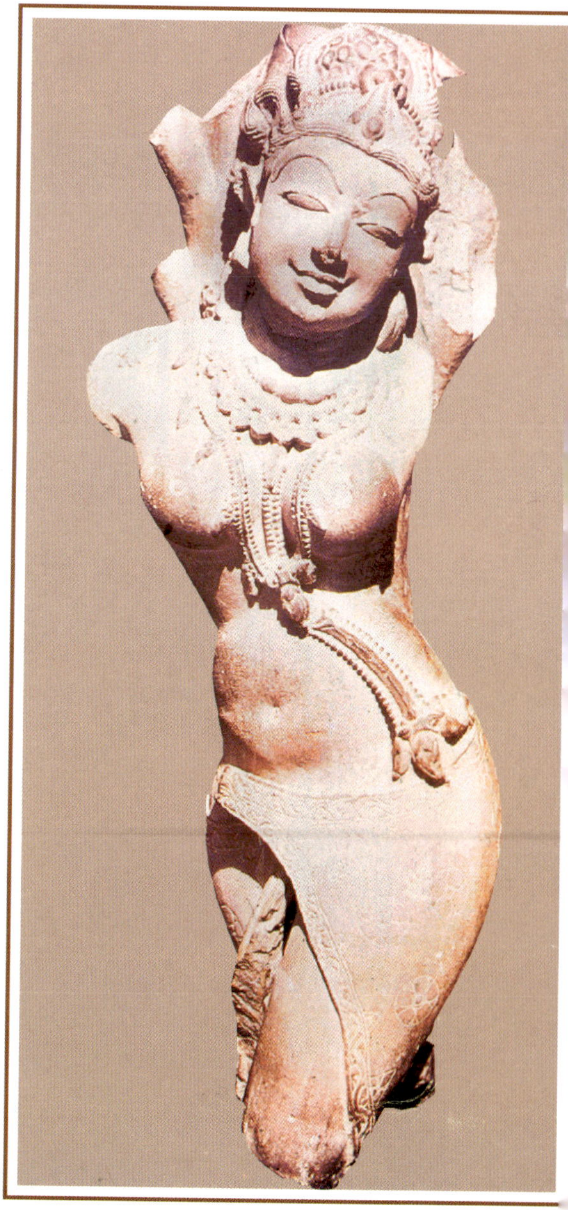

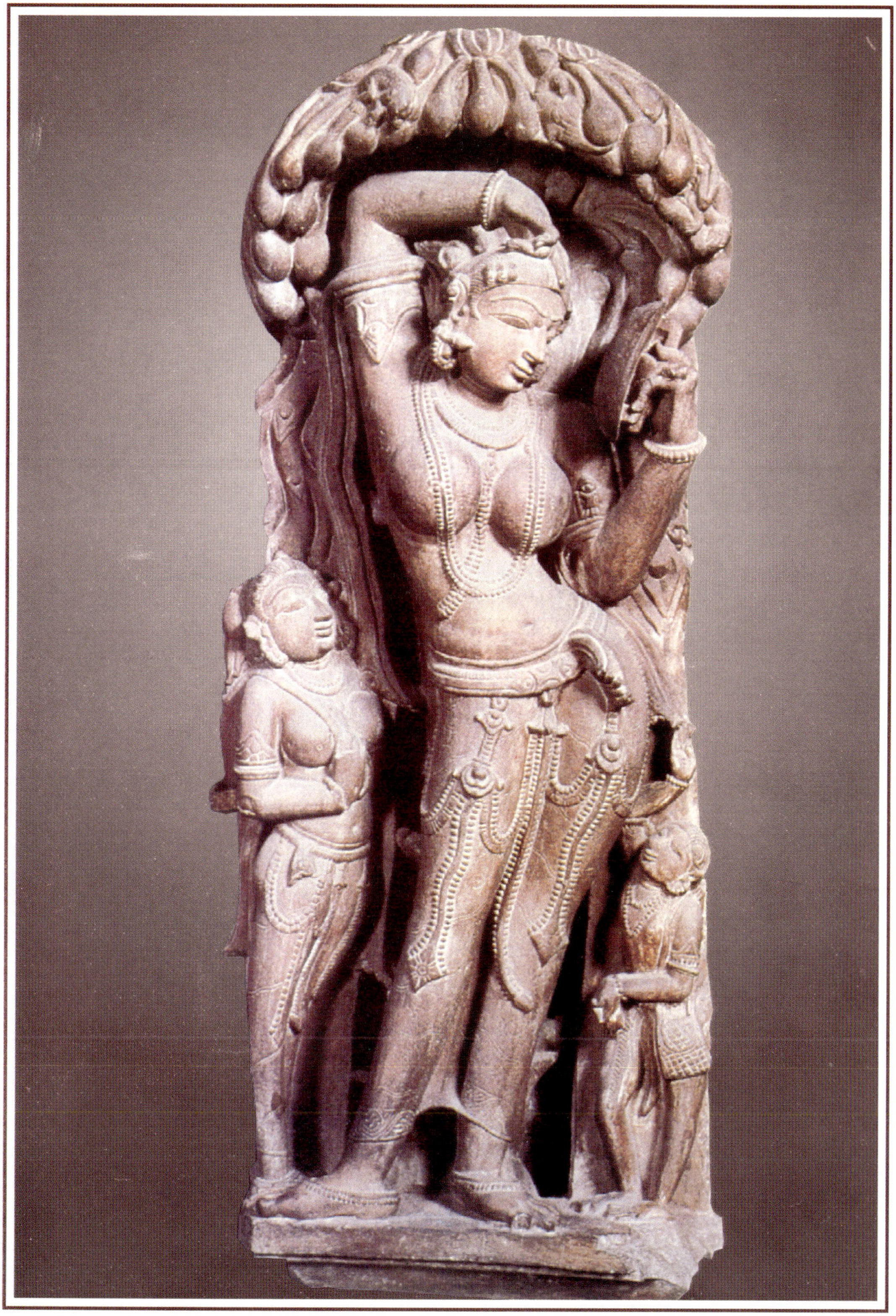

15. Lady with Mirror, sandstone, eleventh century AD.

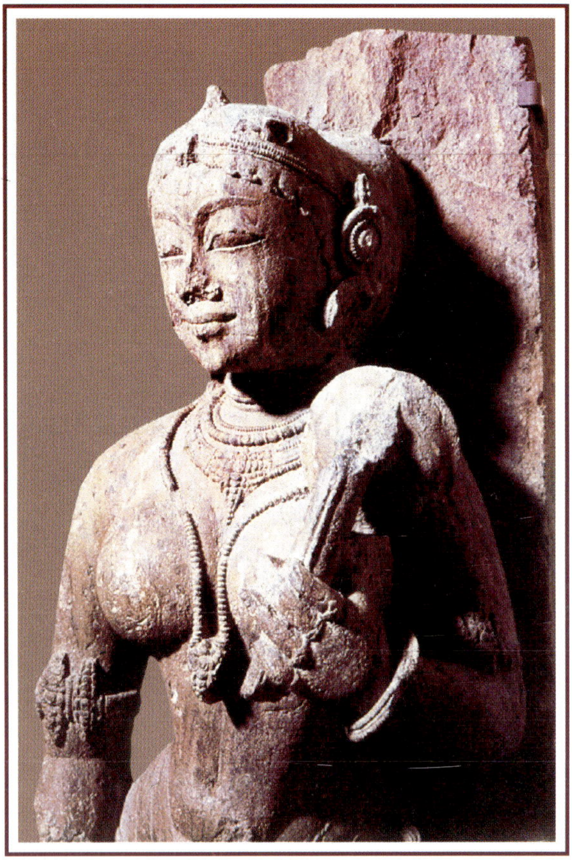

16. Surasundarī, sandstone, eleventh century AD.

17. Couple in Embrace, sandstone, eleventh century AD.

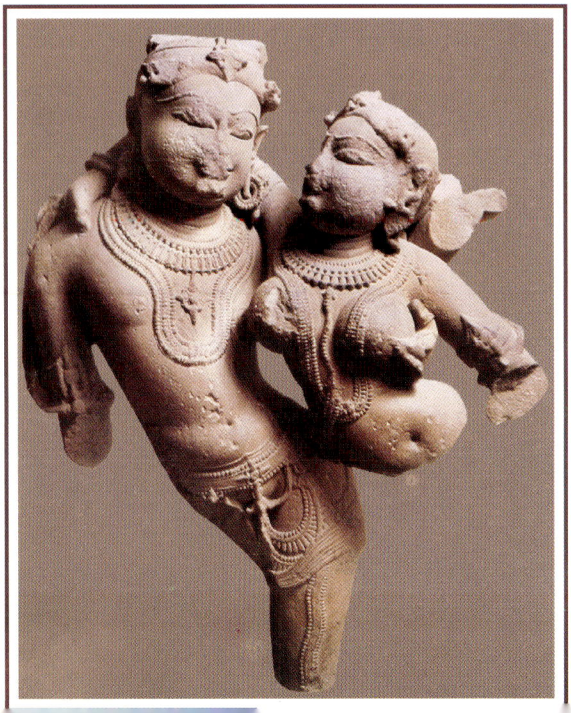

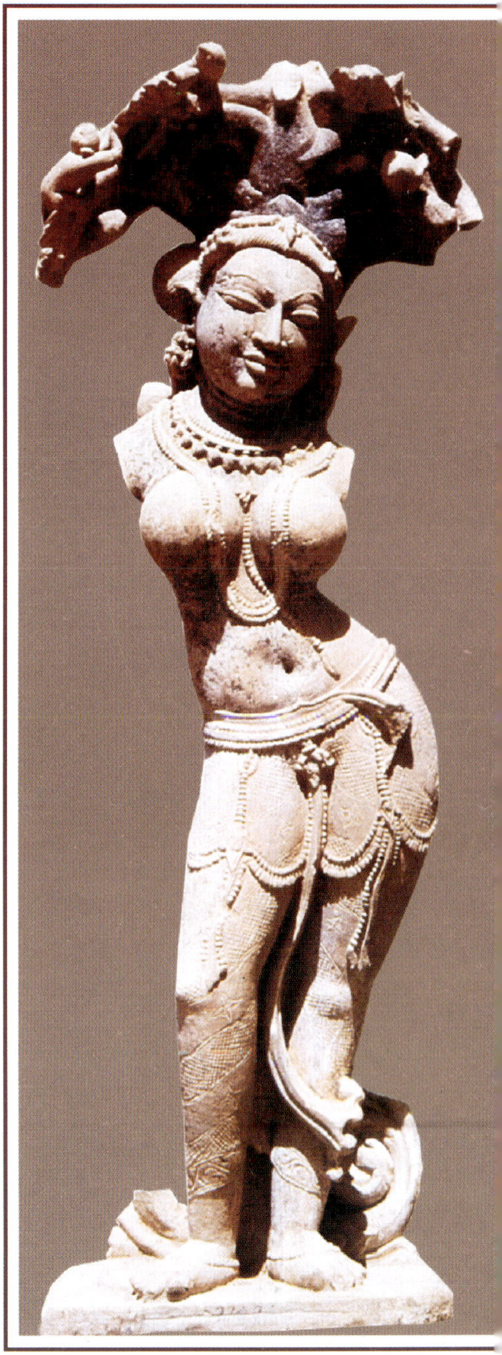

18. Mohinī (A temptress), sandstone, eleventh century AD.

Glossary

Ācāra : Rule.

Ādinātha : Primal lord.

Advaita : Non-dualism.

Advaya/Advaita : Non-dualism.

Ādya-Śakti : Primordial energy conceived as a goddess.

Aghora : One of the five forms of Śiva.

Agni : Fire.

Ahaṅkāra : Egoism.

Ahiṁsā : Non-injury.

Aikya : Unity.

Ajapā : A special form of meditation.

Ājñā-cakra : One of the six nerve-plexuses situated between the eye-brows.

Ākāśa : Space.

Ākāśa-tattva : Space element.

Akula : The Śiva aspect of Śakti. According to Abhinava-gupta that which is manifested from *kula* or Śakti is *akula* and it is endowed with the elements of Śiva.

Amṛta : Nectar.

Anādi : That which has no beginning.

Anāhata : One of the six nerve-plexuses (*ṣaṭ-cakra*) situated in the heart region. *Anāhata* is also the name of a particular form of sound.

Ānanda : Bliss.

Ānandamaya kośa : Sheath of bliss.

Āṇava : Egoism.

Aṇimā : The power of becoming as small as an atom.

Annamaya kośa : Sheath of food.

Aṅśa : Part.

Antaraṅga : Inner.

Antarātmā : Inner soul.

Anugraha : Grace.

Apakva : Unripe.

Apāna : Vital wind; current (which throws things out).

Aparā : The term for material or lower knowledge.

Aparigraha : Disowning of possessions.

Ardhanārīśvara : The half-woman and half-man (Śiva).

Artha : One of the four *puruṣārtha*s denoting wealth or material prosperity. The term is also used to denote 'meaning' and expression.

Asamprajñāta : Ultra-cognitive.

Asamprajñāta-samādhi : Concentration in which there is no consciousness of objects; gross or subtle.

Āsana : Posture.

Asmitā : The sense of personality.

Asteya : Abstention from stealing or misappropriation of others property.

Ātmadarśana : Self-realization.

Ātmaśakti : Power of the self.

Avadhūta : The aspirant who commands universal reverence.

Avidyā : Ignorance.

Avyakta : The unmanifested. A synonym of *prakṛti* or primordial.

Āyurveda : Indian indigenous system of medicine.

Bahiraṅga : Exterior.

Bandha : Different kinds of arrest.

Bhakti : Devotion.

Bhāṇḍa : Body.

Bhāva : Emotion, disposition, mental certitude and state.

Bhāvanā : *Bhāvanā* is a Pāli word, and it means culture on mental development.

Bhoga : Enjoyment.

Bhūmi : Planes.

Bhūta : Śiva, living being, the world, one of the five elements.

Bīja : Seed, in Tantra it signifies the germ-syllable which takes the form of a deity. It is also the term for semen.

Bindu : A term used in a variety of senses. As a dot denotes Śiva and as a double dot (*visarga*), Śakti, both being alphabetical signs. The former stands for solar power, the later for lunar. In Śaiva conception, *bindu* is an evaluate of *nāda* which is produced owing to the *kriya-śakti* of Śiva. It also stands for the male organ while *visarga* denotes the female organ.

Bodhi : Wisdom.

Bodhicitta : Enlightenment.

Bodhisattva : Who requires certain *pāramitā*s to qualify himself for the attainment of Buddha-hood.

Brahmacarya : Celibacy.

Brahmāṇḍa : Universe or cosmic egg.

Buddha : Perfect enlightenment.

Buddhi : Intelligence.

Caitanya : Consciousness; in internal worship the aspirant has to think that the goddess is enshrined within his body as pure-consciousness or the self.

Cakra : Cycle of world process. The word *cakra* is used with references to sun (Sūrya) and the earth, and human body is defined or compared with *cakra*. *Ca* indicate unsteady mind, and *kra* means the series of events or the process.

Candra : Moon.

Caryā : Observance.

Cit : Intelligence, consciousness or knowledge.

Citśakti : The principle of consciousness.

Cittabhūmi : The plane of mind.

Cittaśuddhi : Purification of mind.

Cittavṛtti : Intellectual feeling.

Deha : Body.

Dhairya : Steadiness of mind.

Dhāraṇā : Steading the mind or concentration; fixed attention.

Dharma : Religion.

Dharma-kāya : Word of Buddha.

Dhauti : Inner washing.

Dhvani : Sound.

Dhyāna : Contemplation or meditation.

Dhyāna-rūpa : Nature of formation.

Dīkṣā : Initiation as an precondition of *sādhanā*.

Divya : Divine, superior.

Divya-deha : A divine body.

Dṛḍhatā : The attainment of strength.

Ekāgra : One-pointed.

Garimā : The power of becoming as heavy as one likes.

Grāhya : Perceivable.

Grāhaka : Perceiver.

Granthi : Knots.

Granthi-bhedana : Piercing of knots.

Guhya : Secret.

Guṇa : Quality.

Guru : *Guru* is one who dispells darkness. The preceptor or teacher who is the pivot of *sādhanā*.

Haṁsa : A symbolic *mantra* in the form of breath. *Haṁ* is the symbol of *bindu* (*puruṣa* = Male principle of creation) and *saḥ* of *visarga* (*prakṛt* = the female principle of creation).

Haṭh-Yoga : A form of physical exercise for making the body so disciplined as to serve all spiritual purposes. It is regarded as the source of all forms of Yoga.

Icchā : Will.

Icchā-śakti : Volition, will-power.

Iḍā : One of the four principle nerves. As the symbol of moon, it is situated on the left side of the spinal cord.

Indriya : Organ of sense.

Īśāna : One of the Rudras.

Iśitva : The power of obtaining supremacy over things.

Iṣṭa : Desired.

Īśvara-praṇidhāna : Devotion of God.

Jāgrat : Wakefulness.

Jala-tattva : Water element.

Jīva : Soul.

Jīvanmukti : Liberation with span of bodily existence, a very important Tāntric or Yogic concept. He who has complete grasp of the knowledge of the self, has dispelled from within the darkness of false knowledge by constant practice and meditation and is reaping the fruits of his *karma*. He may be called a *jīvanmukta*.

Jīvātmā : Individual soul.

Jñāna : Knowledge; philosophical knowledge.

Jñāna-śakti : Cognition, knowledge.

Jñāna-sattva : Attainment of wisdom.

Kaivalya : Isolation, detachment of soul from matter or further transmigration. Absolute independence or oneness.

Kalā : Evolutes of *varṇa*, it denotes *prakṛti*, Śakti and *māyā*; absolute transcendental power.

Kāla : Time.

Kālacakra : *Kālacakra* denoting the wheel of time, wheel of destruction.

Kālacakrayāna : The vehicle for protection against the wheel of destruction.

Kālāgni : The principle of destruction, the fire, fire of time.

Kālātīta : Timeless.

Kāma : Desire, passion.

Kāma-bīja : Vital fluid.

Kāma vāyu : Wind-passion.

Kāraṇa : Tāntric term for wine.

Kāraṇa-śarīra : The material body.

Karma : Action, deeds and activity.

Karuṇā : Universal compassion.

Kāyā : Body.

Kāya-sādhanā : Disciplining the body.

Kleśa : Suffering.

Kriyā : Action or activities.

Kriyā-śakti : Administration, activity.

Kṣipta : Wandering.

Kṣudra brahmāṇḍa : Microcosm.

Kumbhaka : A form of breath control.

Kuṇḍalinī : The serpent power remaining latent in the *mūlādhāra*.

Laghimā : The power of assuming excessive lightness at will.

Lalanā : The name of nerve, it is also known as the *āli* (left) and represents a vowel.

Latā : The female partner of the aspirant.

Latā-sādhanā : *Pañca-makāra* rituals with female partner.

Lāulikī : Whirling of belly from side to side.

Laya : *Laya* means absorption of the mind or deep concentration or the state of absolute bliss. Dissolution.

Laya-yoga : The higher form of Haṭha-Yoga which destroys (*laya*) all form of desire. It is an experience of eternal bliss in which the mind totally merges with the Supreme Being.

Liṅga : Male generative organ worshipped in phallic symbols.

Liṅga is the symbol of Śiva.

Madhyamā : Name of a special type of sound which is between *paśyanti* and *vaikharī*. It is also called as a state of equilibrium of *parā* and *paśyanti*.

Mahā : Supreme or great.

Mahābhūta : Gross element.

Mahārāga : Intense emotion.

Mahārajas : Ovum.

Mahārasa : Great juice.

Mahāsattva : Attainment of wisdom.

Mahāsukha : Supreme bliss, blissful condition or great bliss.

Mahāsukha-sthāna : The place of great bliss.

Mahāyāna : Great vehicle, theistic form of Buddhism, with emphasis on divine Buddhas and *bodhisattvas*.

Maheśvara : Great lord.

Mahimā : The power of becoming big.

Maithuna : Sexual intercourse which is regarded as one of the five *makāra*. For spiritual interpreation see *Kulārṇva*.

Mala : Taints.

Manana : Logical thinking.

Maṇḍala : A special gathering of aspirants for collective rituals of the five *makāras*, mystic circle.

Maṇipūra : A nerve (*cakra*) plexus near the naval region. It is also called *nābhi-cakra*.

Manomaya kośa : Sheath of lower mind.

Manomūrchā : A process of breath control.

Mantra : The mystic sound or the ultimate reality in the form of the sound. Power (*śakti*) in the form of sound, words and letters.

Mātṛkā : Divine mother. It is also the name of mystic letters.

Māyā : Illusion, false knowledge, material cause of creation, immersion in the material world.

Mithuna : Amorous couple.

Mokṣa : Salvation, liberation.

Mūḍha : Forgetful.

Mudrā : *Mudrā* is also the name of one of the five *makāras*. In Tantra, *mudrā* is used exclusively for the woman, posture and gesture.

Mukti : Salvation (*nirvāṇa*).

Mūlādhāra : The first of the six nerve plexuses, situated in the lowest extremity of the spinal cord, where the *kuṇḍalanī* is coiled.

Nāda : (a) Sound, (b) A term used in Tantra in a variety of senses. Its simple meaning is sound. In Tāntric concepts, the Supreme Being (Para-Śiva or Para-Śakti) is soundless and without any vibration. When this Para-Śakti goes to express itself in creation, its first vibration is known as *nāda*. It is the manifestation of the consciousness of the Supreme

Being revealed as sound. This manifestation is thought of as the terms of the copulation of Śiva and Śakti (the static and kinetic aspects, also known as *prakāśa*, and *vimarśa*, of the same ultimate reality) and the thrill of the pleasure of this union (*maithuna*) is known as *nāda*.

Nāda-Brahman : *Nāda* conceive of *Brahman* in the form of primordial sound expressed in *parā*, *paśyanti*, *madhyamā* and *vaikharī*.

Nāḍī : Nerves of the human body, pulse.

Nāma-rūpātmaka : Made up of name and form.

Neti : Cleaning of nostrils.

Nirākāra : Formless.

Nirañjana : Speckless.

Nirātmā : Essencelessness.

Nirguṇa : Attributeless.

Nirliptatva : Detachment.

Nirmāṇa-kāya : Nomenal body.

Nirodha : Restraint state.

Niruddha : Restrained.

Nirvāṇa : Salvation, non-duality.

Nirvikalpa-samādhi : In which nothing is perceived except the universal soul.

Niṣkala : Undifferentiated.

Nivṛtti : Return current.

Niyama : Observance.

Nyāsa : Identifying deities in different parts of the body of the devotee.

Pada : Word.

Pakva : Ripe.

Pañca-bhūta : Five material elements.

Panth : Way, cult.

Parā : Higher knowledge; *parā* is motionless casual sound conceived as existing in the *kuṇḍalinī* in the *mūlādhāra-cakra* in dreamless state of deep sleep.

Parabrahman : Supreme Being, the absolute, the ultimate reality in the form of pure consciousness.

Paramahaṁsa : The one who has attained success in *haṁsa mantra*.

Paramānanda : Supreme bliss or realization of full bliss.

Paramasukha : Supreme bliss.

Parā-mukti : Liberation.

Parā-Śabda : Motionless casual sound.

Parā-Śakti : *Parā-śakti* is the energy of Śiva which is regarded as the instrumental cause of creation. The term is also used to denote the power of independence of the Supreme Being. In the Śaiva and Śākta outlook, *parā-śakti* is the *vimarśa*, that is, vibrating or kinetic energy of the Supreme Being. It is equated with *kuṇḍalinī* and its functioning.

Parā-saṁvit : Pure consciousness.

Parā-vāk : It is the first stage of sound

expressing itself only at *mūlādhāra*. It is without any vibration, it is like flame of light, unmanifested yet indestructible.

Pāśa : Fetters.

Paśu : Fettered individual.

Paśu-bhāva : Ordinary human state.

Paśyanti : One of the constituents, which is regarded as the second stage of development. This form of sound belongs to the naval region. It has little vibration and is connected with *nāda-tattva*.

Piṇḍa : The visible body.

Piṅgalā : One of the major nerves. Together with its sister nerve *iḍā* it rises from *mūlādhāra* and ends in the right nostril. It is also known as *sūrya-nāḍī* — having the masculine characteristics of the sun.

Prajñā : Insight, knowledge, wisdom; insight into the nature of things by concentration.

Prakāmya : The power of obtaining all objects of pleasure at will.

Prakāśa : The static aspect of the ultimate reality.

Prakāśaka : Revealer.

Prakāśya : Revealed.

Prakṛti : (a) Female principle of creation, variously conceived as primordial matter or energy. Often identified with Śakti and Supreme Being of the Śākta. (b) Nature.

Pralaya : Dissolution (*saṁhāra*).

Prāṇa : Vital wind or life force (which takes things in).

Prāṇamaya kośa : Sheath of life.

Prāṇāyāma : The process of breath control, Regulation of breath.

Prāpti : The power of obtaining everything at will.

Prasāda : Divine grace.

Pratyāhāra : Withdrawal of senses or abstraction.

Pratyakṣa : The realization.

Pravṛtti : Moving around.

Pṛthag-jana : Lay people.

Pṛthivī : Earth.

Pṛthivī-tattva : Earth element.

Pūjā : Worship.

Puṇya : Merit.

Pūraka : A form of breath control.

Puruṣa : Male or principle of creation.

Puruṣa-prakṛti : Male and Female, principles of creation, later equated with the principles of sound and matter.

Puruṣārtha : *Dharma* (Religion), *artha* (Money), *kāma* (Desire), *mokṣa* (Liberation) being the four *puruṣārtha*.

Pūrva : Earlier.

Rāga : Attachment; emotion.

Rajas : Energy.

Rasa : Sentiment, sap, elixir, taste and

juice. *Rasa* is also conceived in terms of intense emotional attachment between the male and female principles, symbolizing two aspects of Śakti and impersonated by the aspirant and his partner.

Rasanā : The name for nerve; it is also known as the *kāli* (right) which represent consonants.

Rati : Sexual pleasure; the wife Kāma.

Ṛddhi : Supernatural power.

Recaka : A form of breath-control.

Ṛṇas : Debts.

Rudra : The other name for Śiva, indicating the shedding of tears.

Rūpa : Form.

Rūpa-kāya : Material elements.

Śabda : Sound; word.

Śabda-Brahman : Brahmā or Śakti conceived as the substratum of sound.

Sādhaka : Spiritual aspirant; seeker.

Sādhanā : Term for spiritual exercise.

Sādhya : The goal to be sought.

Saguṇa : With attributes.

Sahaja : (a) The way (*mārga*) of spiritual exercise which is the earliest and most natural. It is also the term for ultimate reality among the Sahajīyas, i.e., those who believe in the *mārga,* (b) Non-duality, natural.

Sahajānanda : Non-duality, perfect bliss, more intense bliss.

Sahaja-Yoga : Sahaja-Yoga is that final state, where all kinds of duality are absorbed in a principle of non-duality.

Sahasrāra : The highest cerebral region above; all the *cakra* or neve-plexuses where *kuṇḍalinī* meets its source. For its description, see *Ṣaṭcakra-Nirūpaṇa,* XLI-XLIII.

Śakti : Energy, female partner of the aspirant; it is the power of the Supreme Being conceived as the female principle through which the manifestation of the universe is effected. The important aspects of this power are *cit* (will), *jñāna* (knowledge), and *kriyā* (action).

Sālokya : This is one of the four stages of beatitude.

Samādhi : Concentration, state of perfect bliss in which the world of senses disappears from the mind of the aspirant. It is the aim of all Yogic exercises; non-duality; trance contemplation.

Samādhi-prajñā : Concentrated insight.

Samāna : Vital wind (which assimilates).

Sāmantabhadra : Entirely auspicious.

Sāmānya-spanda : A non-particularized motion.

Samarasa : The state of unity of emotion or oneness of emotion.

Sāmarasya : Equilibrium of Śiva and Śakti, male and female principles.

In Buddhism it is that of *upāya* and *prajñā*. Very often this equilibrium is conceived of in sexual terms. Its spirit is felt by the aspirant within his own self. Complete understanding of this equilibrium leads to the experience of non-duality.

Saṁbhoga-kāya : Body of bliss.

Sāmīpya : This is one of the four stages of beatitude; proximity (in space and time).

Saṁprajñāta : Cognitive.

Samprajñāta-samādhi : Conscious concentration.

Samprajñāta-yoga : *Samprajñāta-yoga* is that in which the mind is concentrated upon some object, external or internal.

Saṁsāra : World.

Saṁskāra : Mental state; impression.

Saṁyama : Constraint.

Sānanda : Where the reflection is on the mind which is full of *sattva* (that is a *samādhi* of joy).

Sanjñā (*Saṁjñā*) : Perception, name or conceptual knowledge.

Saṅkleśa : Adherence.

Santoṣa : Contentment.

Sārūpya : Conformity with the deity; one of the grades of *mukti* or beatitude.

Sāsmitarūpa : Where there is only a sense of personality in which the knower himself is the object of perception.

Sat : Existence.

Ṣaṭ-cakra : The six nerve-plexuses, i.e., *mūlādhāra, svādhiṣṭhāna, maṇipūra, anāhata, viśuddha* and *ājñā*.

Ṣaṭa-karma : The six processes.

Sattva-guṇa : Intelligence stuff.

Satya : Truth speaking.

Śauca : Purity of cleanliness.

Savicāra : Where there is a reflection over a subtle object such as *tanmātras*.

Savitarka : Deliberation over or realization of a gross object like the image of a god.

Siddha/Siddhi : *Siddhi* is spiritual attainment. The term is also used to denote the attainment of miraculous power. He or she who has attained *siddhi* is known as *siddha*.

Śiṣya : Disciple.

Skandha : Elements.

Smṛti : Mindfulness or capacity to call up the desired object before the mind repeatedly by that energy.

Śodhana : Cleansing.

Spanda : Motion.

Sparśa : Touch.

Śraddhā : Faith in the efficacy of concentration.

Śrī : A goddess of abundance, fertility, blissful prosperity, luck and beauty.

Sṛṣṭi : Creation.

Sthāna : Place.

Sthiratā : Fortitude.

Sthiti : Substance.

Sthūla : Gross.

Sthūla-deha : Gross body.

Sukha : Bliss.

Sukhamaya : Incessant Bliss.

Śukra : Semen.

Sūkṣma-deha (*śarīra*) : Subtle body.

Śūnya : Reality.

Śūnyatā : Perfect knowledge, void; the Buddhist idea of vacuity conceived in terms of the Female principle. It is also known as *prajñā* and symbolized in the form of different goddesses. The male principle is thought of as *karuṇā* or *upāya*.

Sūrya : Sun.

Suṣumnā : The most important nerve, also known as *brahma-nāḍī*. It is said that universe itself is contained in this nerve. It extends from the *mūlādhāra* to *brahmarandhra*. It is the route by which *kuṇḍalinī* marches upwards.

Suṣupti : Deep sleep.

Svādhiṣṭhāna : The nerve-plexus situated above the *mūlādhāra*.

Svādhyāya : Study.

Svapna : Illusion, dream.

Svarūpa : Own true nature.

Svecchayā : Own free will.

Tamas : The gross material stuff.

Tanmātra : Subtle, potential elements.

Tapas : Right aspiration.

Tattva : Essential principles.

Tejas : Fire, Fiery energy.

Teja-tattva : Fire element.

Trāṭaka : Cleaning the eyes.

Turīya : A very high state. The *sahasrāra-cakra* is supposed to contain a field of knowledge which is also known as *turīya*.

Udāna : Vital wind (which expresses, especially in speech).

Ulṭā-sādhanā : Regressive process.

Upabhogya : Food.

Upāsanā : Worship.

Upāya : Method or means.

Uttara : Later.

Vācaka/Vākya : *Śakti* or power of *mantra*; the former is denoting or signifying aspect, while the latter is the basic one. *Vākya* is contained in the *vācaka* and formally there is no distinction between them. Denoter and denoted.

Vaikharī : One of the four ingredients of sound, other being *parā*, *paśyanti* and *madhyamā*. It is that sound which is carried by the wind inside the body and becomes articulated in the throat. It is the gross sound.

Vaikharī-spaṣṭatara-spanda : Clearly articulated speech.

Vajrayāna : A form of Tāntric Buddhism.

Vāk : Speech.

Vākya : Sentences.

Vāsanā : Inherent tendencies that we are carry with us.

Vaśitva : The power of subduing, fascinating or bewitching.

Vasti : Contraction and expansion of the anus in water.

Vāta-karma : Removal of phlegm by inhalation and exhalation or water drawn through nostrils and ejected through the mouth.

Vāyu : Wind.

Vāyu-tattva : Air element or the science of the vital wind.

Vedanā : Feeling; sensation.

Vibhūti : Supernatural power.

Vicikarṣa : Desire to create.

Vicitra : The moment when the realization of pleasure is resulting from physical union (*ānanda*).

Vidyā : *Vidyā* denotes knowledge.

Vijñāna : Ego-consciousness/ consciousness.

Vijñānamaya kośa : Sheath of higher mind.

Vijñapti-mātratā : Pure consciousness or pure wisdom.

Vikṣipta : Occasionally steady.

Vilakṣaṇa : The realization of bliss is free from any emotion of attachment or detachment (*sahajānanda*).

Vimarda : When realization of bliss is attended with the consciousness of the ego as the realizer of the bliss (*virāmānanda*).

Vimarśakhya : Differentiating aspect.

Vipāka : A kind of mental state when the bliss is matured to knowledge (*paramānanda*).

Vīra : Tāntric aspirant of the second grade whose mental faculties are of an advanced nature.

Virāmānanda : Detachment from the worldly pleasure.

Visarga : Alphabetical sign of double-dot which is symbolically regarded as the complementary Śakti of *bindu*. It signifies both the *parā* and the *aparā* aspects of Śakti. It is Female Principle (*saḥ*) as complementary to the Male Priciple (*haṁ*).

Viśuddha : *Viśuddha* means 'pure'. The nerve plexus above the *anāhata* in the neck.

Viśvādhik : More than the universe.

Viśvamāyā : Immanent.

Viśvatṛṇa : Transcendent.

Vyakta : Manifest or form.

Vyāna : Vital wind (which circulate and distributes).

Vyavadhāna : Distinction.

Vyoma : Ether.

Yama : Self-restraint.

Yāna : Way (Paths).

Yoga : Disciplining of the body for various purposes — physical, mental and spiritual and mediation.

Yogācāra : One who practices *yoga*.

Yoni : Female generative organ.

Yugala : Non-duality.

Yuganaddha : Male principle in union with the female principle. It is the non-dual state of unity of *śunyatā* and *karuṇā*.

Bibliography

Abhinavaguptacharya, *Śrī Tantraloka*, Part IV, Srinagar, Govt. Publication, 1922.

Acharya, Narendra Deo, *Bauddha Dharma Darśana*, Patna, 1956.

Agrawal, Vasudeo Sarana, *Harṣacarita, Ek Sāṁskṛtik Adhyayana* (Hindi), Patna, 1964.

———, *Śiva-Mahadeo*, Patna, 1966.

Anand, Mulk Raj, and Lance Dane, *Kāma-Sūtra of Vātsyāyana*, New Delhi, 1982.

———, *Kāma-Kalā*, New York, 1958.

Apte, Vamana Shivrama, *Sanskrit-Hindi Kośa*, Varanasi, 1966.

Aśvaghoṣa, *Buddhacarita*, tr. E.H. Johnston, Reprint, Delhi, 1972.

Bagachi, P.C., *Studies in the Tantras*, Part I, Calcutta, 1939.

———, *Pre-Dravidian and Pre-Aryan in India*, Calcutta, 1929.

———, *Kaulajñānanirṇaya and Some Minor Texts of the School of Matsyendranath*, Calcutta, 1934.

Banerjea, J.N., *The Development of Hindu Iconography*, Calcutta, 1956.

———, *Paurāṇic and Tāntric Religion*, Calcutta, 1966.

Barua, B.M., *Pre-Buddhistic Indian Philosophy*, Reprint, Delhi, 1970.

Basham, A.L., *A Cultural History of India*, London, 1975.

Basu, Manoranjan, *Tantra — A General Study*, Calcutta, 1976.

Benjamin Rowland, Jr., *The Evolution of The Buddha Image*, New York, 1963.

Bhandarkar, R.G., *Vaiṣṇavism, Saivism and other Minor Religious Systems*, Reprint, Varanasi, 1965.

Bharati, Agehananda, *Tāntric Tradition*, New Delhi, 1983.

Bharati, Dharmavir, *Siddha-Sāhitya* (Hindi), Allahabad, 1950.

Bhattacharya, B.T., *An Introduction to the Buddhist Esoterism*, London, 1932.

———, *Indian Buddhist Iconography*, Calcutta, 1959.

Bhattacharyya, Dipak Chandra, *Tāntric Buddhist Iconographic Sources*, New Delhi, 1973.

———, *Studies in Buddhist Iconography*, New Delhi, 1978.

Bhattacharya, N.N., *The History of Śākta Religion*, Delhi, 1974.

———, *Ancient Indian Rituals*, New Delhi, 1975.

———, *The History of the Tāntric Religion*, New Delhi, 1982.

———, *The History of Indian Erotic Literature*, New Delhi, 1975.

———, *Tāntric Buddhism*, New Dehi, 1999.

Bhattacharya, Tarapada, *The Canons of Indian Art*, Calcutta, 1963.

Bose, D.N., and Hira Lal, Haldhar, *Tantra: Their Philosophy and Occult Secrets*, Calcutta, 1981.

Brahma, Nalani Kant, *Philosophy of Hindu Sādhanā*, London, 1932.

Briggs, G.W., *Gorakha Nātha and the Kanphaṭa Yogīs*, Calcutta, 1938.

Brunton, Paul, *A Search in Secret India*, London, 1947.

Chakravarti, C., *Tantras, Studies on their Religion and Literature*, Calcutta, 1963.

Chatterjee, S.C. and D.M. Datta, *An Introduction to Indian Philosophy*, Calcutta, 1939.

Chaturvedi, Sita Ram., *Kālidāsa Granthāvalī* (Sanskrit-Hindi), Varanasi, 1980.

Coomaraswamy, Anand K., *Art and Craft of India and Ceylon*, London, 1917.

———, *Elements of Buddhist Iconography*, London, 1935.

Dasgupta, S.B., *An Introduction to Tāntric Buddhism*, Calcutta, 1974.

———, *Aspects of Indian Religious Thought*, Calcutta, 1957.

———, *Obscure Religious Cults*, 2nd edn., Calcutta, 1962.

Dasgupta, Surendra Nath, *Yoga as Philosophy and Religion*, New Delhi, 1978.

———, *Yoga Philosophy* (in relation to other systems), New Delhi, 1979.

Datta, R.C., *Prācīn Bhārat Kī Sabhyatā Kā Itihāsa* (Hindi), Allahabad, 1966.

De, Sushil Kumar, *Ancient Indian Erotics and Erotic Literature*, Calcutta, 1959.

Desai, Devangana, *Erotic Sculpture of India : A Socio-Cultural Study*, New Delhi, 1975.

Deussen, Paul, *The Philosophy of the Upaniṣad*, Reprint, New Delhi, 1979.

Dvivedi, Hazari Prasad, *Nāth Sampradāya* (Hindi), Allahabad, 1959.

———, *Kabeer* (in Hindi), Allahabad, 1947.

Eliade, Mircea, 'Yoga, immortality and freedom', translated by Willard R. Rask, London, 1958.

Eggeling, J., *Śatapatha Brāhmaṇa*, 1963.

Fouchit, Max Pol, *The Erotic Sculpture of India*.

George, Christopher, *The Candamaharasana Tantra*, New Haven, 1974.

Gichner, Lawrence, *Erotic Aspects in Hindu Sculpture*, USA, 1949.

Gopinath Rao, T.A., *Elements of Hindu Iconography*, vol. I & II, Madras.

Gordon, D.H., *Pre-Historic Background of Indian Culture*, Bombay, 1958.

Gosh, Aurobindo, *The Synthesis of Yoga*, Arya, 1918.

Guenther, H.V., *Yuganaddha, The Tāntric View of Life*, 2nd edn., Benaras, 1964.

Gupta, Sanjukta, *Prapanchasar*, Leiden, 1972.

———, *History and Culture of Indian People*, vol. I-X, Bombay.

———, *The Age of Imperial Kanauj*, vol. IV, Bombay.

———, *Indian Archaeology — A Review*, 1958-59, 1962-63.

———, *Indian Historical Quarterly*, March, 1933.

Havell, E.B., *Ideals of Indian Art*, London, 1911.

———, *Ancient and Medieval Architecture of India*, 1915.

John Woodroffe, *Principles of Tantra*, Madras, 1952.

Joshi, Lalmani, *Studies in Buddhist Culture of India*, Benaras, 1967.

Joshi, Pandit Harishankar, *Vedic Viśvadarśana*, Benaras Hindu University, Varanasi, 1966.

Kane, P.V., *History of Dharmaśāstra*, 5 vols., Poona, 1962.

Kaviraj, Gopinath, *Journal of Ganga Nath Jha Research Institute*, vol. III, Allahabad.

———, *Tāntric Sāhitya* (Hindi), Lucknow, 1972.

———, *Gopinath Kaviraj Abhinandan Grantha*, Lucknow, 1967.

———, *Bhāratīya Sanskṛt aur Sādhanā*, PartI & II (IIindi), Patna, 1963 and 1964.

———, *Tāntric Vāṅgamaya aur Śākta Dṛṣṭi* (Hindi), Patna, 1963.

Kazi, Dawa Samdup, *Cakrasambhavatantra*, Calcutta, 1919.

Keith, A.B., *The Religion and Philosophy of Veda and Upaniṣad*, Varanasi, 1965.

———, *Taittirīya Saṁhitā*, Varanasi, 1967.

———, *Ṛgveda Brāhmaṇas, and Aitareya and Kauṣītaki Brāhmaṇas of the Ṛgveda*, 1920.

———, *The Karma Mīmāṁsā*, London, 1921.

Kern, H., *Manual of Indian Buddhism*, Strassbourg, 1996.

Kosambi, D.D., *Myth and Reality*, Bombay, 1962.

———, *The Culture and Civilization of Ancient India*, New Delhi, 1962.

Lesson, Francis, *Kama Shilpa*, Bombay, 1962.

Lorenzen, D.H., *The Kāpālikas and Kālāmukhas* (Two Lost Śaivite Sects), New Delhi, 1972.

Mallick, Kalyani, *Nātha Sampradāya Itihās Darśana O Sādhanā-praṇālī* (Bengali), Calcutta, 1950.

Marshall, J., *Mohenjo-daro and Indus Civilization*, London, 1930.

———, *Buddhist Art of Gāndhāra*, London, 1961.

Max-Müllar, *The Upaniṣad*, Delhi, 1965.

Mishra, Ram Prasad, *Sahajayāna*, Calcutta, 1991.

Mishra, T.N., *Bhāratīya Prācya Sāhitya Me Śiva kā Svarūpa*, *Pariṣad Patrika*, Verse 25, Ank 3, Patna, 1985.

———, *Impact of Tantra on Religion and Art*, New Delhi, 1997.

———, *Buddhist Tantra and Buddhist Art*, New Delhi, 2000.

Mookerjee, Ajit, *Tantra Asana*, New Delhi, 1971.

———, *Tantra Art*, New Delhi, 1971.

———, and Madhu Khanna, *The Tāntric Way*, London, 1977.

Novonemes, M.M., *Gopinath Kaviraj Smṛti Grantha* (Hindi), Varanasi, 1987.

Pal, Pratipaditya, *The Sensuous Immortal*, London.

Pant, Ramesha Chandra, *Early Hindu Civilization*, Calcutta, 1963.

Pathak, V.S., *The History of Śaiva Cults in Northern India*, Varanasi, 1960.

Pusalkar, A.D., *Studies in the Epics and Purāṇas*, Bombay, 1955.

Radhakrishnan, S., *Indian Philosophy*, vol. II, London, 1931.

———, *Principal Upaniṣads*, London, 1953.

———, *The Hindu View of Life*, London, 1957.

———, *The Brahma Sūtra: The Philosophy of Spiritual Life*, London, 1960.

———, *History of Philosophy: Eastern and Western*, London, 1952.

Randhawa, M.S., *The Cult of Trees and Tree-Worship in Buddhist-Hindu Sculpture*, New Delhi, 1964.

Ray, Niharranjan, *Idea and Image in Indian Art*, New Delhi, 1973.

Rale, J.G., *The Mysterious Kuṇḍalinī*, Bombay, 1927.

Rockhill, W.W., *The Life of Buddha*, Reprint, Varanasi, 1972.

Rhys-Davids, T.W., *Buddhism*, London, 1920.

Saraswati, S.K., *Tantrayāna Art — An Album*, Calcutta, 1977.

Sastri, Hari Prasad, *Advaya Saṁgraha*, Gayakwada Oriental Series, Baroda, 1927.

Sastri, Gopal, *Manu-smṛti*, Varanasi, 1982.

———, *Manu-smṛti or Law of Manu*, tr. G. Buhler, S.B.E., vol. XXV, 1964.

Sastri, Mahadeva, *Brahma Sūtra (Śāṅkara Bhāṣya)*, 1915.

Sastri, Manamatha Nath, *Agni Purāṇa*, Varanasi, 1967.

Satavalekar, Sripada Damodar, *Mahābhārata*, Paradi.

Sharma, L.N., *Kaśmīr Śaivism*, Varanasi, 1972.

Sharma, Shiva Dutta, *Nirukta*, 1904.

Sharma, R.S., *Aspects of Political Ideas and Institutions in Ancient India*, New Delhi, 1959.

———, *Indian Feudalism: 300-1200*, Calcutta, 1965.

Sharma, Ram Swarupa Z., *Śvetāśvatara Upaniṣad*, Bombay, 1913.

Shukla, Vanshidhar, *Vāmamārga* (Hindi), Allahabad, 1951.

Sinha, B.C., *Hinduism and Symbol Worship*, Delhi, 1983.

Sinha, Amar, *Amarakośa*, Chowkhamba Sanskrit Series, Varanasi, 1970.

Singh, Bhagawati Prasad, *Maṇiṣī kī Lokayātrā* (in Hindi), Varanasi, 1980.

Singh, Ram Dular, ed., *Aghora Granthāvalī* (in Hindi), 1986.

Sivaramamurti, C., *Sanskrit Literature and Art — Mirrors of Indian Culture*, Delhi, 1955.

Snellgrove, D.L., *The Image of Buddha*, New Delhi, 1978.

Srinivasachari, P.N., *Advaita and Viśiṣṭādvaita*, Bombay, 1961.

Tatia, N., *Studies in Jaina Philosophy*, Bombay, 1951.

Thomas, P., *Kama Kalpa on the Hindu Ritual of Love*, Bombay, 1959.

Upadhyaya, Baldev, *Bhāratīya Darśana* (Hindi), Varanasi, 1966.

———, *Bauddha Darśana Mīmāṁsā*, Varanasi, 1954.

Upadhyay, Nagendra Nath, *Tāntric Bauddha Sādhanā aur Sāhitya* (Hindi), Kasi, Saṁvat, 2015 (1958).

———, *Bauddha Kāpālika Sādhanā aur Sāhitya* (Hindi), Allahabad, 1983.

Verma, Savaliya Behari, *Visvadharma Darsana*, Patna, 1953.

Waymen, Alex, *Female Energy and Symbolism in the Buddhist Tantra, History of Religion*, vol. II, no. 1, 1962.

———, *Buddhism, in Historia Religion*, ed. C. Jouco Bluker and Geo Widengren, vol. 2, Leiden, 1971.

———, *Yoga of the Guhyasamaja-Tantra*, Delhi, 1977.

William, M., *A Sanskrit-English Dictionary*, London, 1956.

Williams, R., *Jaina Yoga*, London, 1963.

Winternitz, M., *History of Sanskrit Literature*, 3 vols., Delhi, 1972.

Woodroffe, J., *The Serpent Power, being the Ṣaṭcakra Nirūpaṇa*, Madras, 1958.

Zimmer, H., *The Art of India Asia*, New York, 1955.

———, *Myths and Symbols in Indian Art and Civilization*, U.S.A., 1963.

Original Sources

Advayavajra Saṁgraha, G.O.S. no. 40, 1927.

Atharvaveda (Hindi), ed. Satavalekar, Paradi, 1989.

Bhagavad Gītā, Gorakhpur, Vikram Saṁvat, 2040.

Bṛhadāraṇyaka Upaniṣad, Varanasi, 1983.

Chāndogya Upaniṣad, Gita Press, Gorakhpur, Vikram Saṁvat, 2013.

Devī Bhāgavata, Sastri Ram, Tej, Varanasi, 1965.

Gorakṣa-Saṁhitā.

Guhyasamāja-Tantra, Gaekwada Oriental Series, no. 53, Baroda, 1967.

Gorakṣa Siddhānta Saṁgraha, edited by M.M.P. Gopinath Kaviraja, Sarasvati, Bhavan Texts Series, no. 18, Kashi, 1925.

Haṭha-Yoga-Pradīpikā, tr. Pancham Singh, Allahabad, 1955.

Hevajra Tantra, ed. and tr. D.L. Snellgrove, London, 1959.

Jaiminīya Brāhmaṇa.

Jñānārṇava Tantra, ed, G.S. Gokhale, Poona, 1952.

Jñānasiddhi, G.O.S. no. XLIV, 57, Baroda, 1929.

Kabīr Granthāvalī (Hindi) edited by Babu Shyam Sundar Das, Kashi Nagari Pracharani Shabha, 1928.

Kalyāṇa — (Yogāṅka) and Sādhanā aṅka, Gorakhpur.

Kālacakra-tantra : Exposition of Dalai Lama, XIV, ed. Jeffery Hopkins, Dharamasala, 1985.

Kāma-Sūtra, tr. by Indra Singh, London, 1980.

Kaṭhopaniṣad, Varanasi, 1983.

Kaula-Jñāna-Nirṇaya, ed. by P.C. Bagachi, Calcutta, 1934.

Kauṣītaki Brāhmaṇa.

Kena Upaniṣad, Varanasi, 1983.

Kulārṇava Tantra, Tāntric Text, vol. V, London, 1917.

Mālatī Mādhavam, ed. by M.R. Kale, Bombay, 1928.

Māṇḍūkyopaniṣad, Gita Press, Gorakhpur.

Mantra Mahodadhi.

Muṇḍaka Upaniṣad, ed. Vidya Nand Giri, Rishikesh, 1978.

Niṣpannayogāvalī, ed. B. Bhattacharyya, Gaekwada Oriental Series, no. CIX, Baroda, 1949.

Paraśurāma Kalpa Sūtra, Gaekwada Oriental Series, vols. XXII-XXIII.

Ṛgveda (Hindi), ed. Satavalekar, Paradi, 1983.

Rudra-Yāmala, Calcutta, 1937.

Śakti Saṅgam, G.O.S. nos. LXI, CIV, Baroda, 1932-47.

Śāradātilaka, Tāntric Texts, vols. XVI, XVII, Calcutta, 1933.

Saundarya-Laharī, ed. A. Kuppuswami, New Delhi, 1991.

Siddha-Siddhānta Saṁgraha, edited by M.M.P. Gopi Nath Kaviraja, Sarasvati Bhavana Texts, 13, Kashi, 1925.

Śivamahimna Strotram (Puṣpadanta), Varanasi, 1964.

Śrī Kālacakra-tantra.

Śrī Tattva-Cintāmaṇi.

Taittirīya Upaniṣad, Gita Press, Gorakhpur.

Sacred Book of the East: The Vedānta Sūtras, vol. 34, 38 (2 vols.) with commentary by Śaṅkarācārya.

———, *The Vedānta-Sūtras with Rāmānuja Śrībhāṣya*, S.B. E. vol. XLVIII (48), Delhi.

Sacred Books of the Hindus, ed. B.D. Basu.

Sādhanamālā, Gaekwada Oriental Series, no. 26, 41, Baroda, 1968.

Standard English-Hindi Dictionary, 2nd edn., Allahabad, 1983.

Yogapravāha, ed. by Sampurananand, Kashi, Saṁvat, 2003.

Yoga Upaniṣad, ed. by Mahadeva Sastri, Adyar Library, Adyar, 1920.

'Yoga Technique in the Great Epic', by W. Hopkins, in *Journal of the American Oriental Society*, vol. 22, 1901.

Index